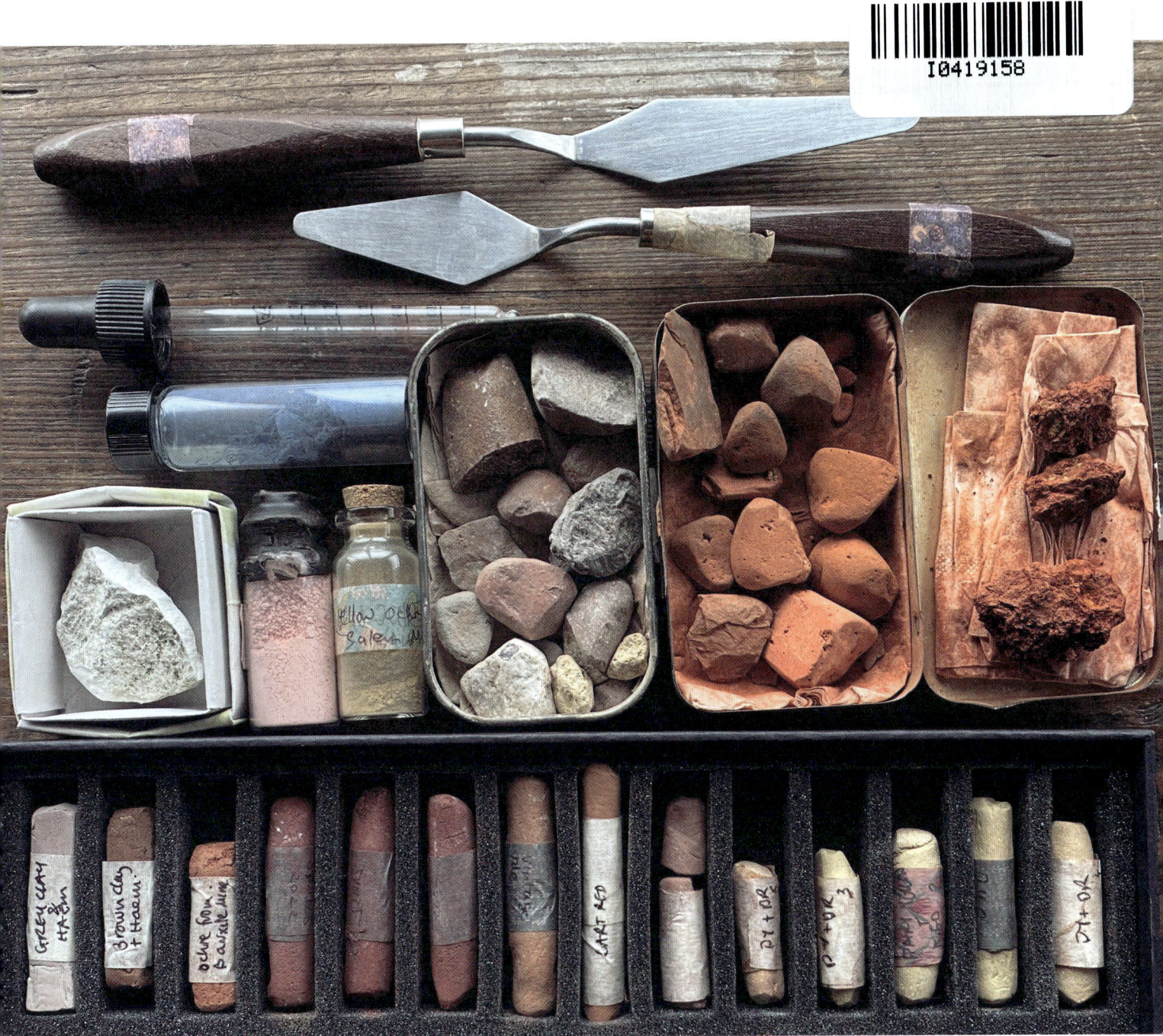

DRAWN FROM
THE WILD

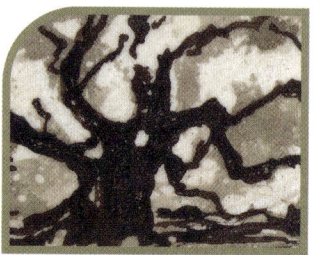

FOUND AND GROUND
www.foundandground.com
@foundandground

DRAWN FROM THE WILD

A practical guide to making your own foraged art materials

Caroline Ross

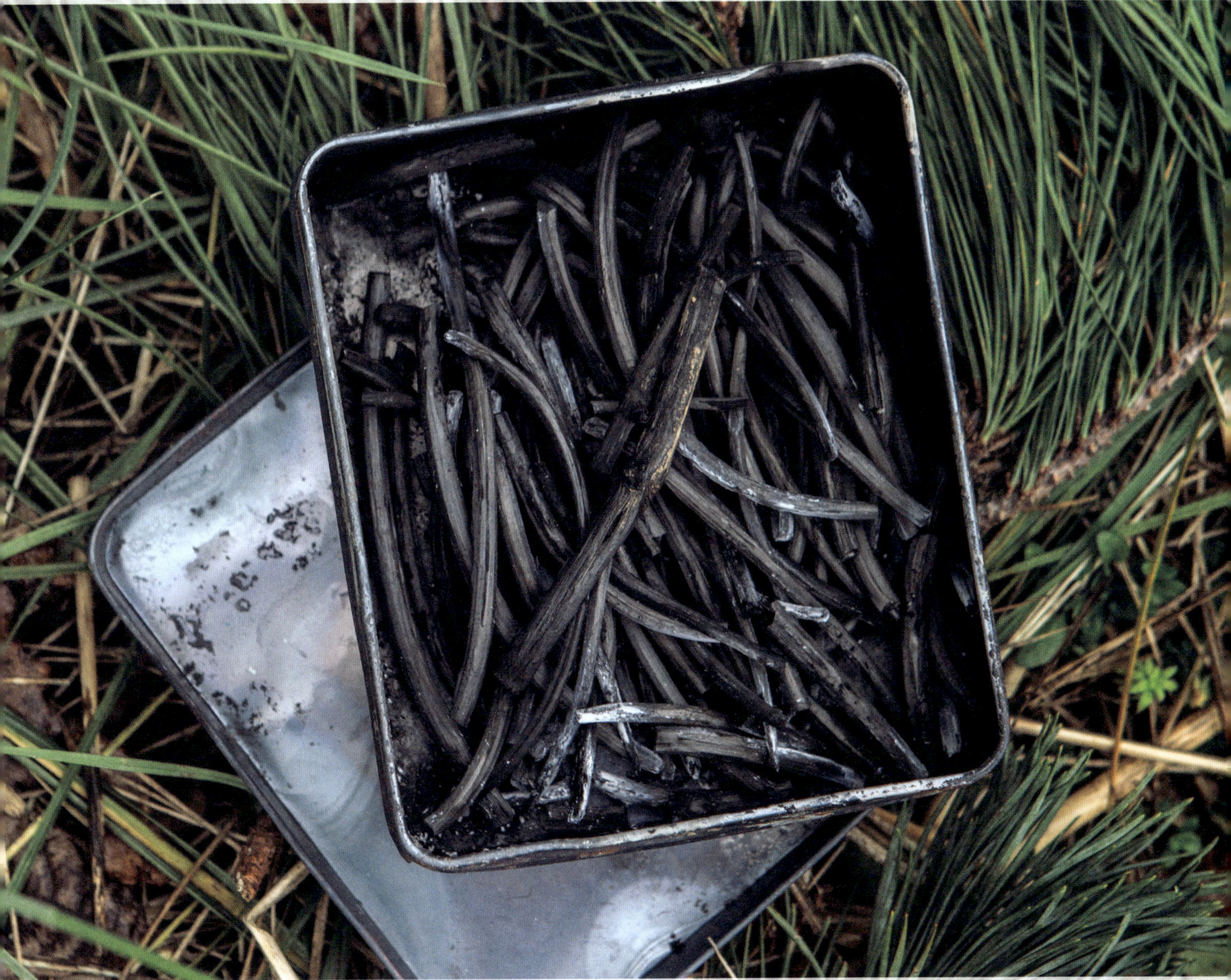

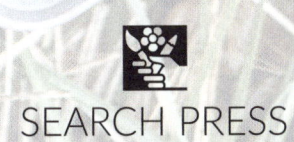

SEARCH PRESS

First published 2025

Search Press Limited
Wellwood, North Farm Road,
Tunbridge Wells, Kent TN2 3DR

ISBN: 978-1-80092-259-4
ebook ISBN: 978-1-80093-258-6

The Publishers and author can accept no responsibility for any consequences arising from the information, advice or instructions given in this publication.

Publisher's note
All the step-by-step photographs in this book feature the author, Caroline Ross, demonstrating how to create artistic media. No models have been used. Caroline Ross created all her original text, art and concepts for this book without the use of AI.

Suppliers
If you have any difficulty obtaining any of the materials and equipment mentioned in this book, visit the Search Press website for details of suppliers: www.searchpress.com

You are invited to visit the author's website at:
www.foundandground.com

Bookmarked Hub
For further ideas and inspiration, and to join our free online community, visit www.bookmarkedhub.com

DEDICATION

To my mother, Jean Ross, whose beautiful, detailed, natural studies of teasels and shells inspired me to spend hours drawing in my room.

And to my late grandmother, Isabella Steed, who took up oil painting late in life and somehow managed to capture the Scottish mountains she missed so much and recreate them in her Dorset bedroom, in oil on canvas.

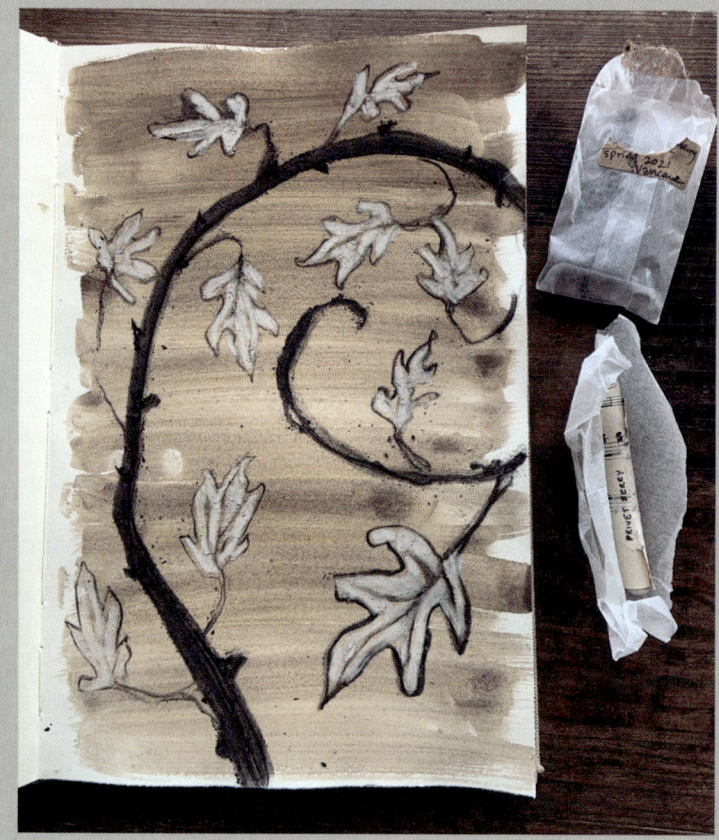

VINE 21 x 30cm (8¼ x 11¾in)
*Gifted charcoal and privet berry lake pastel on
ochre-wash ground.*

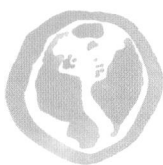

CONTENTS

FOREWORD

by Stewart Lee

> **" What are these,**
> **So withered and wild in their attire,**
> **That look not like inhabitants o' the earth,**
> **And yet are on't? "**
>
> *Macbeth 1.3.38–47, William Shakespeare*

I'm finishing this foreword in Stratford-upon-Avon, where I'm closing outstanding business on a production of Macbeth I wrote some jokes for last year, from whence the appropriate quote above is culled. Today I will drive from the remnants of the great green Forest of Arden to a cabin in Bannau Brycheiniog to view the Orionids at night, traversing twin poles of a Caroline Ross landscape, crossing the lower steppes of the wet Welsh Marches to the Brecon Beacons; via mossy ancient monuments and furzed foothills. It's a world that would look to Caroline like nothing more than a massive natural artist's larder, a branch of an art supplies shop carved from oak, rock and peat, and staffed by the spirits of her ancestors.

I first spoke to Caroline thirty years ago, when she worked in a book shop off the Charing Cross Road, where so many great stories started in the now-dead book dealer days, and she invited me to see her band that weekend at the Water Rats in King's Cross. Delicate AWOL played a jazzy avant-rock, both ahead of and behind the times, and Caroline quivered at its centre in a costume she had made, hanging rags and torn wings, a black angel defenestrated, like something vibrant and natural rising from the ground, unearthly and yet on't. Finally, this book fulfils that first impression.

In the three decades I have known Caroline she has gradually reduced her life to a short shopping list of bare essentials, moving from a flat in Balham to a ruined rat-roofed highland lodge, to a succession of boats and beach huts, returning from every shared riverbank or seashore stroll with pocketfuls of edibles – wild garlic and mysterious berries – and handfuls of raw art materials – red ochre, brown bark, and flakes of black rock. When my children were little they thought Caroline was magic, and I did nothing to disabuse them of that notion.

My home is full of things Caroline has made; a truthful impression of the Uffington White Horse, grubbed from moss and chalk; a vulvic pouch sewn from deerskin; a perfectly cylindrical pot, hollowed from birch branch. To me they are totems, a last gesture on behalf of imperilled nature, and a tribute to humanity's creative potential. I'm going to a woodland cabin this weekend, struggling to scrape together a new stand-up comedy show that opens in mere weeks. But doubtless Caroline will be under a raw shelter of branches somewhere, doing something infinitely more worthwhile, showing me the clear line between her charcoaled antlered celebrants and the rock art paintings of palaeolithic people I once saw flickering through firelight deep in a Pyrenean cave.

We grow distant from the dying world. Caroline Ross reminds us that the instruments of our re-enchantment are arrayed in abundance all around us.

Stewart Lee, writer/clown, Warwickshire, October 2024

Stewart Lee is a stand-up comedian, writer, filmmaker, would-be musician and failed hermit. His world can be accessed at www.stewartlee.co.uk

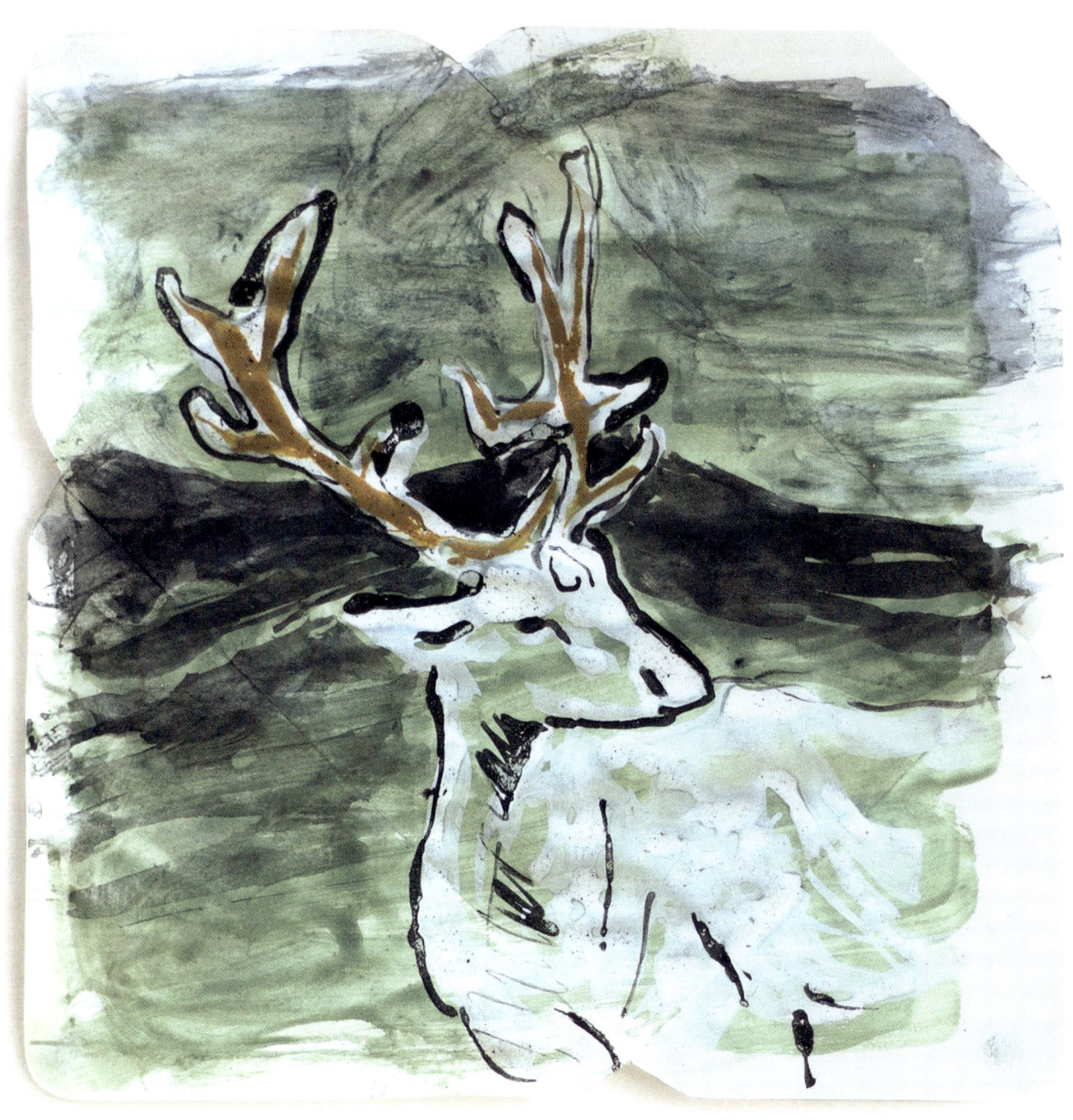

STAG WITH THE GOLDEN HORNS   20 x 20cm (8 x 8in)

Chalk, terre verte and gold ochre paint with oak gall ink on reused envelope. An illustration for Paul Kingsnorth's book, The Wake.

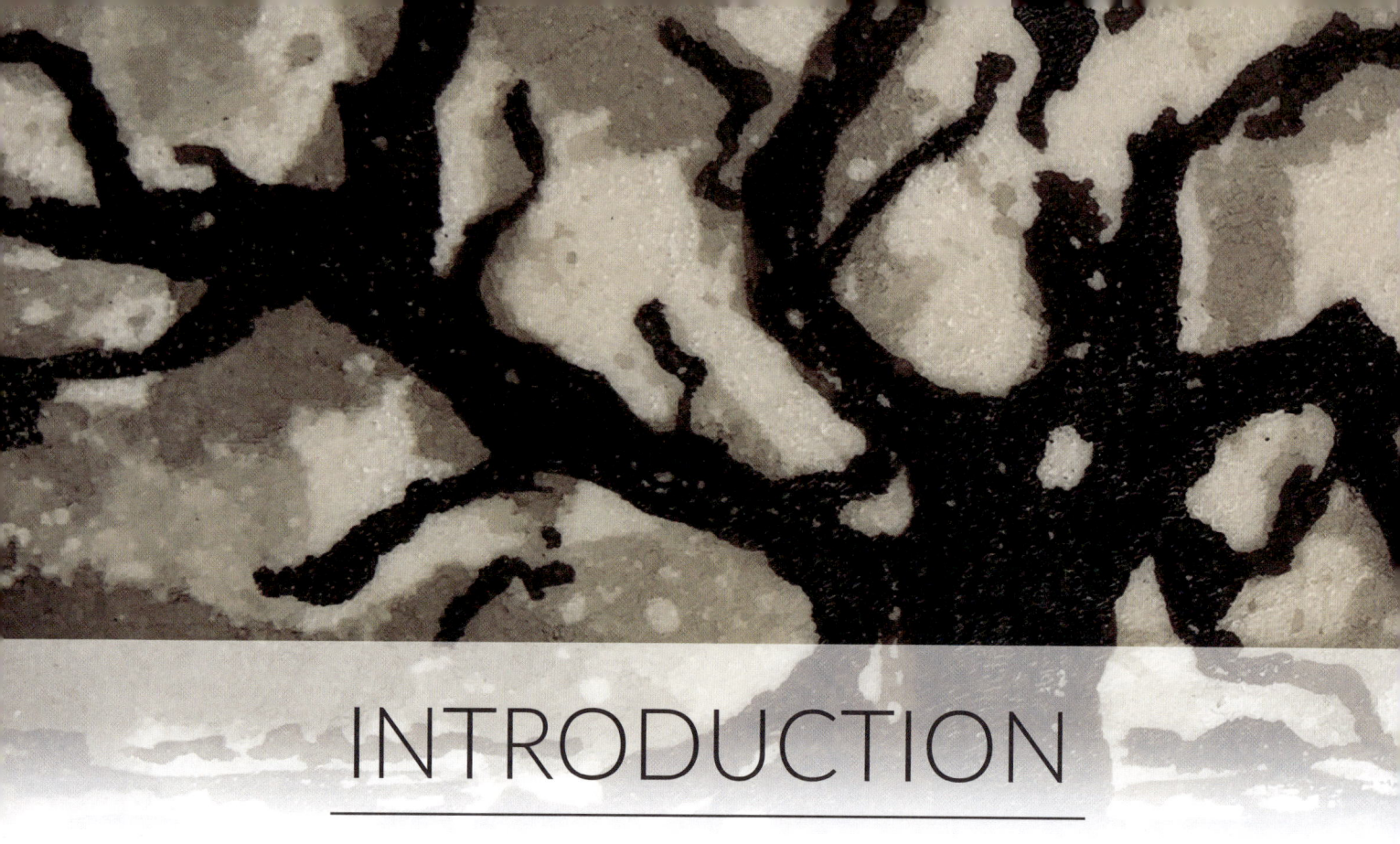

INTRODUCTION

Making your mark

It's late January and the bare branches of oak, lime and chestnut trees across the road are lit by low bright winter light, making the trees look like drawings made with dip pen and black ink. I went out earlier and picked up fallen lime twigs from the pollarded street trees to gather their inner bark fibre. It comes off easily from the sticks, after my neighbours have driven over them while parking their cars. I twist these fibres into cordage and sew up a quick sketchbook, made from discarded envelopes and packing materials from things my flatmate bought online. You can always be foraging, even in a town, or in your own home and garden.

You don't have to live in a rural idyll to make beautiful, useful art supplies from foraged, natural, discarded or repurposed materials. In this book I'll bring together ancient techniques and modern waste streams, plus introduce novel twists with traditional materials so that you can make art without it costing the Earth.

As in *Found and Ground,* my first book on foraged paints, we'll use easily found natural materials, and this time we'll bring our magpie mindset back to town, to bring a bit of wildness to the drawing board. *Drawn from the Wild* invites you to pick up sticks, rusty iron and stray feathers, to make brushes, ink and pens from old bones the fox left in the garden, and sheep's wool you find on hedgerows or fences on a country walk.

Are none of those near you? No matter; thistle down and hollow plant stems will make a stippling brush fit for a Pointillist. Garden vine prunings and an old tin are a source of artists' quality charcoal to make the finest sketches. Discarded wooden chopsticks will make the best dip pens you've ever used. Windfall walnut husks and gums from neighbourhood fruit trees make rich brown ink for calligraphic sweeps or atmospheric washes. And you won't believe the bold indelible marks you can make with leftover kitchen

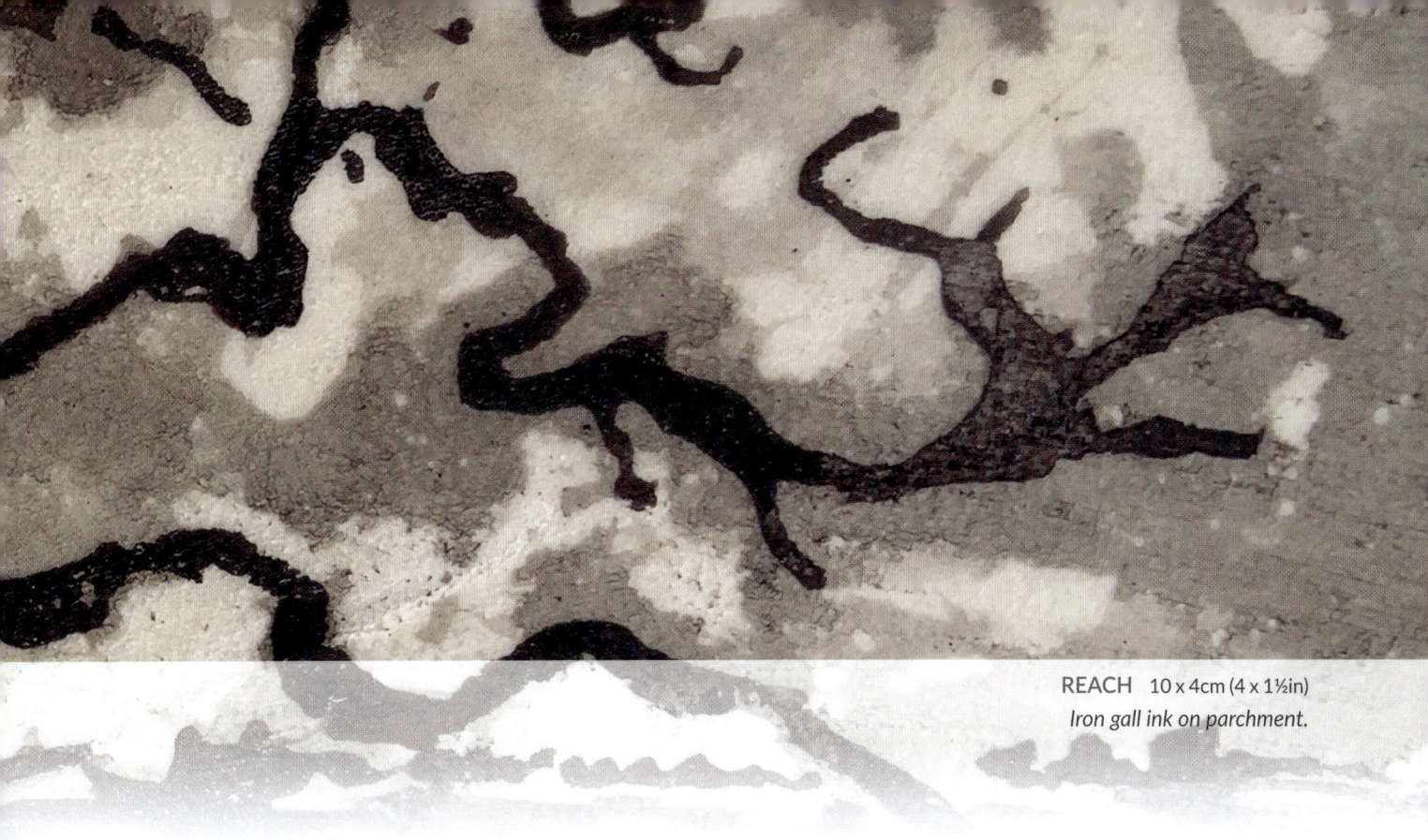

REACH   10 x 4cm (4 x 1½in)
Iron gall ink on parchment.

foil, or the subtle textures left by cheap old metal beads, once you know how to prepare the paper.

Drawing is found in every culture throughout history, from building plans to detailed tattoos, from sketched portraits to illuminated manuscripts, via wild beasts running across a thousand cave walls. Carefully incised drawings on small stones and bones, that were then rubbed with ochre, are some of the earliest drawings that still survive – and across the whole world, astounding drawings have been found in caves and on rocks. Their subtle mark-making and bold designs still speak to us, even after tens of thousands of years. It seems humans have always been drawn to make their mark.

Who this book is for

Wildness, ingenuity and creativity are part of all of us. I have planned this book to be as accessible as possible to everyone, whether young or old, novice or experienced. Themed around the traditional Chinese five elements – earth, fire, water, wood and metal – each chapter explores ancient materials seen from a contemporary angle, and includes projects that will give both newcomers to drawing and professionals alike plenty of inspiration.

If, like me, you love culture but know in your bones you are also part of nature, you'll want to make your art practice more ecologically sound and sustainable. You've come to the right place.

Welcome to *Drawn from the Wild.*

Drawing kings with kids

I've always loved drawing, but for a long while I stopped sketching for my own pleasure. Some years ago, my friend Stewart and his son Luke came to visit and we met at Hampton Court Palace, a few hundred metres from my houseboat, where I lived at the time. After exploring, we sat and drew pictures of a very grumpy King Henry VIII, as the café provided paper and pencils for kids (of all ages). It was years since I'd sat and drawn with someone else. Why didn't I do this more often?

Some time later, I got a lovely card from Stew's family when they came to stay for our annual Winter Solstice get-together. Luke had drawn a wonderful Green Man, based on the one from the front of Paul Kingsnorth's *The Wake*. You can see it to the right. More than any work by a famous artist, Luke's lively figure made me really want to draw again, and soon I was illustrating *The Wake* and getting back to my own art practice – this time using my own homemade inks, pens, charcoal, sketchbooks and paints. I put *The Green Man* in a frame and hung him in pride of place among my wild art materials, where he still lives now.

Inspiration can come from almost anywhere: art, nature, design, costume, history, folk traditions, science, religion, books, and of course, raw imagination. Drawing is for everyone, not just children and artists. In this book you'll get to try lots of different materials, styles and methods, so there is something for everyone to enjoy.

Some of the techniques were used historically, but have fallen out of favour. I want to bring them back! Drawing is a living, developing tradition. If you've been used to felt tip pens and permanent markers, then I can't wait to see what you'll do with metalpoint and oil charcoal.

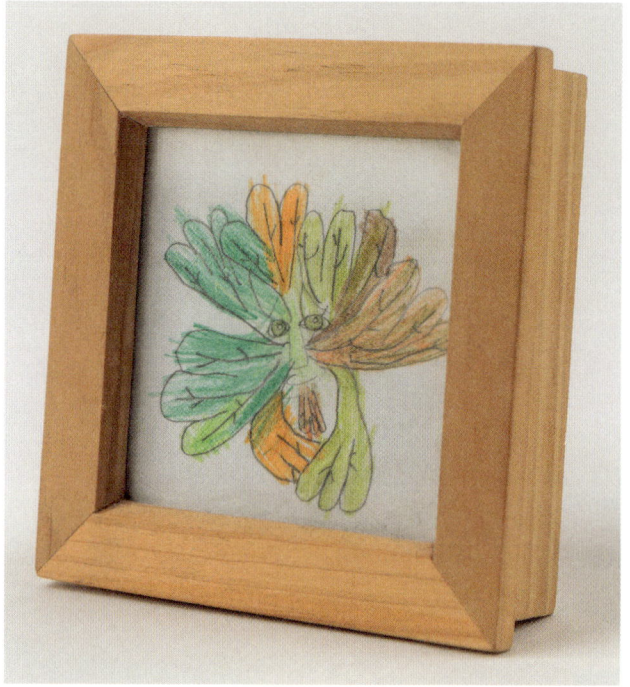

THE GREEN MAN   12 x 12cm (4¾ x 4¾in)
Artist: Luke Lee.
Coloured pencil on paper.

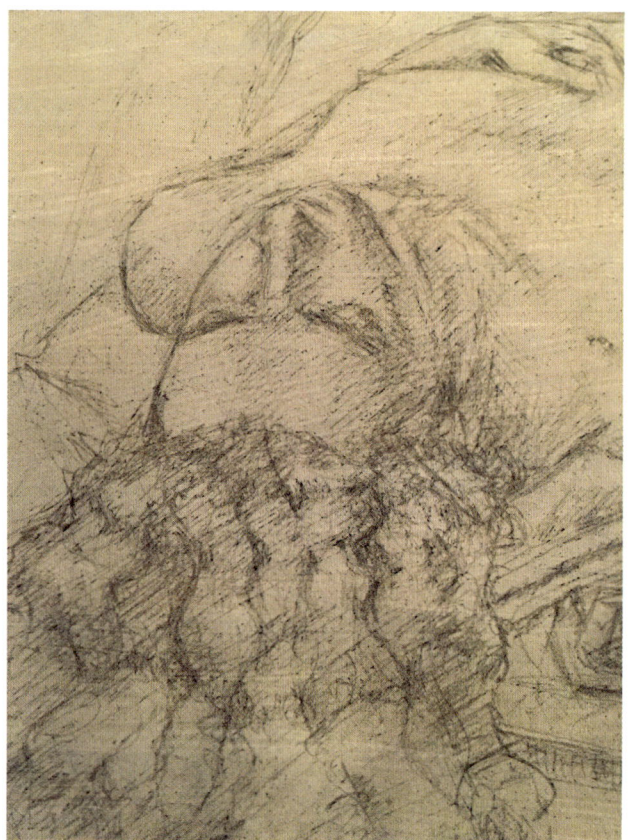

RECLINING MODEL   35 x 50cm (13¾ x 19¾in)
Silverpoint on prepared ground.

Fantastic beasts and painted people

What are indigenous, traditional, historical, folk and contemporary arts like where you live? A little research into local traditions and arts will open a world of inspiration. There is nothing better than a day spent with a sketchbook at a museum, cultural site or gallery – except perhaps a day out sketching in nature. The simple sketchbooks you'll be learning to make on pages 101–103 are perfect to stash for such adventures. And because they don't cost much, you'll be far more likely to experiment freely in them.

In my case, the Scottish side of my family all come from Aberdeenshire, home to at least 99 stone circles and megalithic sites. When I lived there, I visited many of them and also fell in love with the carved stones of later eras. The name of their creators, the Picts, comes from the Latin *pictus*, which literally means 'painted', as they were reported by contemporaneous Roman writers to have loved decoration. A passion for drawing has certainly continued in my clan down the generations and is strong in my youngest niece, too.

SKETCHES FOR COVER OF DARK MOUNTAIN 13   10 x 15cm (4 x 6in)
Charcoal on handmade sketchbook paper.

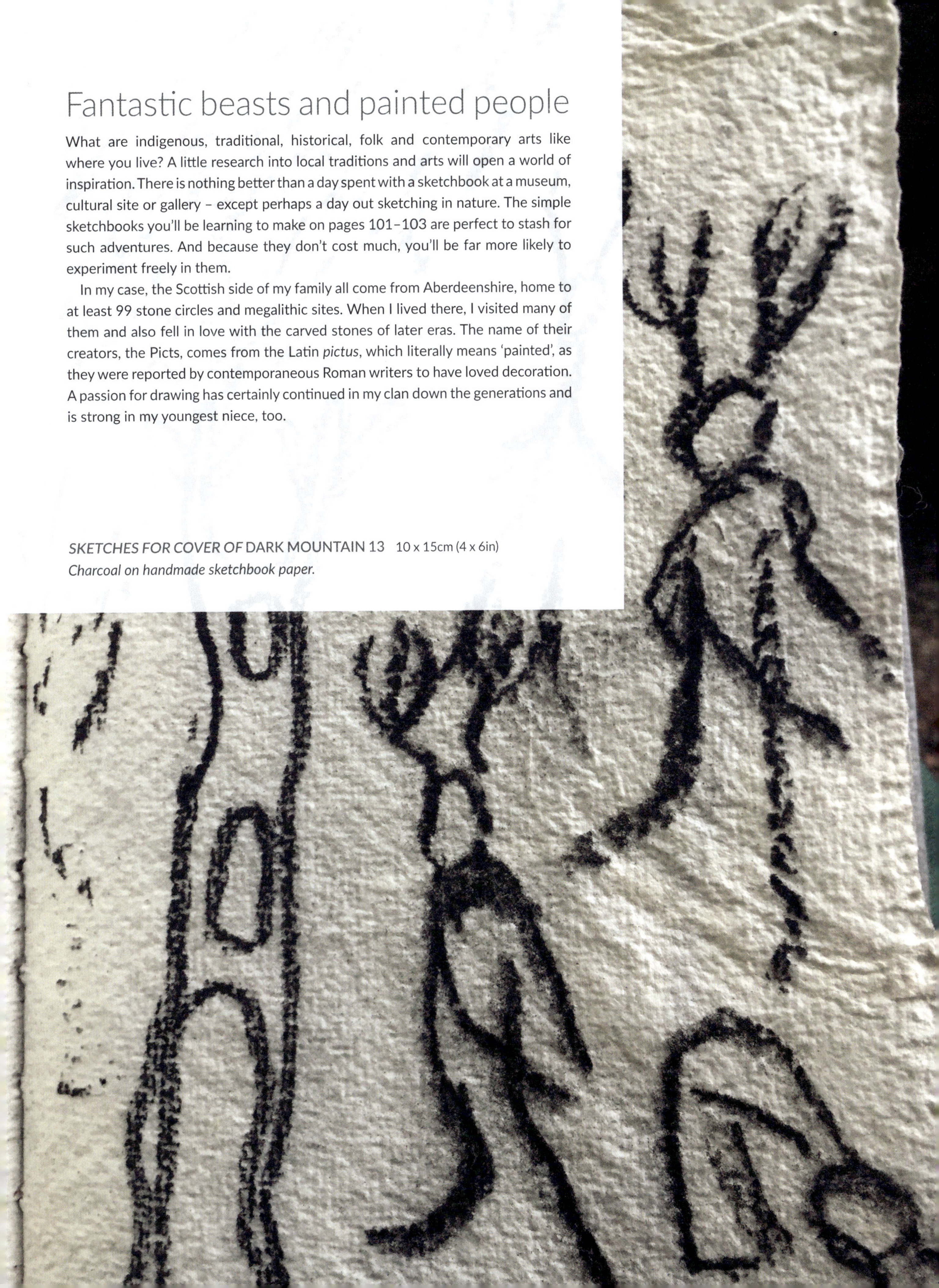

Chalk figures and jousting rabbits

Painter Paul Klee wrote about drawing as 'taking a line for a walk'. Depending on who and where you are, that walk could be as contrasting as a walkabout in the Outback or a stroll in Sherwood Forest. By making and finding our own materials, our drawings can become as unique as our home territory.

In southern England, where I grew up and live now, long-hidden red and yellow ochre drawings and paintings can be seen emerging from behind the flaking Reformation-era whitewash applied to the walls of ancient churches. Sinuous vines and rich abstract patterns adorn illuminated manuscripts, while cheeky snails, rabbits and other, stranger, creatures peer from the margins, drawn with great humour in ink by mediaeval scribes. Graphic richness even oozes from the hilltops here: giants, horses and other figures are the subjects of truly monumental chalk figures – colossal drawings that are the result of many people working together. We will explore all these materials, and more, over the coming pages for you to make your own drawings.

I concentrate mostly on materials from my locality and cultural traditions, not because I think they're best, but out of deep love and respect. I share these methods widely and simultaneously learn about other lineages, some of which you'll see featured later in this book. It is for this reason that I have invited contributions from artists across the world, whose practices draw from hugely different traditions. I have gathered them together in the hope that their drawing materials or methods spur you on during your own wild drawing journey.

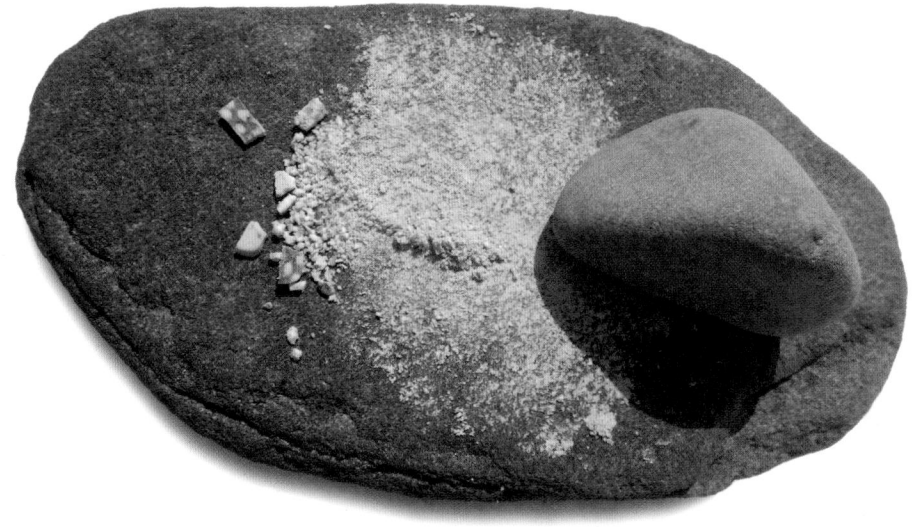

Sea urchin shell.

Think like a watershed

I used to think I should be more single-minded and focussed, to avoid splitting my attention across so many things. I thought I should be more like the classic picture of a river, with a single 'V'-shaped valley and a clearly defined stream. I looked up to people who specialized in one thing and had mastered it, especially in art – and while I still do, I also see the value in breadth of learning. At school I loved art and chemistry – and now I know that there is no real need to choose between them.

We need to get a bird's-eye view of our artistic terrain, in order to take in the whole watershed. All the different tributaries and springs of our interests do eventually make their way down to the same estuary, and out to sea. When I started to teach natural art materials to others, Found and Ground was where my artistic landscape finally came together, including nature, science, experimentation, history and more.

I encourage you to cross-pollinate by bringing ideas from other aspects of your life – such as cookery, gardening, archaeology or other hobbies – into your drawings and art materials. Draw from your own experience to help pose yourself fun questions, and explore to find the answers. Here are some of mine, as examples: How can we make a cheap, natural pastel fixative that doesn't come in a spray can? Now, how can we make a vegan version? What happens when we combine waste household metals, a love of Stone Age cave art and Renaissance drawing techniques? What can we do with an overabundance of stone dust, blown into a ditch from a local quarry? What happens when we treat an old leather skirt like an ancient sheet of parchment?

Read on, and find out!

I overlapped washes of neighbourhood-foraged mahonia and elderberry inks on paper and then worked on top in watercolour pencil to create this abstract study based on local geology.

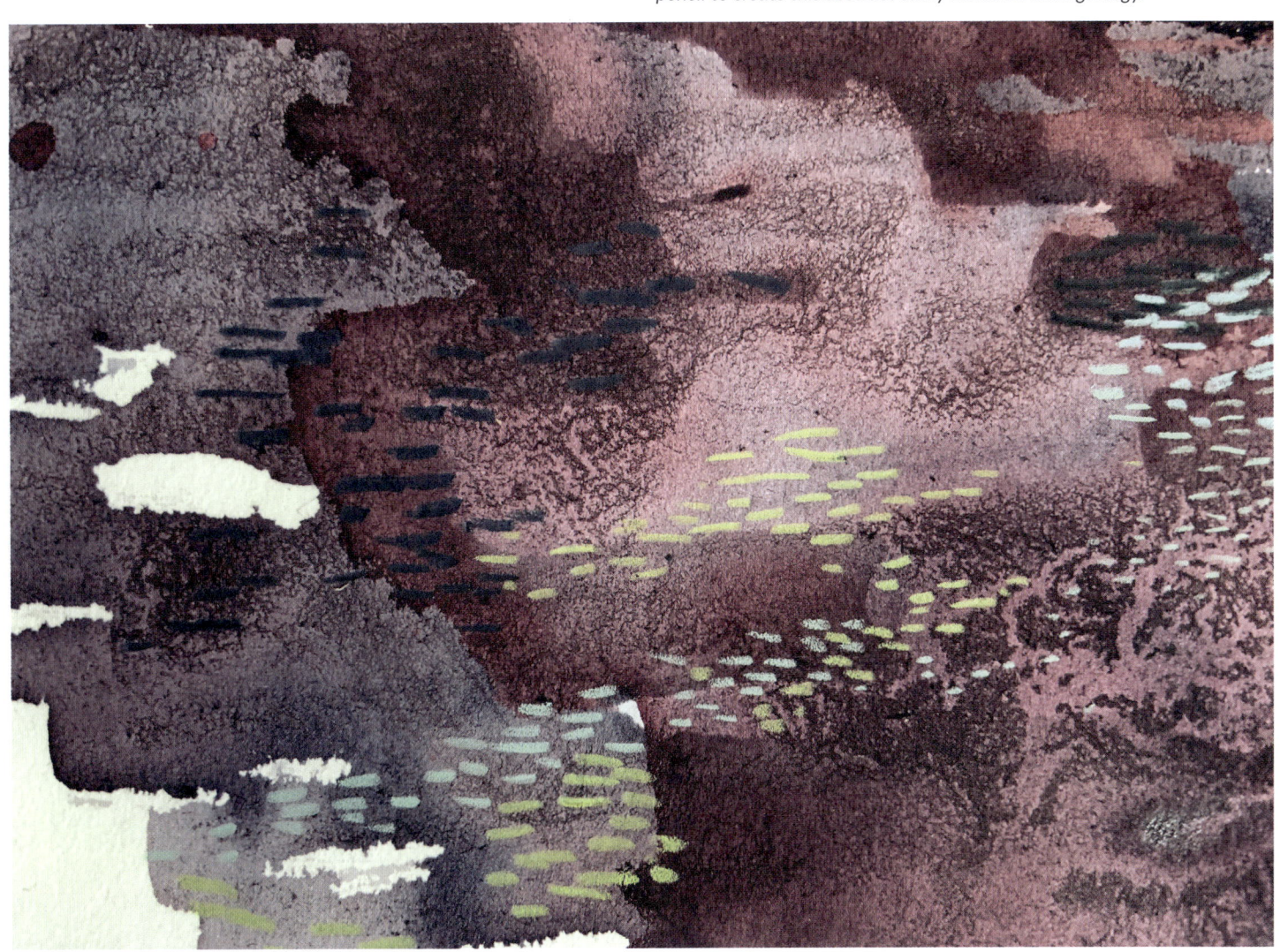

FORAGING

How to start

The best way to forage is with an open mind, a peaceful heart and a sense of adventure. An open mind helps, as preconceived ideas can severely limit both your ability to find things and your fun. A peaceful heart is best, as if we go out with an acquisitive, grasping attitude, we'll not treat the natural world – or even our neighbourhood – with the care and appreciation they deserve. A sense of adventure is essential, as you never know what you might find.

In a world where screens and algorithms mediate so much of what we do, the possibility of surprise and delight are more important than ever before.

Where to start

Right where you are is as good a place as any to start looking for your raw art materials. For the projects in this book, sources may be as diverse as your garage or garden, the street you live in, woodlands, seashores, urban sites and the countryside.

If you're new to foraging, plan a walk without a specific goal in mind beyond looking more closely at the familiar. See how many new things you notice on your walk: you will likely be pleasantly surprised.

Once you've looked through the book and have seen something you'd like to find, you can plan your next foray. For instance, if you want thin straight sticks for charcoal-making, then a winter woodland wander with a pair of secateurs and some gloves is just the ticket. If it's rusty old iron you need to blacken ink, then you might find just what you need under the shelves in your garage, or along the side of the road.

This practice might coincide with some edible foraging – while looking for sticks you might also find some oyster mushrooms, and while gathering old iron, you might spot a glut of ripe but unwanted pears in a neighbour's front yard.

Reusing and repurposing

Much to some people's surprise, my life isn't all fairytale woodland baskets and cute animal helpers. I live in a big seaside town in an ordinary flat, so my practice reflects that. While I'd love a completely plastic-free art life, I don't drive, and rely on public transport to teach. If I carried everything in birch bark or balsawood tubs, cardboard boxes and metal tins, I wouldn't be able to lift my rucksack of materials onto my back. I therefore try to find a middle way by reusing and repurposing what is all around me: other people's and my own household 'waste'. Waste stream materials such as wrappers, metal, plastic and packing materials can be a rich source of inspiration and experimentation. It just takes a change of view.

In this book, as well as foraged and found natural materials, we'll be using some everyday items you can find around the home, garden and workshop. We'll also be scavenging in the urban environment for items such as clean used kitchen foil, old bottles, crumbly brick, or even hair from your hairbrush.

People learn best from encouragement rather than shaming. I am inclined towards a gradual approach to rewilding your art practice, rather than throwing everything out all at once, then wondering how to start again. In this book there will hopefully be one or two obvious projects that leap out at you to become part of your new/ancient materials repertoire. There will be others that might need a few bits of equipment, and perhaps a trip to the art suppliers or local quarry for some marble dust, or the thrift store for a pan.

Follow your inclination through the materials and mark-making possibilities on offer between the covers of this book. Treat reading it like a foraging walk, and see what catches your eye.

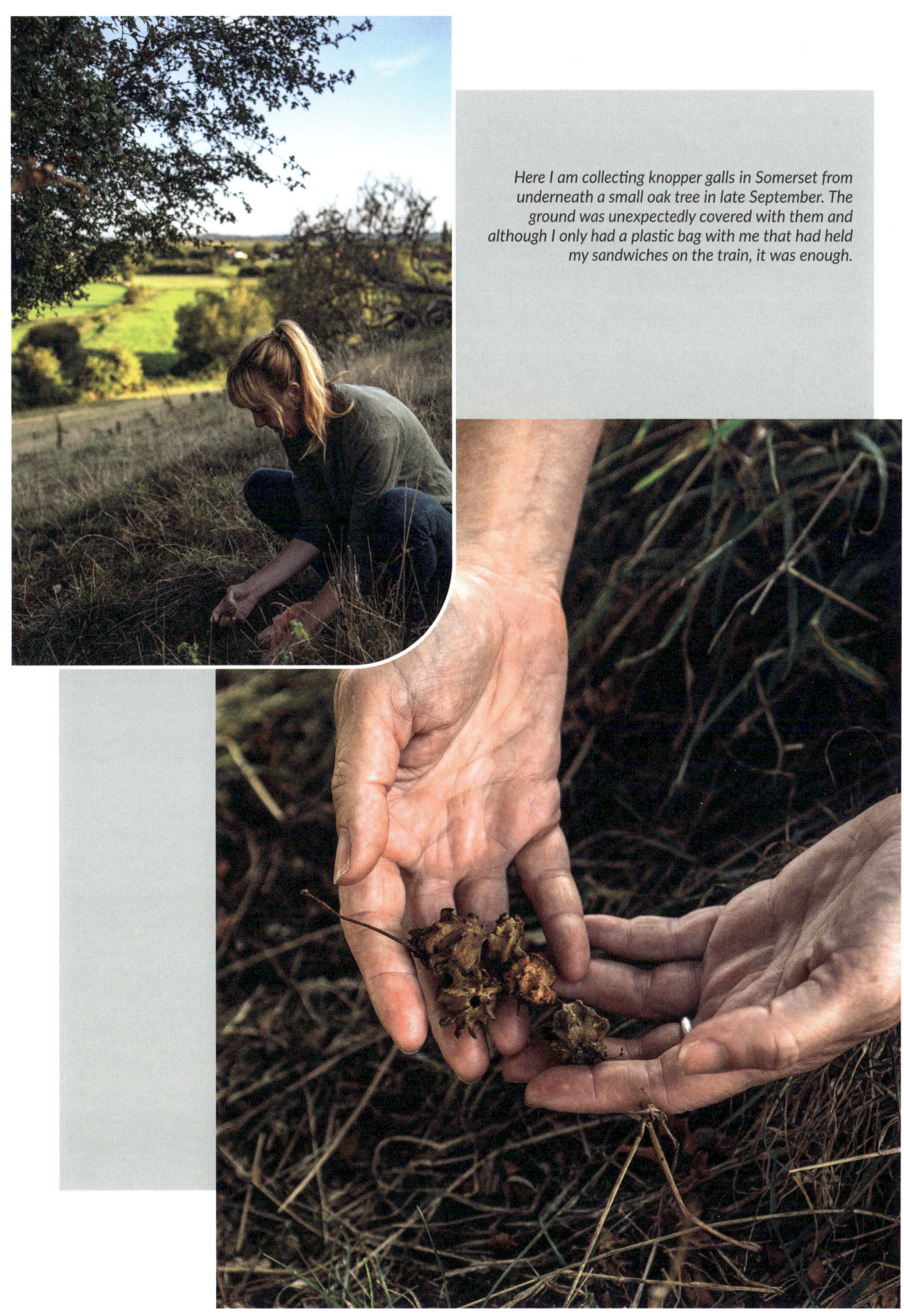

Here I am collecting knopper galls in Somerset from underneath a small oak tree in late September. The ground was unexpectedly covered with them and although I only had a plastic bag with me that had held my sandwiches on the train, it was enough.

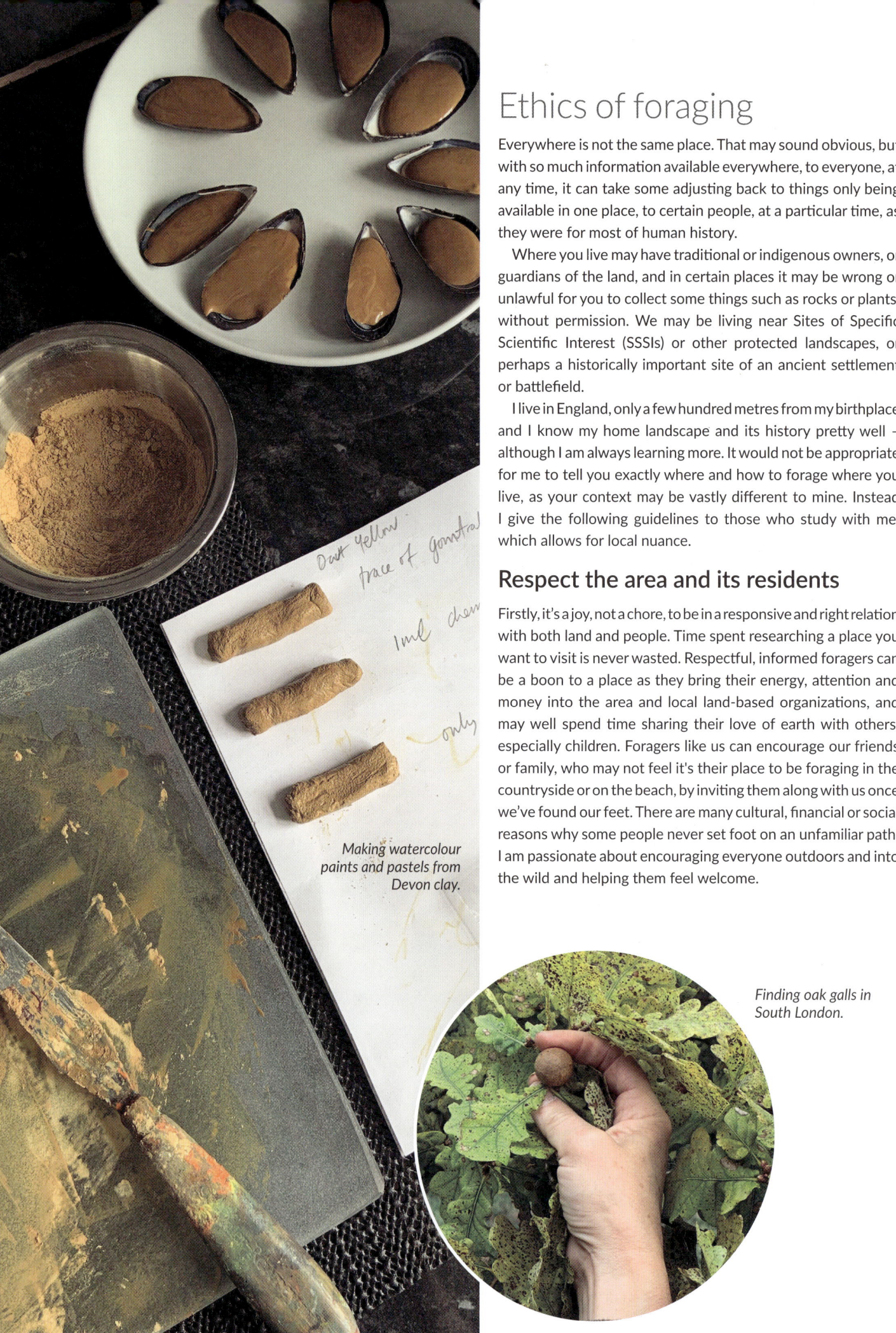

Making watercolour paints and pastels from Devon clay.

Ethics of foraging

Everywhere is not the same place. That may sound obvious, but with so much information available everywhere, to everyone, at any time, it can take some adjusting back to things only being available in one place, to certain people, at a particular time, as they were for most of human history.

Where you live may have traditional or indigenous owners, or guardians of the land, and in certain places it may be wrong or unlawful for you to collect some things such as rocks or plants, without permission. We may be living near Sites of Specific Scientific Interest (SSSIs) or other protected landscapes, or perhaps a historically important site of an ancient settlement or battlefield.

I live in England, only a few hundred metres from my birthplace and I know my home landscape and its history pretty well – although I am always learning more. It would not be appropriate for me to tell you exactly where and how to forage where you live, as your context may be vastly different to mine. Instead I give the following guidelines to those who study with me, which allows for local nuance.

Respect the area and its residents

Firstly, it's a joy, not a chore, to be in a responsive and right relation with both land and people. Time spent researching a place you want to visit is never wasted. Respectful, informed foragers can be a boon to a place as they bring their energy, attention and money into the area and local land-based organizations, and may well spend time sharing their love of earth with others, especially children. Foragers like us can encourage our friends or family, who may not feel it's their place to be foraging in the countryside or on the beach, by inviting them along with us once we've found our feet. There are many cultural, financial or social reasons why some people never set foot on an unfamiliar path. I am passionate about encouraging everyone outdoors and into the wild and helping them feel welcome.

Finding oak galls in South London.

Know what you can forage

Take only what is plentiful and leave what is scarce. Other creatures may need those berries more than we do. As we become better foragers, we learn about overabundant species that are perhaps out-of-place in our locale, and we should feel free to make copious inks, charcoal or tools out of these.

Improvising is fun when we come across a glut but are not prepared. I've filled a sandwich wrapper with cherry tree sap more than once, and a billy can with chalk when in the Wiltshire woods. It seems to be catching, at least once a year I get a text from a friend with a picture of their coat pockets crammed full of oak galls picked for me.

Trust your feelings

Listen to advice on foraging, but also to your own intuition. Humans have always tended wild places and we belong there: we are nature too! Sometimes it is correct to just walk along and not gather, for no obvious reason. It is worth trusting this feeling. Some people vocally ask permission and give thanks on entering places to forage, others interact silently, or just straightforwardly. The guideline is to do your foraging wholeheartedly, whatever your personal style.

Be prepared

Lastly, have the right kit for the terrain, weather and season. For me, summer on the beach in the southern UK means I need to bring sandals, a sun hat and a bag for shells and stones to forage successfully. In the winter visiting Skye, it means hiking boots, a backpack, full waterproofs, a head torch and telling my friend what time to expect me home – dusk there falls quickly and early.

A dedicated foraging notebook will feed your imagination once you are back at home, so a notebook and camera or phone are handy to record locations and observations. You can switch the phone to airplane mode, so that it doesn't intrude.

A wicker basket, secateurs, scissors, a trowel, yoghurt tubs and reused plastic bags can all be of use when gathering. Masks and gloves can be useful for dusty situations. Carrying some bags with you means you can take litter home with you, too: a kindness to the land.

> " **Welcome to the territory. Now we have the lay of the land, it's time to get elemental.** "

Art can save the day

The history of conquest and colonization is a sorry one. So many wild landscapes and indigenous ways of life, including rich cultural and artistic traditions, were quashed or destroyed across the globe. Others persisted despite these invasions, and many still flourish to this day. Over centuries, the ruling classes of my country, Britain, played their part in this destruction of nature and culture. So, it is my pleasure and duty as an ordinary person of good will, who loves art and people, to play my part in reversing this through my creative practice. For instance, by putting tactile, natural materials back in the hands of everyday people, for almost no cost. By empowering and supporting artists from diverse backgrounds whenever possible, and showcasing their work. By showing that ecologically sound and so-called waste materials can often take the place of the environmentally disastrous plastic tools and paints of modernity. By demonstrating through my books and courses that we are all part of nature, a family that goes far beyond the only-human world, and back in time long before the first person picked up a lump of charcoal from the hearth and drew around their hand.

I trust you to find the best way to use the methods and materials in this book to help you craft a more beautiful world for us all. You get the picture. You can make the picture.

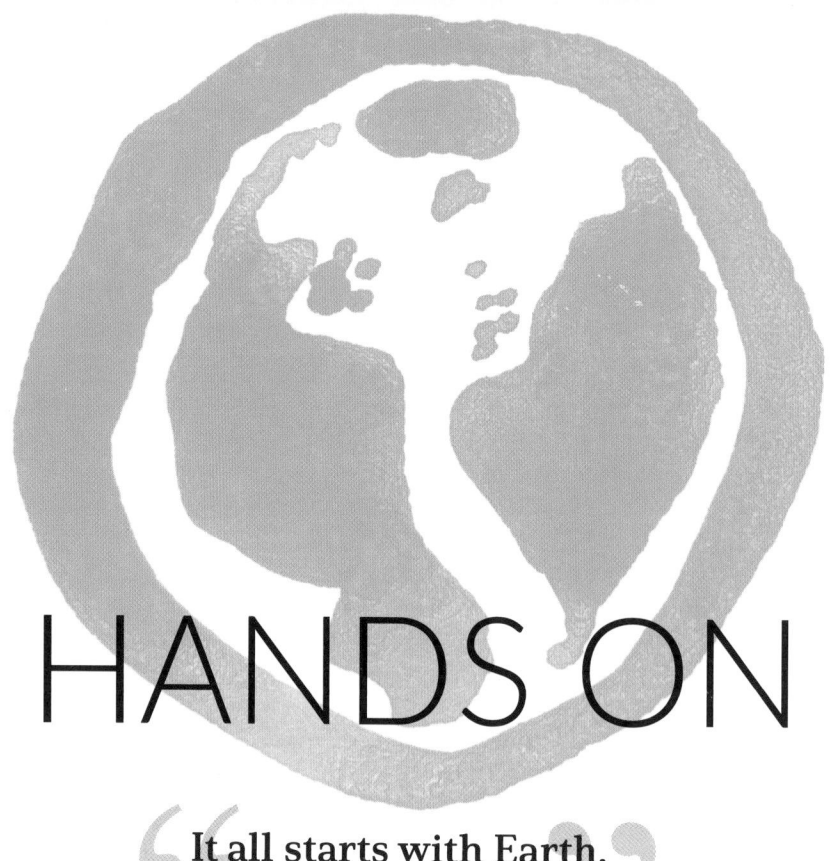

HANDS ON

It all starts with Earth.

It all starts with Earth. The place where we are, the ground beneath our feet, it's what everything we have is made from. Earth is the foundational element so it's a good place to start our materials-making journey.

Transforming earth, clay, rocks, plant materials, charcoal or chalk into pigment can bring us into a deeper connection with the place where we live and the landscapes through which we move. For contemporary people, used to swiping on phones and often starved of tactile richness, the sensation of crushing and refining raw materials can be a source of real delight and awakening.

In my first book, *Found and Ground*, we took earth and gum or eggs and turned them into paint. Here, approaching simple science hands-on through an experiential lens, we'll be turning pigments into pastels via old and new recipes.

Pastels are a great way to make drawings rich with immediacy and colour. The preparation time is spent making the crayons, but once a set is made and dried, there's nothing quicker than pastels for getting a sketch onto paper, as no water is needed. The mixing is done with the hands through blending, or in the eye via optical mixing, as in works by the Impressionists. Pastels are eminently portable, with just a little thought about protective padding.

But first, can we draw with just the raw earth itself, nothing added, no special tools at all? Yes, we can, and it's the oldest way to make art in the world.

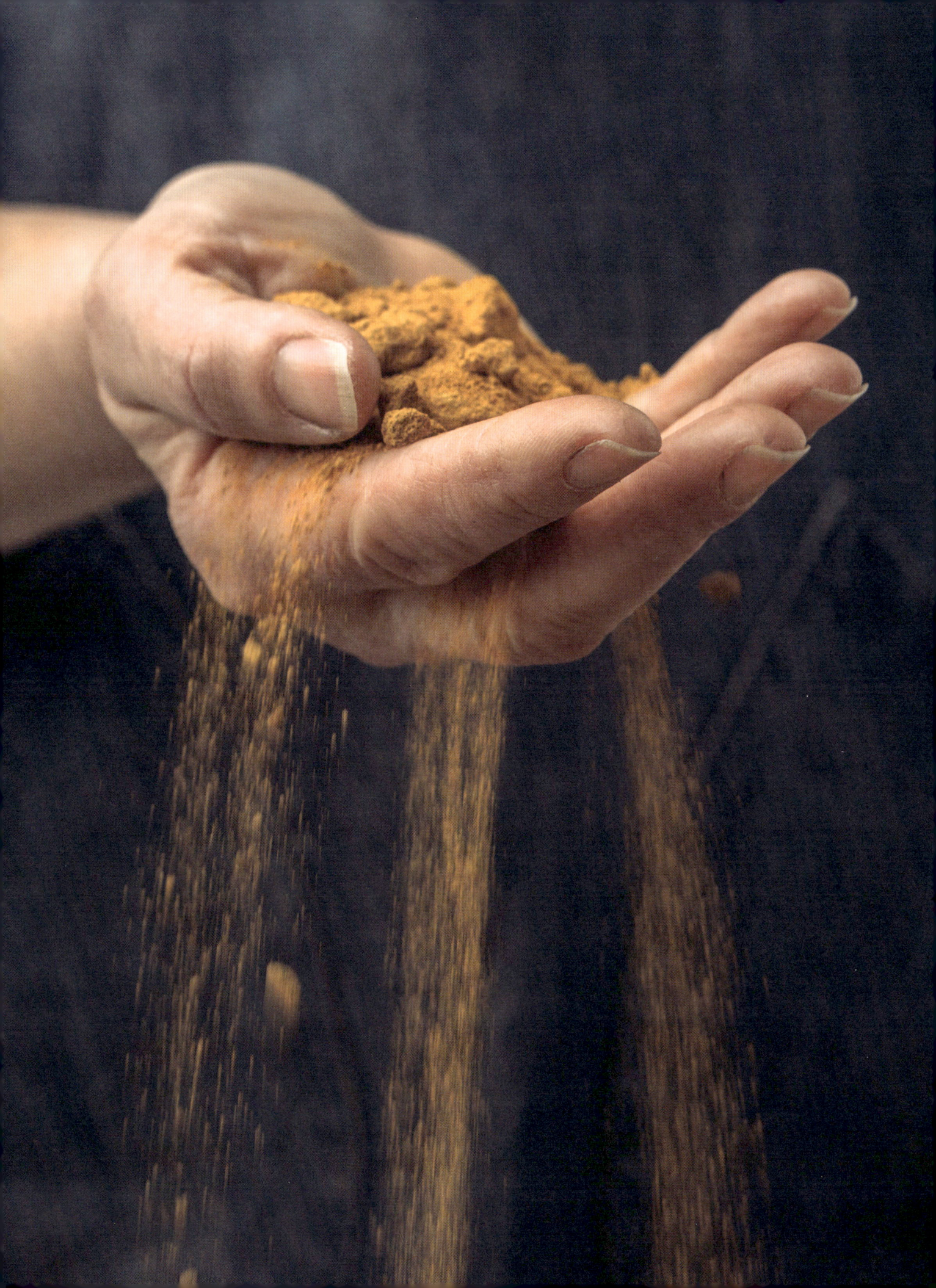

LUMP MEDIA

This is the home of colourful rocks and blackest burnt wood, soft stones and crumbly white chalk. These are often called 'lump media' simply because they are lumps which you hold in your fingers to draw! If you can remember back to being a young child, you may recall the sensation of holding big chunks of chalk to scrawl on the playground to draw hopscotch grids.

If you hail from Italy, France, Iran or England's Forest of Dean, you may be lucky enough to live near huge deposits of colourful ochres, where the lumps of bright earth are both easy to find and deeply pigmented. The famous colours of Sienna, Hormuz, Roussillon or Clearwell are rightly famous and have inspired artists for millennia.

Lump media are often what were used to draw the roving aurochs and galloping horses on rock walls in cave art across the globe. They were also the go-to drawing materials of Renaissance artists in Europe: sanguine, bole and rosso Ercolano allowed them to conjure red chalk sketches of models in complex poses and exquisite detail.

The advantages of simple lump media are their immediacy, simplicity and relative low cost. You may be able to find something to use near you, but even if you buy some sanguine with which to draw, you'll be amazed at the difference between using raw natural materials compared with coloured pencils or oil pastels.

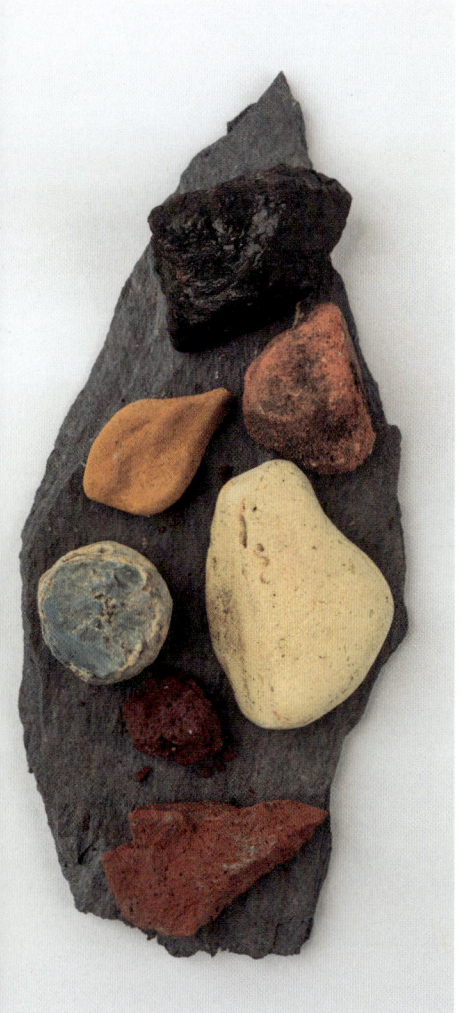

Where to find lump media

It is surprisingly easy to find basic materials in urban, rural and waterside settings.

Urban brick Crumbly brick from beneath old walls and demolitions can be an excellent basic terracotta red drawing tool. If it's too hard to draw with on paper, it can be crushed to make a pastel.

Hillside chalk In many areas of the world, chalk and other soft calcium rich rocks are found near the surface, and can be easily picked up as pebbles. In southern England they are found in ridges running east to west across the country.

Ochre in gravels and paths Look beneath your feet on walks and hikes: orange and yellow ochres are often found among the materials used to make paths in parks. Similarly, footfall on trails often expose brightly coloured soft rocks beneath the soil.

Charcoal This can be found in lumps close to home in your barbecue or firepit. Areas regenerating from forest fires can also be a source of drawing charcoal. They can be a poignant opportunity to reconnect with landscapes you love which have undergone drastic change and renewal.

Clays Clays of many different colours can be found in riverbeds, alongside ditches and beside lakes. Clay is found almost everywhere in the world, and pottery is ubiquitous. Check old maps, and keep an eye out for old placenames like Kiln Road and Clay Lane – the clay is often right under our feet, and a windblown upturned tree can reveal it.

Haematite and ochres These wash up on beaches as pebbles. Just test them against a harder rock to see if they easily leave a mark, or better still, take a sketchbook to the beach!

Other approaches

Kauae Raro Research Collective and Naimeh Ghabaie both delve deeply into the meaning of place-based culture and materials, helping counteract the influence of mass-produced goods by bringing a love of specific land and colour into the heart of their work.

Kauae Raro Research Collective

In *Aotearoa*/New Zealand, this group of indigenous contemporary artists/activists inspire me and thousands of people worldwide with their creativity and writing. This is achieved by diverse means such as reclaiming traditional uses of earth pigments for adornment, or describing how the respectful collection of *whenua* (land), such as ochres or clays, fosters a deeper relationship with *whakapapa* (layers of ancestry, deep connection and belonging to place).

They work with the abundant coloured earths and rocks of their country to create art, to teach and restore knowledge of earth-based art practices, and to create guides for contemporary Māori to reconnect with their *whenua* through art. Their colourful website (see page 128) and instructional videos share great information on pigments, Māori culture, natural paints, plus a host of beautiful rocks and earths in the wild, bringing joy to people as they connect with them.

(see page 128)

Kauae Raro Research Collective are a group of *wāhine* Māori who have been promoting customary paint-making since 2019.

Naimeh Ghabaie

These pictures below give an insight into the materials of Lebanese artist Naimeh Ghabaie – raw rocks, the processed pigments, and the place from which they were collected, Naimeh's birthplace, the Zagros Mountains.

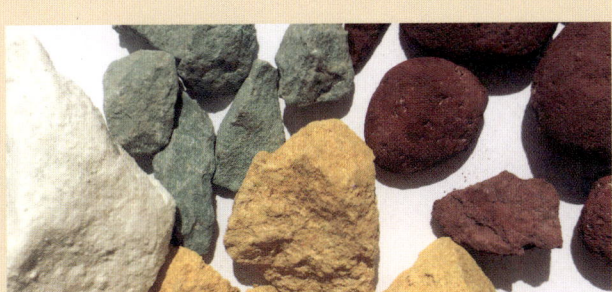

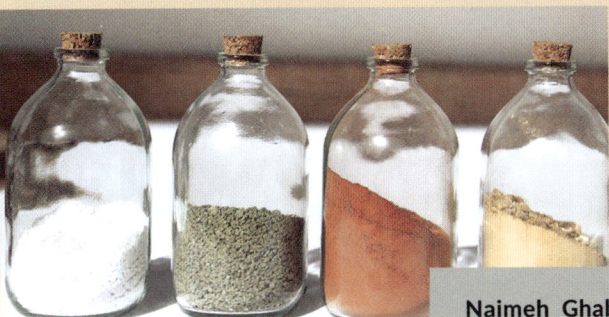

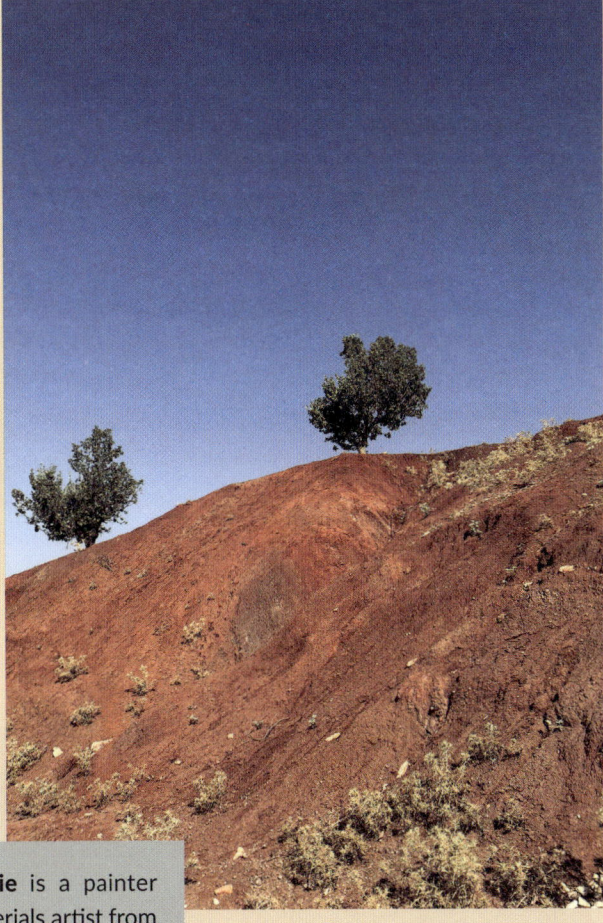

Naimeh Ghabaie is a painter and natural materials artist from Lebanon. She currently lives in Paris, France.

Lump media to try

Chalk, red earths and charcoal are obvious contenders for both the simplest and the most ancient drawing media. You might also find stones soft enough to work with on the sea or lake shore. Clay, however gloopy and wet, will make a lovely lump medium when dry. Even a crumbly old brick can be used as a pigment, the older the better. Although your local geology may be very different, there is sure to be something to find.

 Below are a selection of lump media – most very easily found – and the marks they make. For ease of comparison, these marks are all worked on the same paper: Ingres 160gsm (98lb) pastel paper.

FORAGED OBJECT	RESULTING MARK
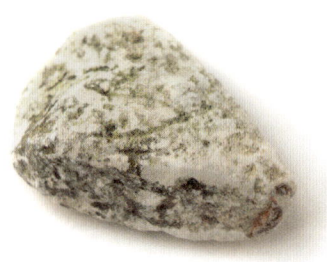 CHALK	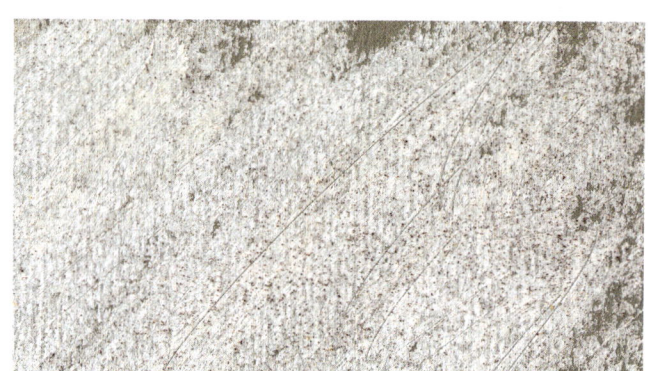
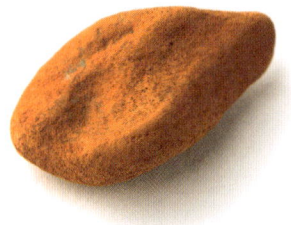 OCHRE	
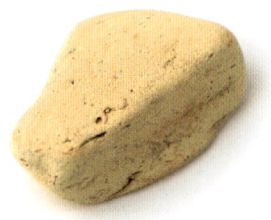 BEACH PEBBLE	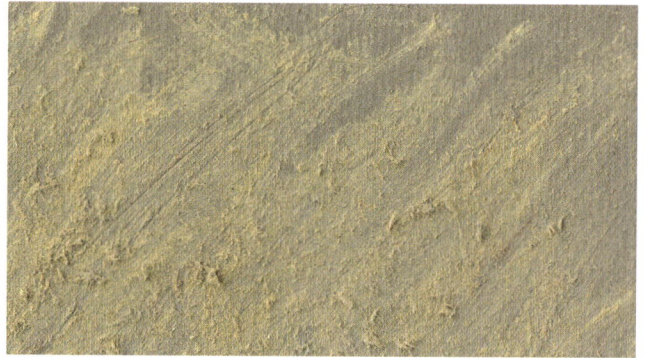

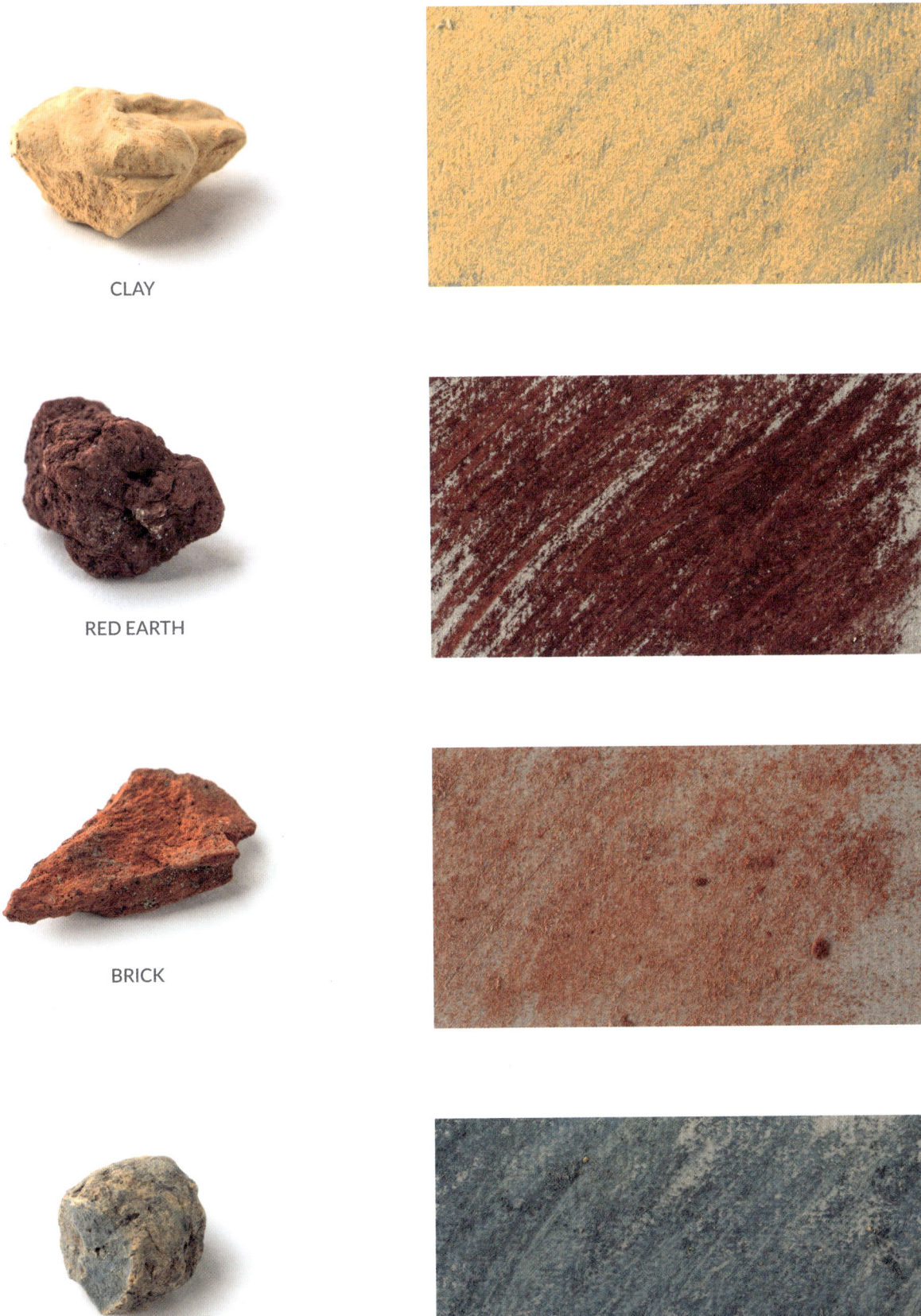

CLAY

RED EARTH

BRICK

VIVIANITE

Using lump media

There really is no limit to how we can use these wild crayons from nature. Break them up into shapes and sizes you like for the drawing you have planned. Renaissance artists often sharpened lumps of red ochre or chalk to a fine point for finer hatching marks – but if you're doing a huge mural, then leave them big. Experiment and see what works for you.

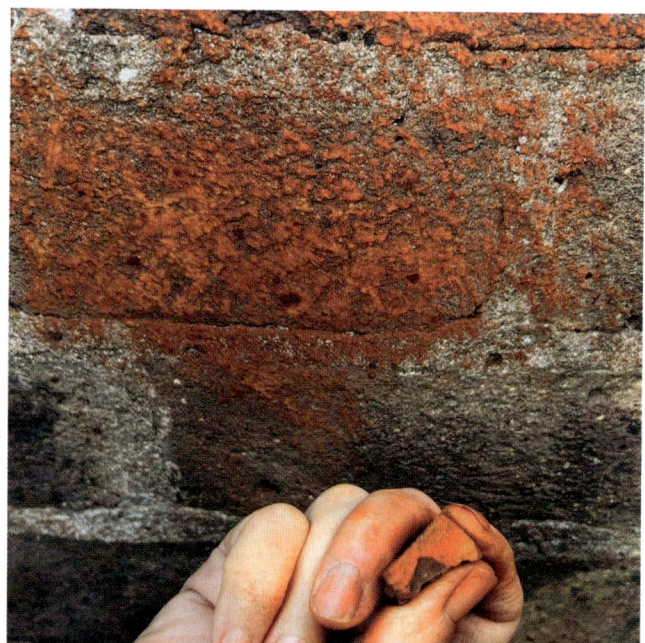

Testing stone

It's handy to have a favourite stone, something with a bit of texture, on which you can test your found stones for colour and softness. Mine, shown to the right, comes from the beach at Burntisland, Scotland. If it leaves a mark on the stone, then try it on good quality paper too. Don't worry if it's not soft enough to draw with on paper; we can still use it for pigment to make pastels.

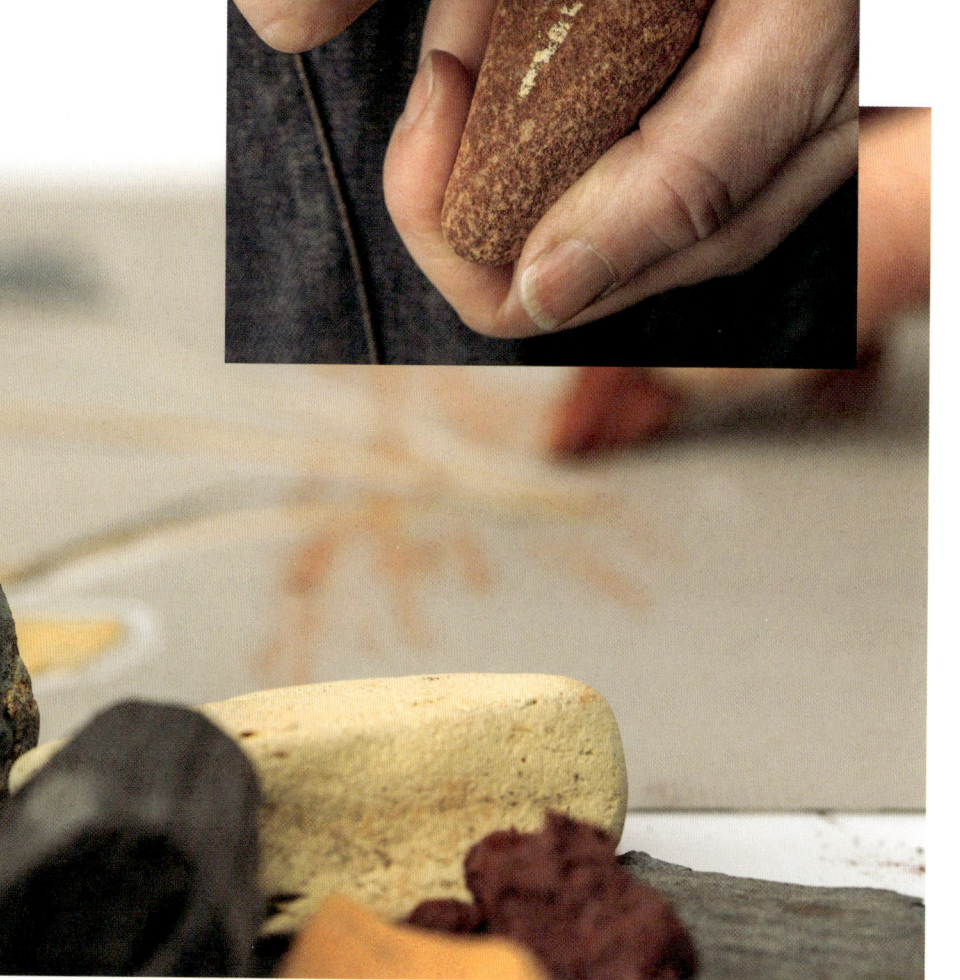

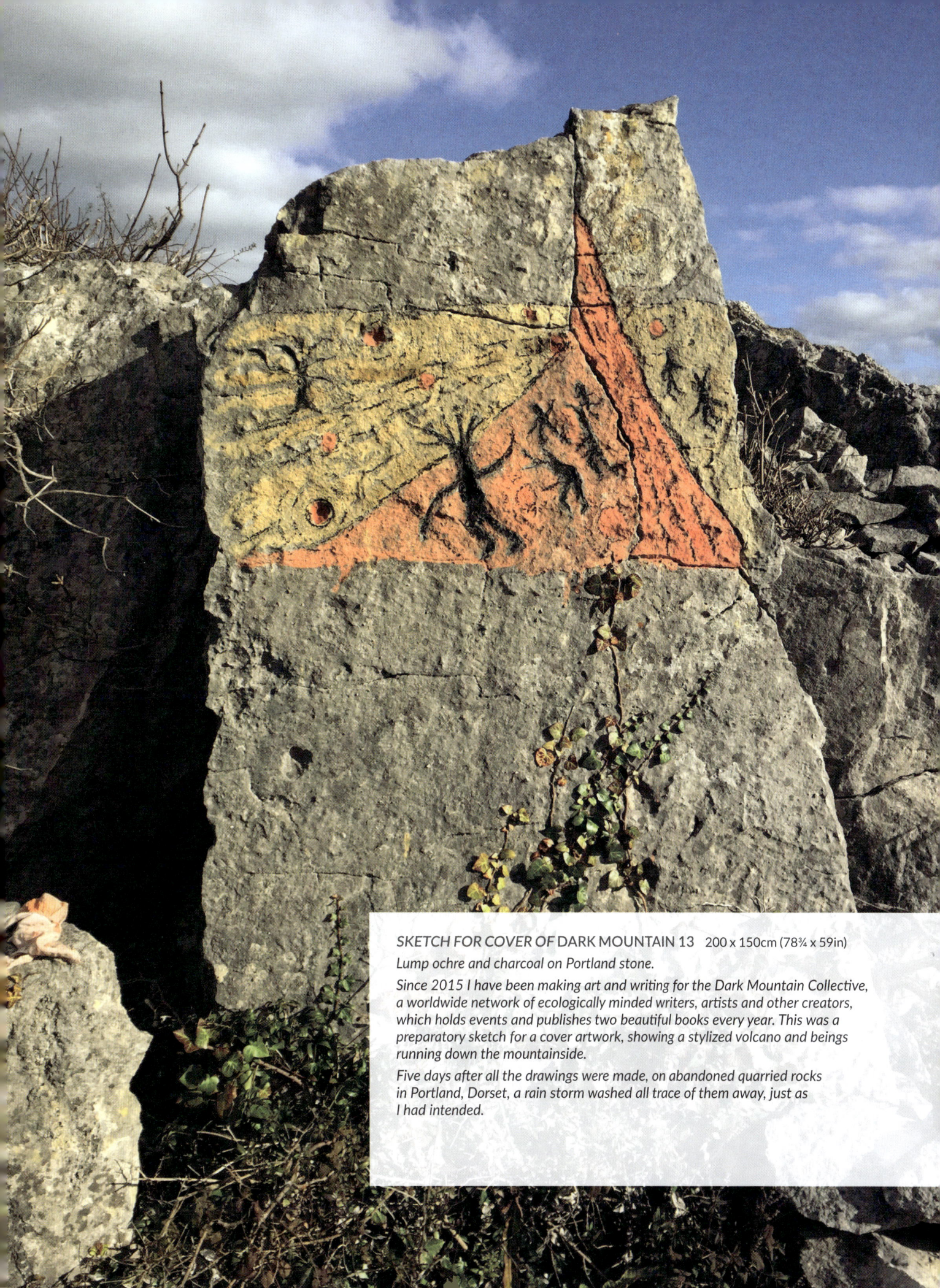

SKETCH FOR COVER OF DARK MOUNTAIN 13 200 x 150cm (78¾ x 59in)
Lump ochre and charcoal on Portland stone.

*Since 2015 I have been making art and writing for the Dark Mountain Collective,
a worldwide network of ecologically minded writers, artists and other creators,
which holds events and publishes two beautiful books every year. This was a
preparatory sketch for a cover artwork, showing a stylized volcano and beings
running down the mountainside.*

*Five days after all the drawings were made, on abandoned quarried rocks
in Portland, Dorset, a rain storm washed all trace of them away, just as
I had intended.*

Preparing pigment

Earth pigments are commercially available from most art and craft stores, and they are identical to what you will gather yourself. You can therefore follow the techniques here with your own foraged pigments, or use bought pigments and skip these stages. All you need to prepare your own pigments is explained here, but for more in-depth information, see my previous book, *Found and Ground*.

The process is simple: grind your pigments as shown below, and either sieve them dry through a flat screen-type sieve, or mix them in plenty of water to pour them through a culinary sieve. Finely-ground earth pigments are best, so use a 100 micron or finer sieve (see opposite) for the smoothest artists' quality pastels.

Put any remaining pigment (which did not pass through the sieve) in a jar of clean water and leave it to settle. You can then gently pour off the excess water, leaving a sediment. This can be reground, or used for paint or more coarsely textured pastels.

Tools needed

Lump media, pestle and mortar, fine sieve, container

Useful extras:

Teaspoon, jar of water, mask (if working indoors)

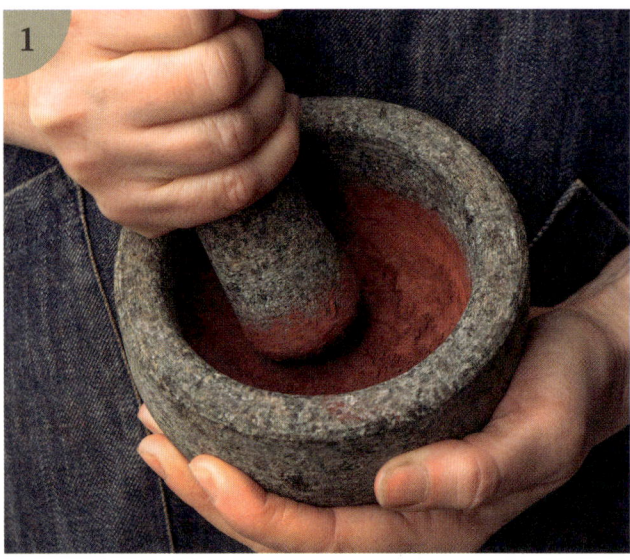

1 Use a pestle and mortar to break up and grind down your gathered lump media.

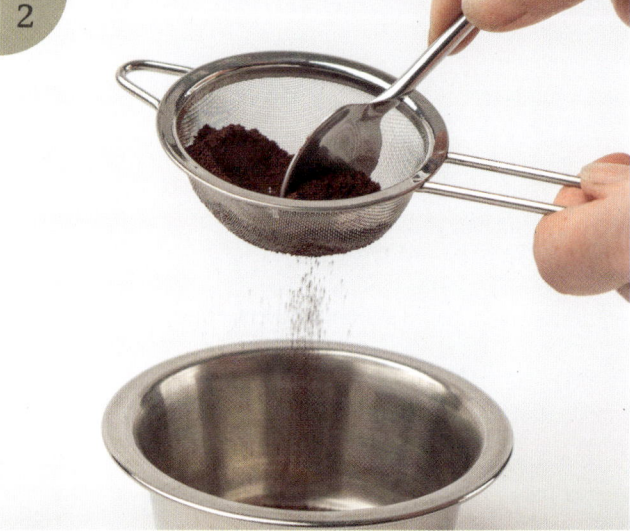

2 Grind down the stone to a fine powder; then run it through a fine sieve. The finer your sieve, the finer the resulting pigment.

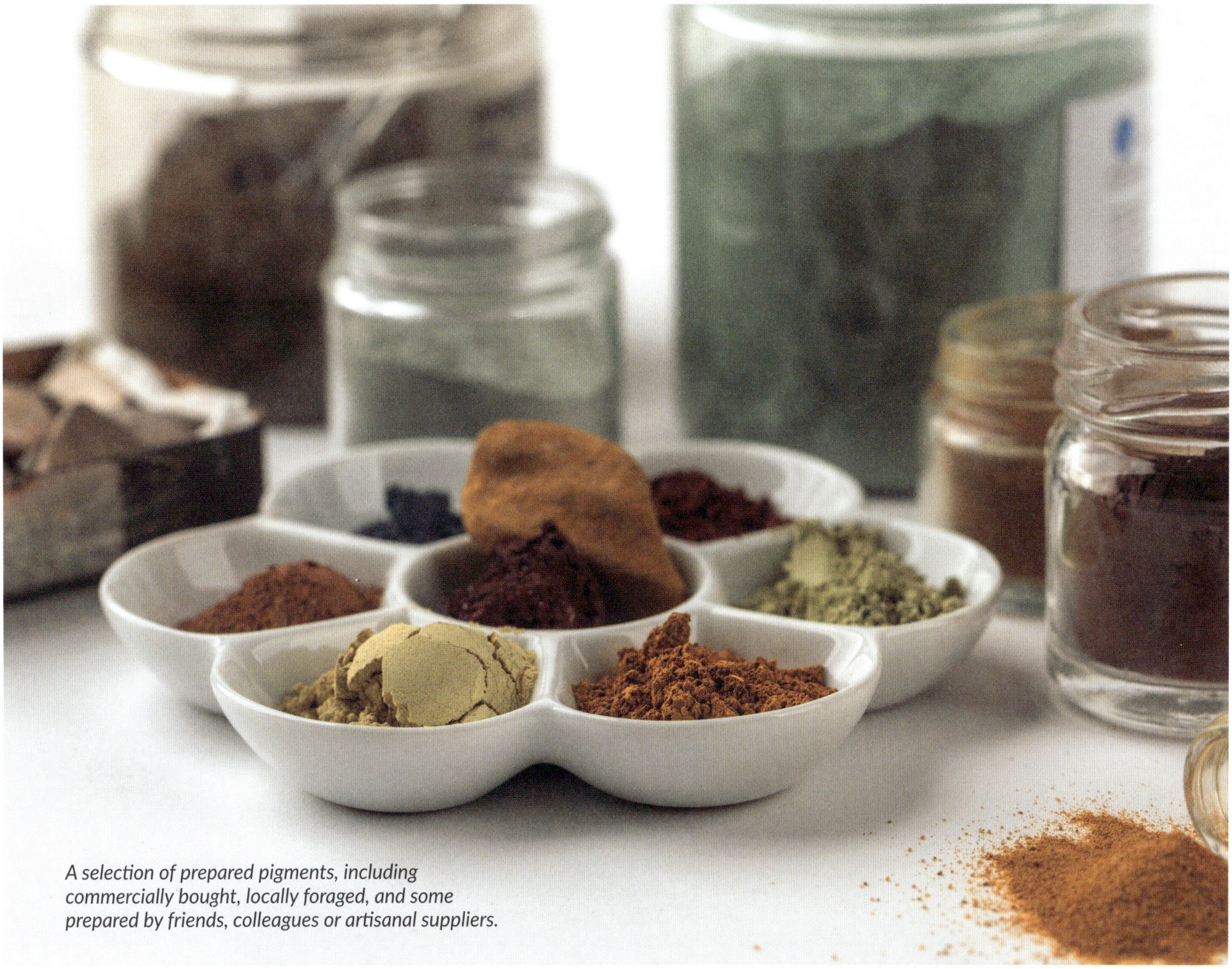

A selection of prepared pigments, including commercially bought, locally foraged, and some prepared by friends, colleagues or artisanal suppliers.

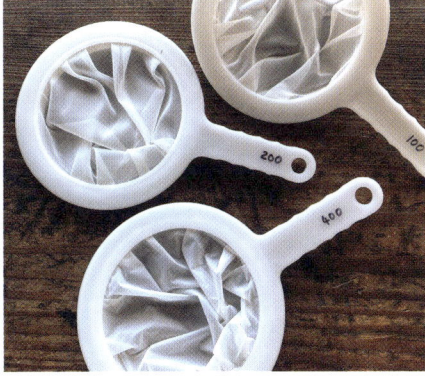

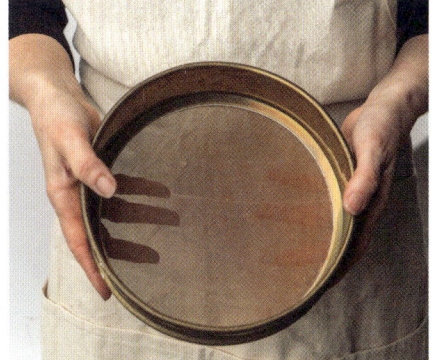

Sieves

Traditionally, pigments were passed through fine muslin cloth, but this is a dusty business. Inexpensive, washable, durable 200 and 100 micron sieves (often labelled 200 and 100 mesh) can be bought from catering suppliers or online and used to refine your freshly ground pigments instead. For a professional quality result, you could buy a 100 micron sieve.

Flora Arbuthnott's approach

You can create simple colourful tools by adding your refined powdered pigments to melted beeswax or soy wax and pouring the mixture into moulds, such as old ice cube trays. The resulting wax crayons are ideal for making interesting resist effects or for use by adults or children, and are a great first step towards making pastels, which we will look at next.

My friend and colleague Flora Arbuthnott brings a wealth of knowledge of growing and using plants for dyes and colour into her art and materials and encourages others to connect to the richness of botanical colour. She uses her pigments to make beautiful wax crayons and her method is shown below:

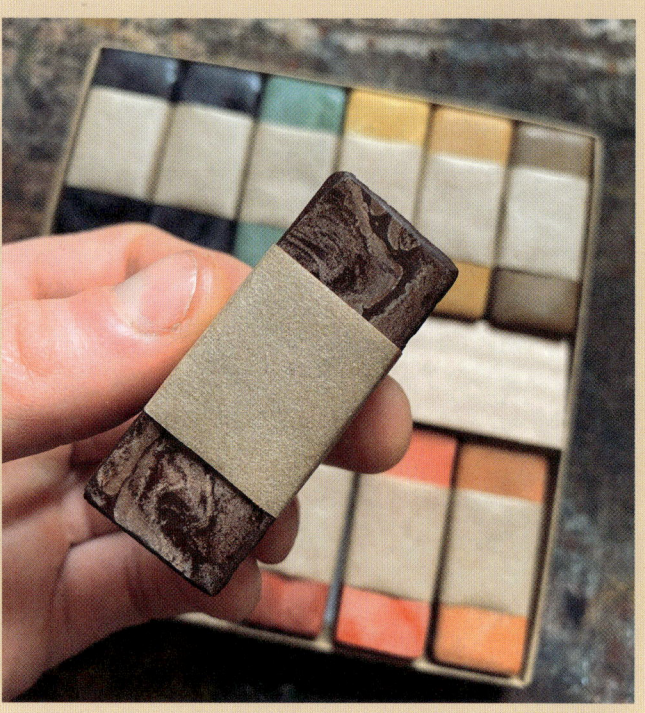

Making wax crayons

To make wax crayons, simply mix dry, finely ground pigment with melted wax and set this wax in a mould. I use a mixture of soy wax and beeswax. Add more soy wax for a softer crayon, or more beeswax for a harder crayon. Not all natural pigments combine well with the wax, so experiment with small amounts first.

1 Find, make, or buy powdered pigment (see pages 26–27).

2 Place the wax in a flat-bottomed plastic container (such as old food packaging), then melt the wax, using a bain-marie or double boiler to ensure you do not burn it.

3 Fill another, smaller, plastic container with the chosen pigment – either pure or a mixture. Retain and reuse a separate small plastic container for each colour so they won't need washing up.

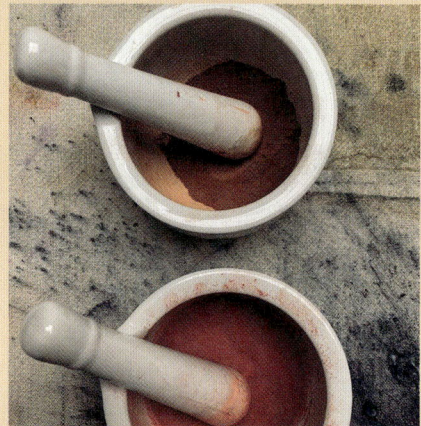

4 Mix the melted wax into the powdered pigment. The optimum ratio depends on the type of pigment you are using; between 1:1 to 1:3 pigment to wax works well. I mix by eye rather than measuring exactly, and tend to start with 1:1 wax to pigment, and adjust. Adding more wax will make the crayons paler.

5 If the wax hardens before you have mixed properly, re-float the container on the bain-marie to re-melt the wax. Once combined, pour the mixture of wax and pigment into a mould. DIY moulds include ice cube trays or the chopped-off fingers of a rubber glove! Silicone moulds also work well. You can buy these in many different shapes.

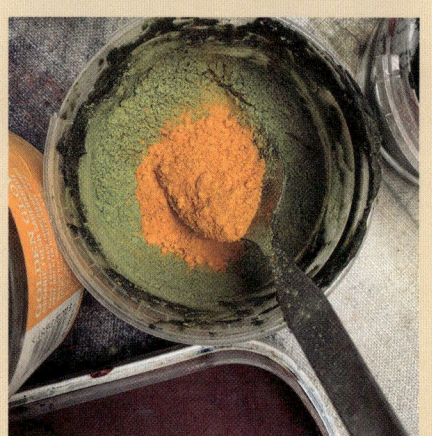

6 Let the wax dry completely in the mould – resist the temptation to put your fingers in the wet wax! Very hot wax added to the mould will shrink in size as it cools. You can pour in more wax to fill the hole if you want an even shape.

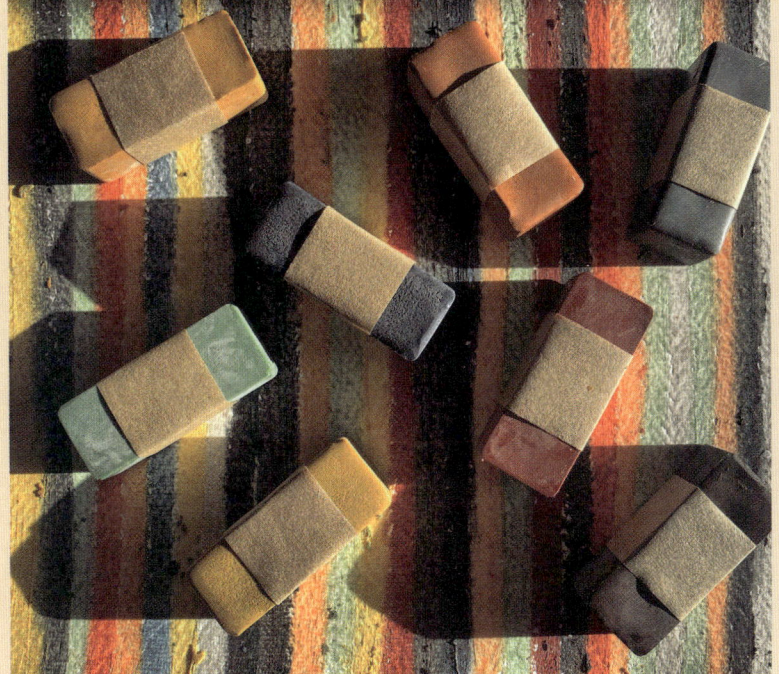
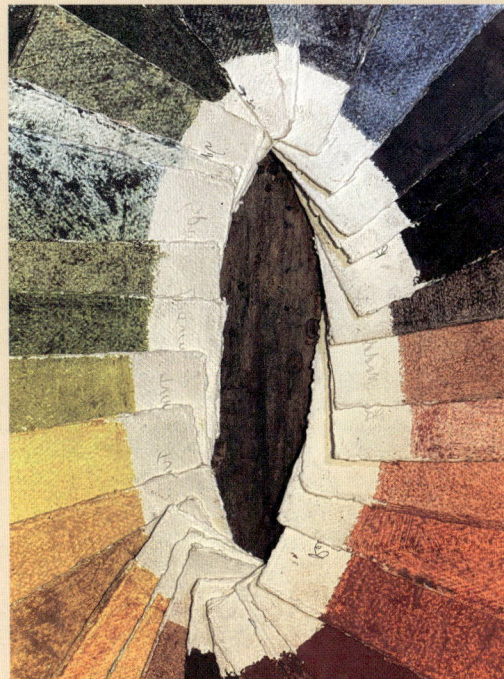

Finished wax crayons, ready to label, are shown above; and swatches made from them can be seen to the right.

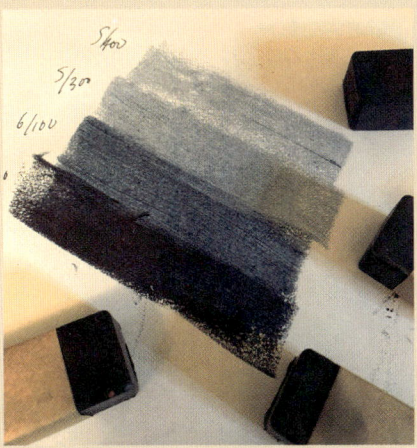
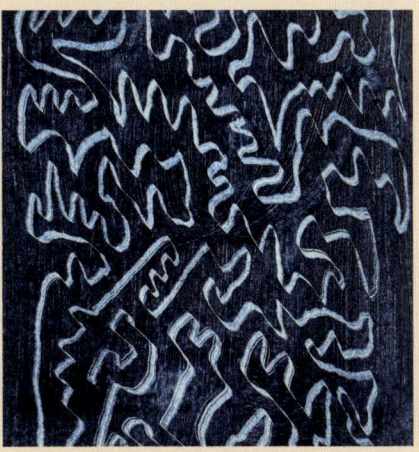
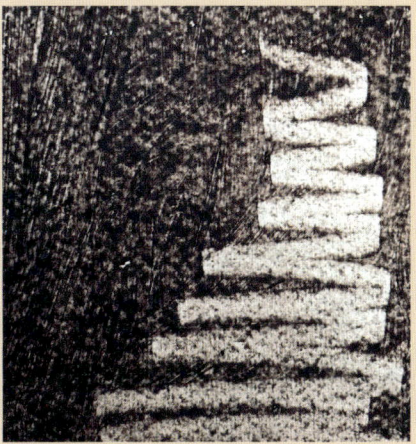

From left to right:

Indigo crayons and swatches; scratching back into an indigo crayon background; marks made with a crayon created from King Alfred's cakes fungus spores.

Flora Arbuthnott is an artist, dye plant grower and expert in botanical colours, living in Devon, UK. She started Plants and Colour as a place to teach her skills both online and in person and now hosts guest tutors, such as Caroline, to share their knowledge on her platform.

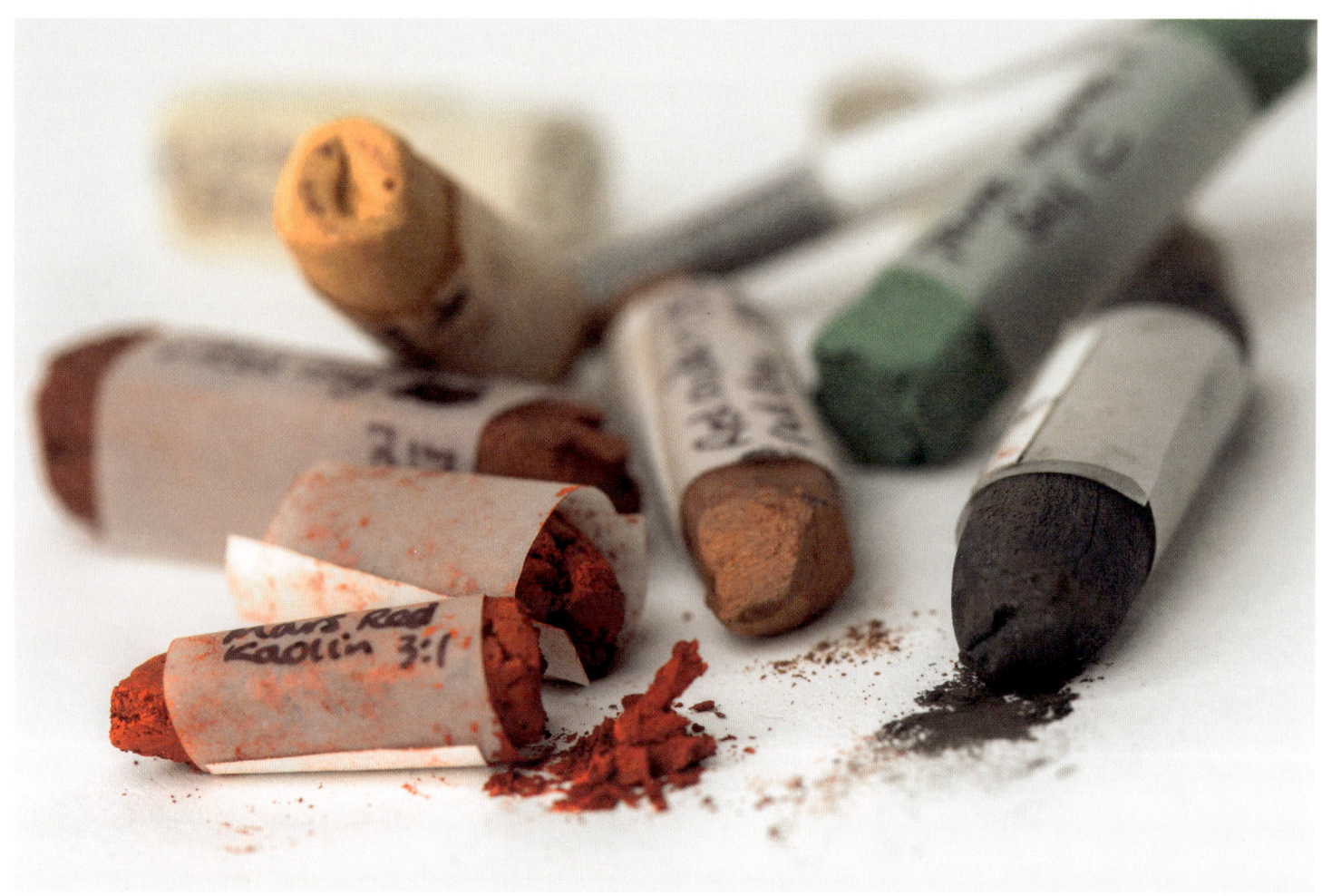

PASTELS

Pastels are simple, highly coloured tools that are easy to make and use. The word pastel derives from the Latin for paste, *pastellus*, which refers to the way in which pastel crayons are made: by mixing pigments with binders and water to form an easily mouldable paste, which is then formed into a stick, cylinder or decorative shape.

Patels have been used by artists since the Renaissance in Europe and have been popular worldwide since the nineteenth century. Earlier artists would often make preparatory sketches with pastel, then continue with paint – but later artists saw the potential in pastels as luminous, expressive painting media in their own right, Amongst the most notable are Odilon Redon, Mary Cassatt, Edgar Degas and, more recently, Paula Rego.

We'll be making a couple of different kinds of pastel. You can incorporate foraged as well as bought pigments, and perhaps add some surprising ingredients from inside the home. First we'll look at a traditional way of making artists' quality soft pastels using gum tragacanth, an easily sourced art and culinary powdered plant gum. Then we'll look at harder clay-based pastels, somewhat like Conté pastels, which are great for creating a wide range of shades for drawing tonal studies.

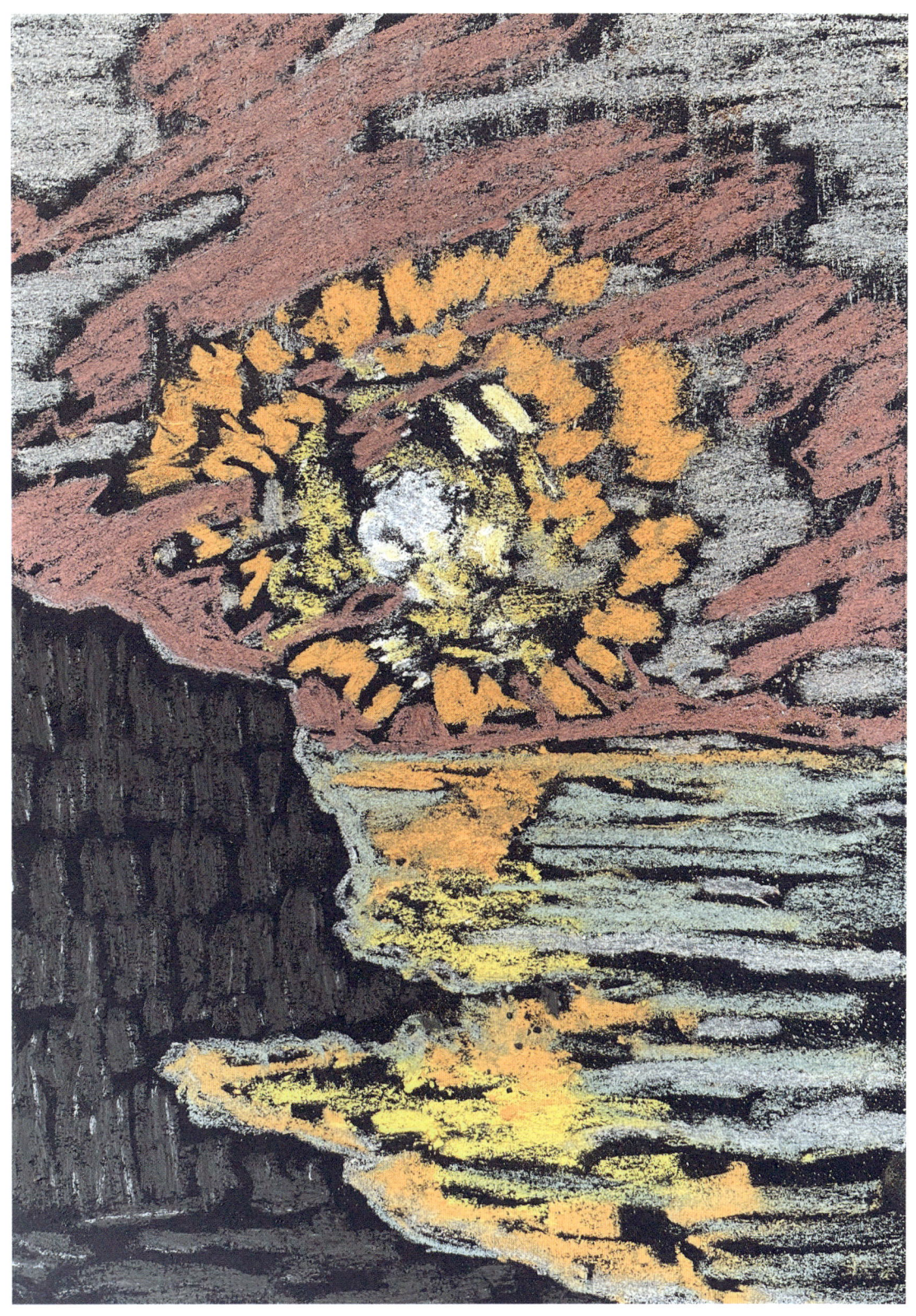

MOONRISE OVER BOY'S ROCK   21 x 30cm (8¼ x 11¾in)
Handmade hard and soft pastels on black paper.

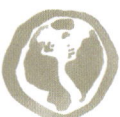

Making soft pastels

There are many recipes for making soft pastels, some dating back to the time of Leonardo Da Vinci. They range from simple pure pigment and water sticks to combinations of powdered gums for binders. The recipes that follow are the methods I use for making my own pastels from pure pigments – whether foraged, swapped with pigment pals worldwide, or shop-bought.

Preparing your binder

Gum tragacanth is a widely used binder for both art and culinary uses. It makes a solution on which to lay colours for marbling papers and forms the basis for ornately sculpted sugar craft as seen on wedding cakes. Extracted from several types of astragalus plant, this useful polysaccharide is not as sticky or shiny as gum Arabic (another binder), so is ideal as a gentle binder that allows soft pastels to leave a mark on paper. Follow the simple instructions below to make a set of solutions of varying strengths with which to bind different pigments.

Tools needed

Pigment, gum tragacanth, water, dropper/pipette, mixing slab, jug, palette knife, measuring spoons, thin cardboard, hand-held or jug-style electric blender

Useful extras:

Water spray bottle, flat-edged culinary scraper (such as for cutting dough or smoothing icing)

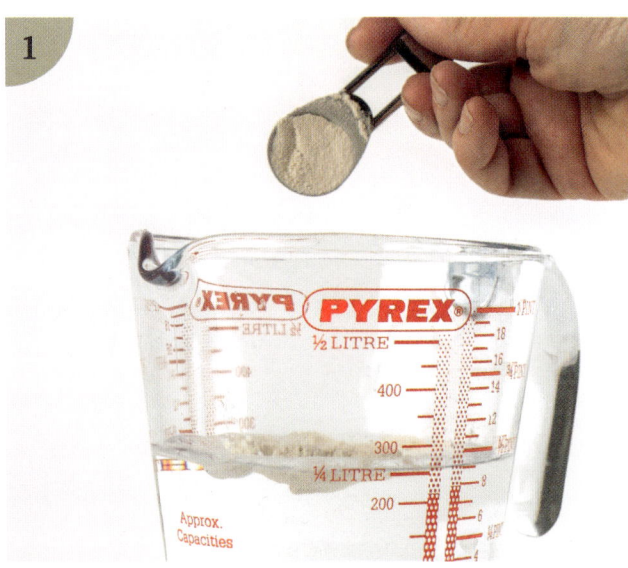

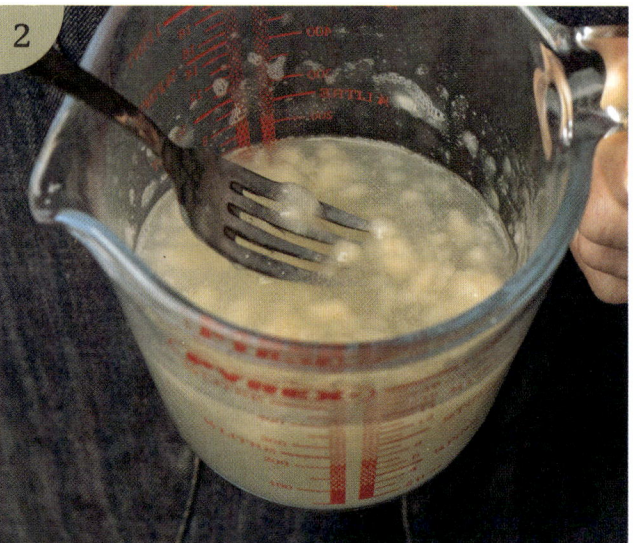

1 In a large jug, add 10g (¼oz) gum tragacanth to 250ml (½pt) of water, and gently stir. Don't worry that it doesn't dissolve. Leave it to absorb the water, ideally overnight.

2 The mixture should look lumpy and gelatinous, as shown. Once it reaches this stage, you need to use a blender to mix it to an even, creamy consistency – a whisk will simply move the lumps about.

Which solution to use

As natural products, both gum tragacanth and earth pigments can vary widely, so there is no firm rule for which solution (see steps 3–4 below) will be right for your chosen pigment. However, you can use the list to the right as a guide for which solution will work best.

Find the listed pigment nearest your own and make small pastels of your pigment using a couple of the likely solutions. Make careful notes about which you used, and test it once dry. This helps to avoid committing a large amount of precious colour to a particular solution, only to find it is too strongly or too weakly bound.

The solutions here follow a centuries-old recipe listed in Ralph Mayer's invaluable book *The Artist's Handbook of Materials and Techniques*, first published in 1940. I have converted the US measurements to metric but do not personally add artificial preservatives, as they are not necessary for dry-stored pastels.

- Sol A: Mars yellow (goethite – yellow iron oxide)
- Sol B: Chalk; burnt umber
- Sol C: Mars black (magnetite – black iron oxide); Mars red (haematite – red iron oxide); graphite
- Sol D: Ivory black (charred blacks such as lamp black, bone black and charcoal); burnt or raw sienna
- Sol E: Red ochre; yellow ochre; clay-like earth colours such as terre verte/green earth; vivianite; raw umber.

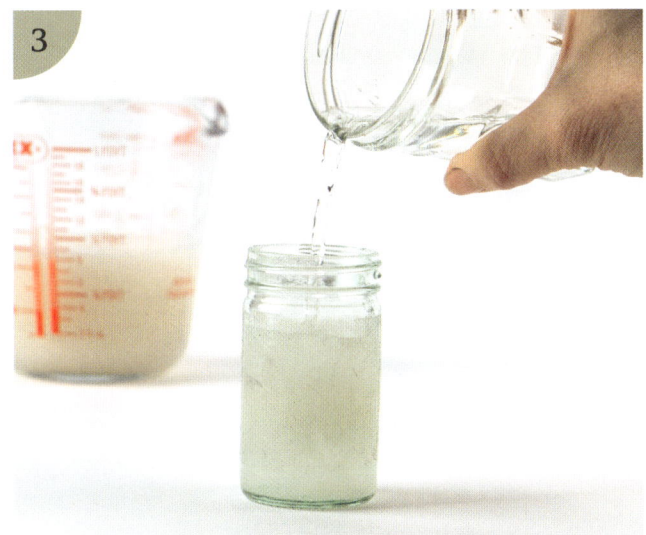

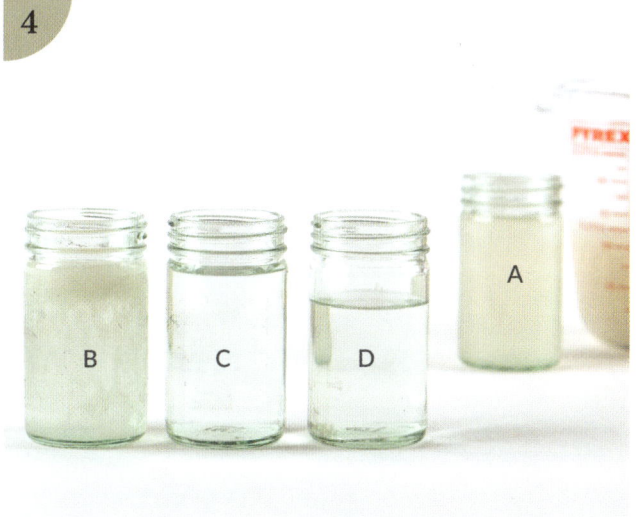

3 We call the resulting liquid 'solution A' or 'Sol A' for short. This is a strong binder and we need to dilute it down to different strengths for different pigments. Combine one part of Sol A with two parts water – this creates Sol B. For instance, mix 125ml (¼pt) of Sol A with 250ml (½pt) water to create Sol B.

4 Repeat the process; combining one part Sol B with two parts water to make Sol C; then combine one part Sol C with two parts water to make Sol D; and repeat the process to create Sol E. Pour the remaining Sol A into another jar, so you have five different binder strength options.

Creating your soft pastel

Professional pastel makers mix large batches at once with pigment almost as wet as a cake batter. They then scoop equally sized dollops of it onto blotting paper, and finish the pastels as a batch when they have dried to a workable consistency. This is a quicker way to make more pastels, once you are sure of your recipe. But for now, we are taking it slowly, one pastel at a time.

The bullet list on the previous page provides a good starting point for which binder to use for your pigment. If you don't see your pigment on the list, or if in doubt, start with Sol C and make a small pastel that will be dry in a day or two, to test. It is important that the paste remains stiff, so start with just a few drops of solution and add it little by little.

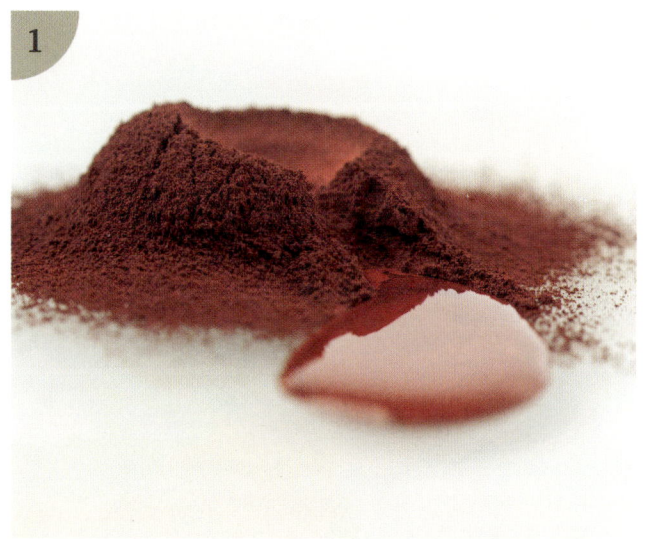

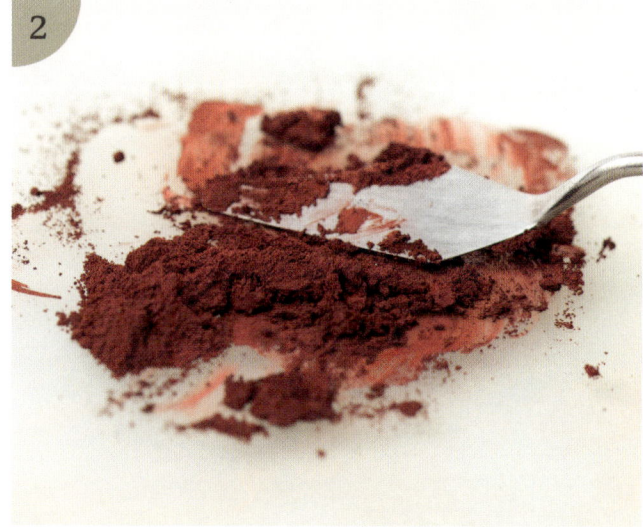

1 On a glass or polished stone surface, sieve around 2tsp of your pigment and form it into a mound. Add ½tsp of binder (refer to the table on page 33 for which solution to use).

2 Use a palette knife to start to combine the two. You are aiming for a stiff paste.

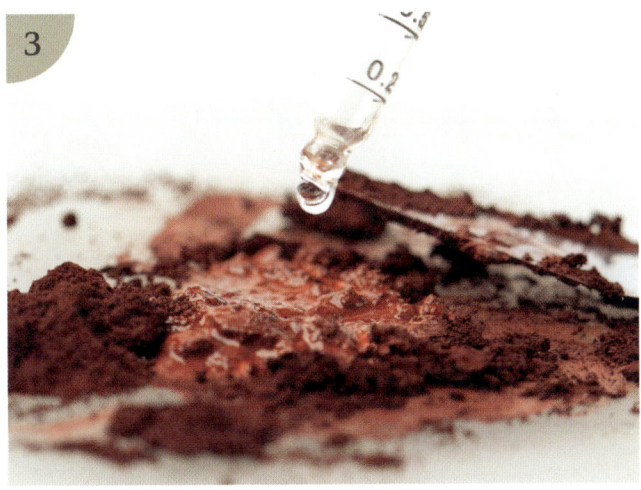

3 Add more solution little by little, then continue to mix, to achieve the correct consistency. A pipette is very useful for this – be careful not to add too much.

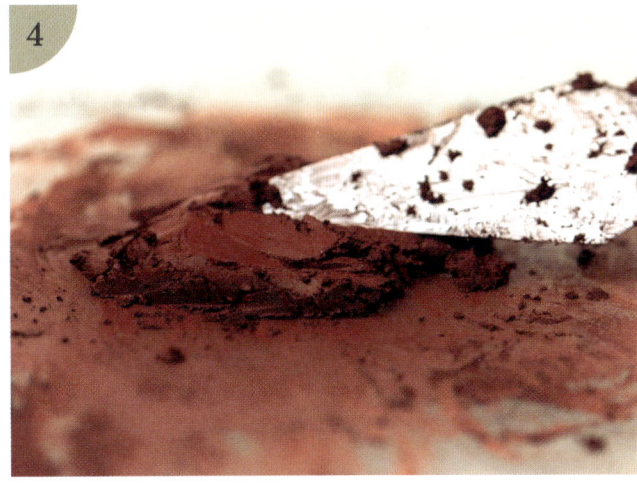

4 Continue working and mixing until you can form it into a block. If it is still matt or crumbly, then it is probably a little too dry. It should be shiny and firm, and hold its shape. A good test is to attempt to polish the surface of the mixture with your palette knife: if it looks nicely glossy and can take a shine, you have the perfect moisture content to form it into your chosen shape.

Tip

If you make the mixture too wet, place it on blotting paper, newspaper or a coffee filter to absorb some of the excess liquid. This will take a couple of hours.

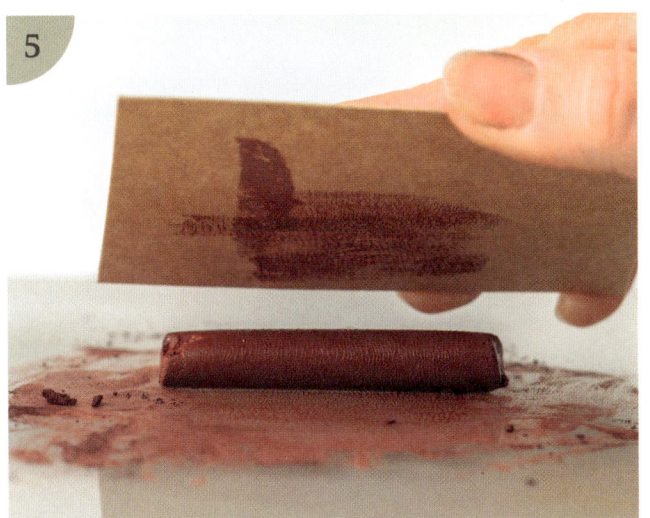

5 Using a piece of packaging cardboard (the shiny surface of a cereal packet or the inside of a milk carton makes them ideal), gently roll the block into the pastel stick shape. Keep your fingers aligned with the pastel to ensure a smooth result.

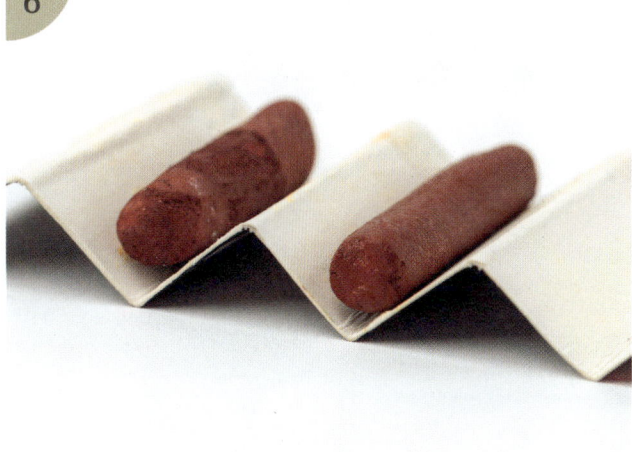

6 Place the pastel carefully on a folded concertina of cardboard, then repeat the process to make more, if you wish to. Leave them to dry in a warm place, out of direct sunlight. They will be ready when they are dry to the touch – generally after a day or two. You can turn them halfway through the process to help speed things along.

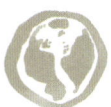

Making hard pastels

When a more accurate line is needed, hard pastels have been used for hundreds of years, as these clay-based pastels sharpen to a point and do not crumble. (Conté-style crayons, developed more recently, work in a similar way.) These hard pastels are also good for drawing on harder surfaces such as stone, found wood or board. The clay you use, whether foraged or bought from potters' suppliers, should be dry, finely sieved and even. See opposite for more information on clays.

Make a test pastel of pure clay from each clay you can find and test them for hardness, colour, mark-making and adhesion. Next, experiment with mixing them with your favourite pigments until you get the perfect hard pastel. As you can see here, it is a wonderfully simple method. It is also very versatile – you can even use old powder eye shadows as pigment: just smash them finely.

Tools needed

Clay, pigment, water, dropper/pipette, mixing slab, palette knife, measuring spoons, thin cardboard

Useful extras:

Water spray bottle, flat-edged culinary scraper

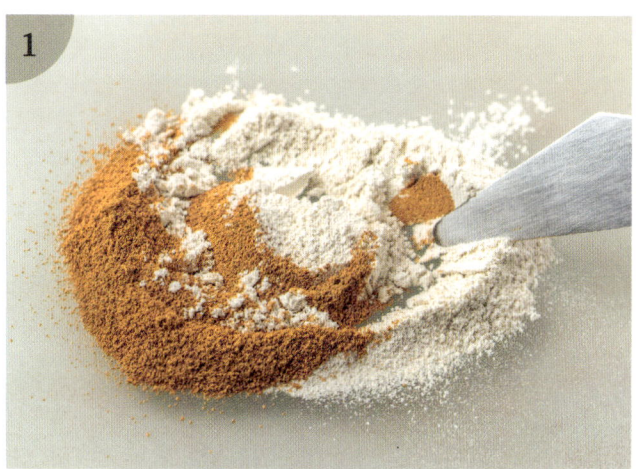

1 Place 1tsp of sieved clay and 1tsp of your sieved pigment on a smooth glass (or stone) surface. Mix these dry ingredients together.

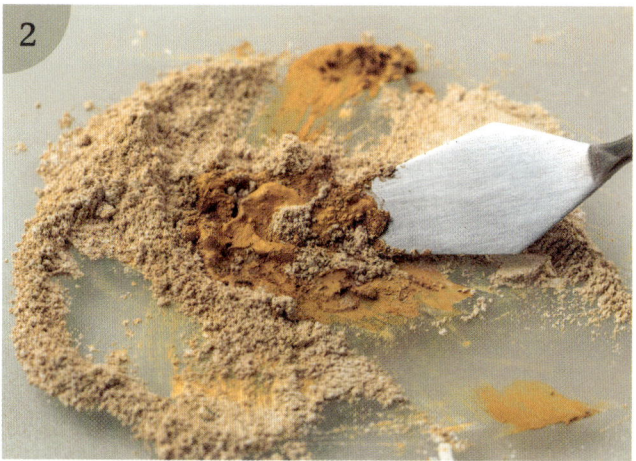

2 Once you have an even mix, add ½tsp of water and use a palette knife to begin to combine the two on the surface.

Clays

Clay can be found somewhere in almost every country – in rivers, pits, geological seams, glacial moraines, gardens, roadworks, fields and ponds. Most clay is suitable for adding to pastels so long as it is clean and not from a polluted source.

To clean natural clay, simply mix it with water into a slurry, then pass it through a fine sieve to remove grit and organic matter. When it settles, pour off the water, divide the clay into easily usable amounts and place it on paper in a warm place to dry.

You can also buy dried clay from your local potters' suppliers very cheaply, alongside red, black and yellow iron oxide pigments at a fraction of art specialist prices. You can also try natural cosmetics suppliers to find kaolin, which will make very soft textured pastels, or bentonite clay for hardening a pastel mix. Stone dust from your local quarry or powdered chalk can take the place of clay, too.

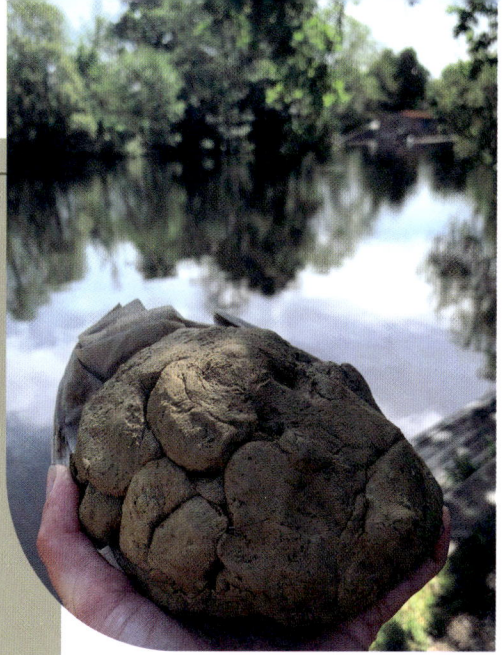

Excess clay from a Found and Ground workshop being returned to the River Dart.

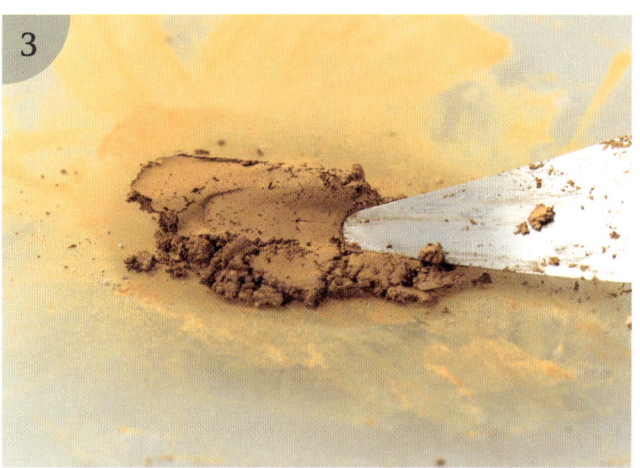

3 Continue adding water drop by drop until the mixture holds together, and you are able to mould it into a stick. The mixture is ready to be shaped when you get a slight gloss on the surface as you draw the knife across it.

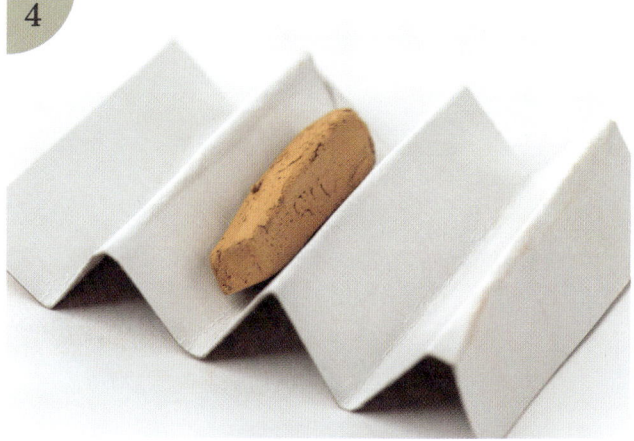

4 Use the knife to shape it into a stick form and place it on a concertina of card to dry.

Subtleties of colour

Tinting and toning soft pastels

Tinting soft pastels is easy and lets you create a pleasingly harmonious set. To minimize the chances of muddying your colours when making several different pastels, start with pale pigments and work towards the darker; finishing with reds and blacks. This helps to make cleaning the slab between pastels much easier. Alternatively, you can deliberately incorporate the last pastel's remnants into the next one, for a truly analogous set.

Creating your own graded pastels is as simple as combining two different pigments in varying proportions. Follow the instructions on the previous pages, but in step 1, make up your 2tsp of pigment from different colours.

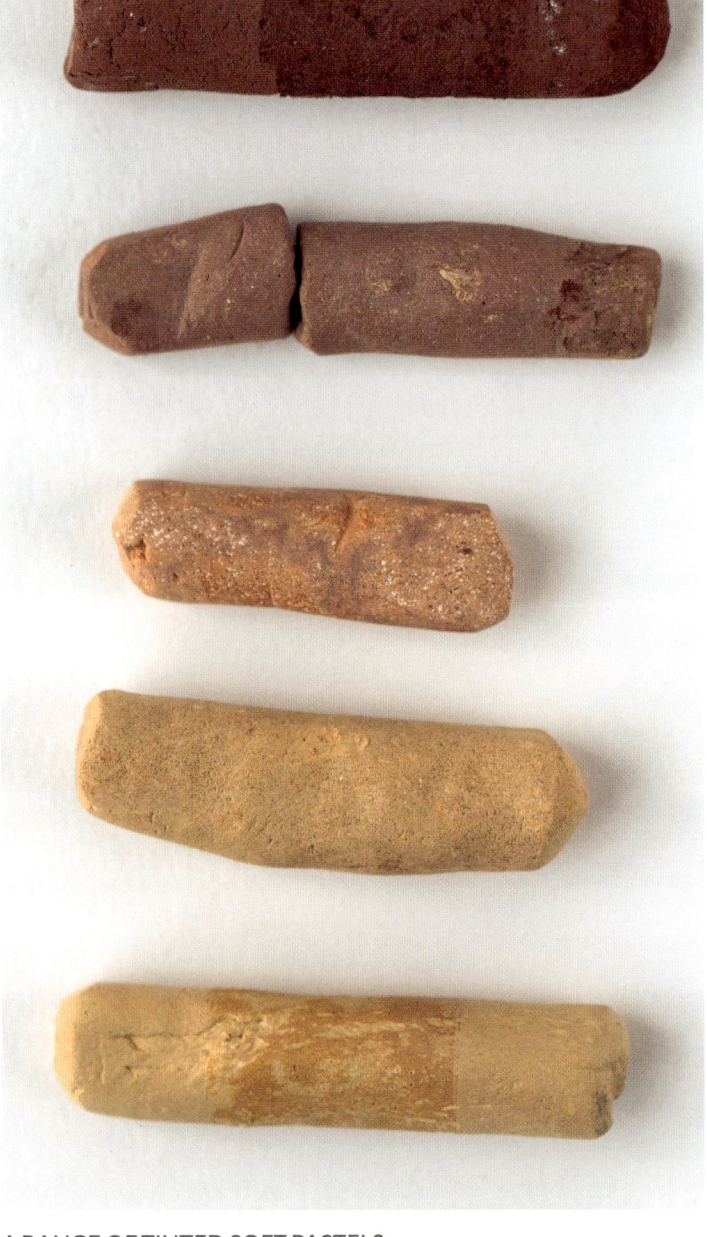

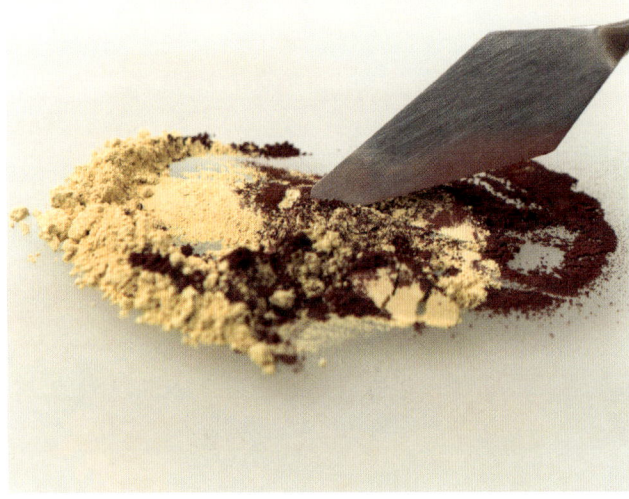

MIXING COLOURS OF SOFT PASTELS

Here I am combining 1½tsp of a yellow pigment taken from Man O' War beach in Dorset, UK, with ½tsp of haematite (a red-tinged iron oxide) from near Bath, UK.

Mix the pigments together until they form a uniform powder and then add the appropriate solution (or just water, if one of the chosen pigments is a clay or clay-like powder).

A RANGE OF TINTED SOFT PASTELS

Top to bottom:

- *Pure haematite red*
- *1½tsp red and ½tsp yellow*
- *1tsp red and 1tsp yellow*
- *½tsp red and 1½tsp yellow*
- *Pure Man O' War beach yellow*

Tinting and toning hard pastels

If you enjoy making tonal studies – for instance when drawing portraits from life or photographs – then a set of bespoke tinted pastels is ideal. Using one chosen clay as our base colour, we can tint it by making increasingly pale mixtures using chalk (or other white pigment). We can also produce a set of toned pastels heading towards a darker colour, whether black or dark brown. Once they have dried, with a few shades between your 'home colour' and your darkest and lightest pigments, you'll have created an all-in-one homemade sketching set, with no need for messy blending to get midtones.

This approach can also be used to blend between different harmonizing pigments, such as red and yellow clay, to make a similarly useful tonal family of pastels. If you can find two contrasting colours in your neighbourhood, such as a pale clay and stone dust from your local quarry or stonemason, you can make a hyper-local graded set of crayons, ideal for drawing the places where the raw materials were found.

To make the gradations really effective, go by proportion rather than equal incremental weights in grams (for instance, make a pastel with a whole, half, quarter and eighth of the stronger colour). The eye will detect the grades better than with machine-like equal percentage differentials. This is an example of the organically human ability to perceive proportion, as shown by the ear with musical tones, the finger tips with grain size, and even the tongue with saltiness!

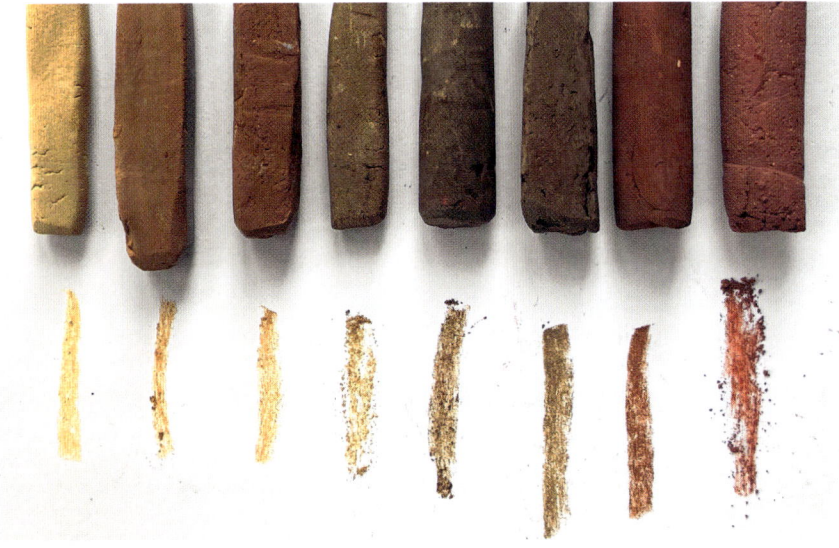

A selection of graded hard pastels from a mixing session; moving from yellow and beige clays through raw and burnt umber pigments and then on towards red ochre.

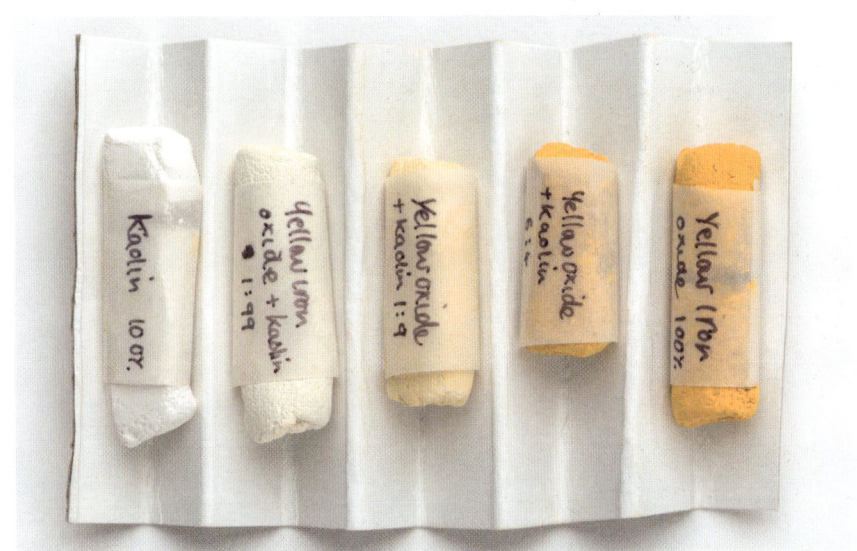

Different proportions of clay to pigment will provide you with a range of different tints. The more clay you incorporate, the firmer the pastel – but the more 'diluted' the pigment will be. For this reason, it's a good idea to pick a clay that is naturally similar in colour to your pigment.

Calcining

Calcining, or burning, is a way to change the colour of ochre. For instance, a yellow ochre (goethite) can be heated to make it change through orange and then eventually to red (haematite). Green earths (terre verte) can be calcined to make a beautiful cool brown. Famous colours such as raw sienna and burnt sienna are simply the uncooked and cooked versions of Italian earth pigments – as the names suggest.

If we have a large amount of ochre, we can produce gradual changes in the pigment and make a beautiful, harmonious set of pastels from just one source. This process is fun to do with only simple tools.

At archaeological sites across the world, evidence of burning ochres can be found going back hundreds of thousands of years, to the beginning of modern humans (*Homo sapiens*). Our Middle Stone Age ancestors used bowl-shaped stones and simple wood fire, or even just put lumps of ochre in the fire itself. We are going to use an old frying pan on a kitchen hob and get the same results.

Tools needed

Cooking pan, wooden or silicone spatula, palette knife

Useful extras:

A ceramic paint palette can be used to separate the colours as they change

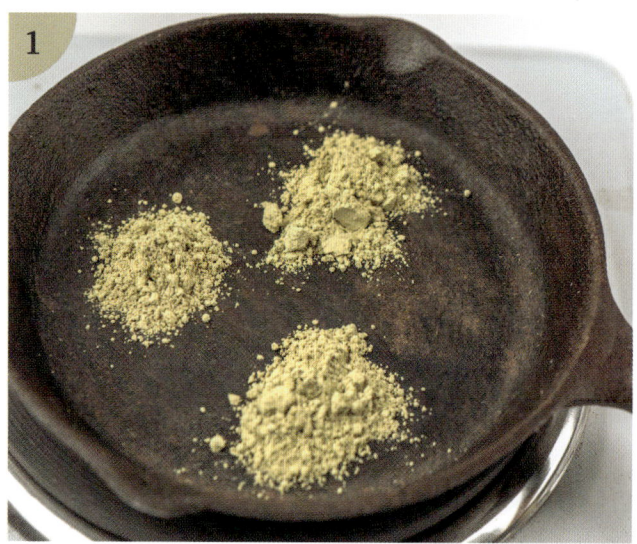

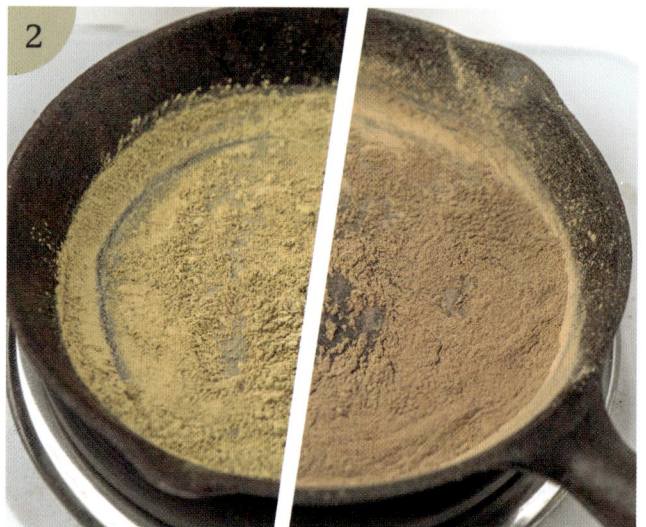

1 Place your ground ochre pigment in to a pan and begin to heat gently. Watch closely for the colour shifts – depending on the ochre you are using, it will start to change from as quickly as 30 seconds.

2 Use a broad flat palette knife (or a spoon) to stir the pigment around the pan, and remove a portion of pigment when you see the colour you are after. The pigment will continue to change for up to 10 minutes.

3

Colour palette

Once you have created a selection of burnt colours from your original yellow or brown ochre, or green earth, you will be able to add your colours to a little clay to bind them, as described on pages 36–37. Alternatively, use the soft pastel method, on pages 32–35, using gum tragacanth solution to bind them with a little chalk.

In your sketchbook, make notes of how long each tone took to create and what original ochre was used. Leave the calcined pigments until they are perfectly dry, then label them ready for storage.

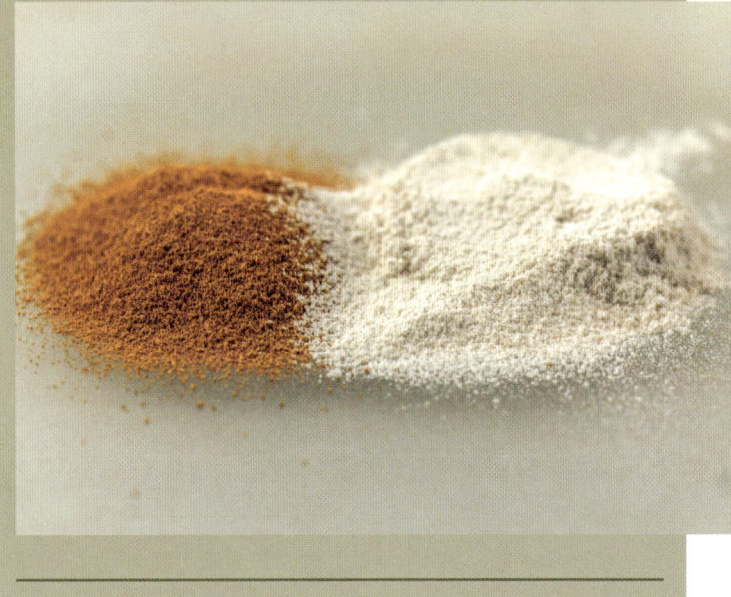

3 This shows three samples of the same pigment (a yellowish green terre verte) which have been calcined for different lengths of time.

Protecting your pastels

Now that you have made some pastels, it's good to label and store them so that you can remember what pigments you used and so that they remain clean and unbroken on trips to draw in the wild.

If you are wondering what to write on your labels, you can name your pastels as you like: descriptively, poetically, or numbered to a key in your notebook – it is up to you.

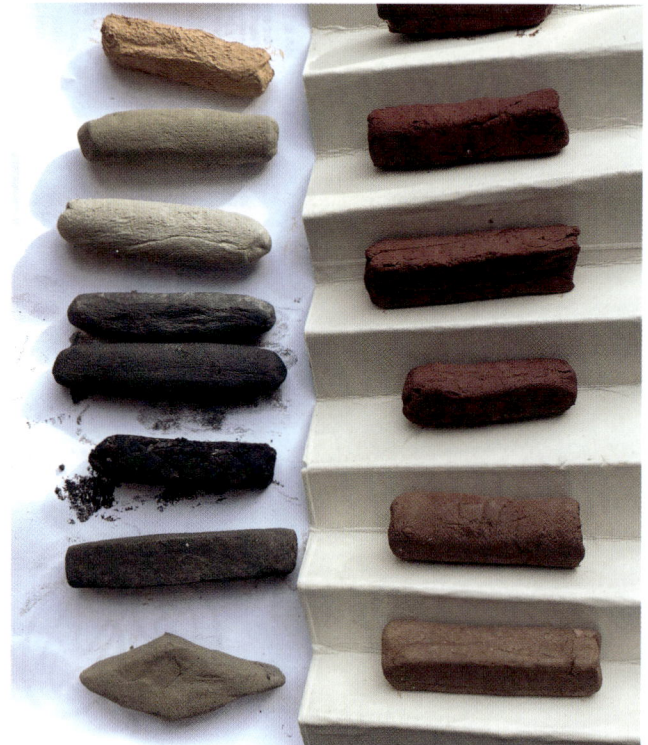

SIMPLE STORAGE
A concertina of cardboard will keep your pastels clean when using or storing them.

Labelling

I label my pastels simply, using a marker pen on a taped loop of tracing paper, as I am often teaching and can note down the colours quickly this way. Students often label their pastels in beautiful and inventive ways, such as by pressing jewellery into the sticks to give them distinct marks. Some use Japanese paper tape to wrap them and write on. Others make swatches in a book and label these rather than the pastels, numbering the swatch and the pastel. American pigment artist Jodi Gear uses a special stamp, like those traditionally used in libraries, to impress the numbers into her pastels, which looks great. Whichever way you choose, you won't regret it when you want to recreate a pastel when it runs out.

Storage

You can buy many purpose-made storage boxes from art suppliers. These needn't be hugely expensive and the padding they contain makes broken pastels in transit much less likely. However, if you like to reuse things then a simple concertina of card tucked into a shallow box topped with a piece of packing cardboard is just as good. In my collection there are old balsawood cigar boxes, chocolate boxes, coloured pencil packs and sweet tins. Christmas or Valentine's chocolate boxes are ideal, and you can have great fun decorating them.

Cleaning

If your pastels become dusty or dingy by rubbing against each other, you can clean them by putting them in a pot with some uncooked white rice and gently shaking them. The dust will cling to the rice and the pastels will be good as new. Don't eat the rice! It can go in the food waste recycling or compost...

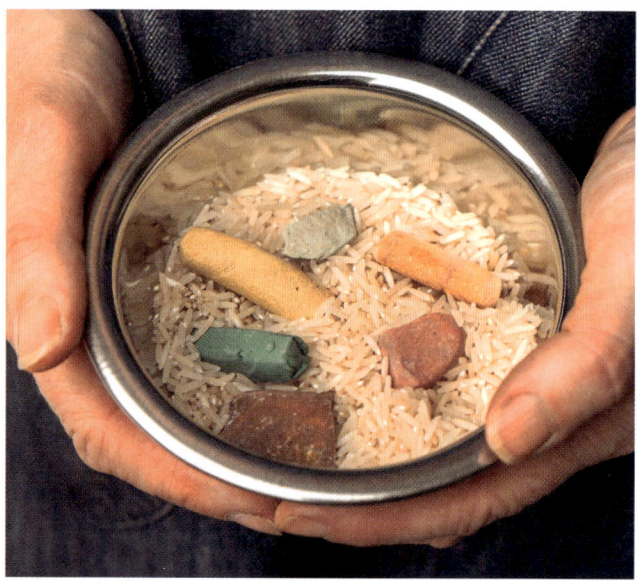

QUICK CLEANING
Shaking the pastels in a bowl of rice makes cleaning them easy.

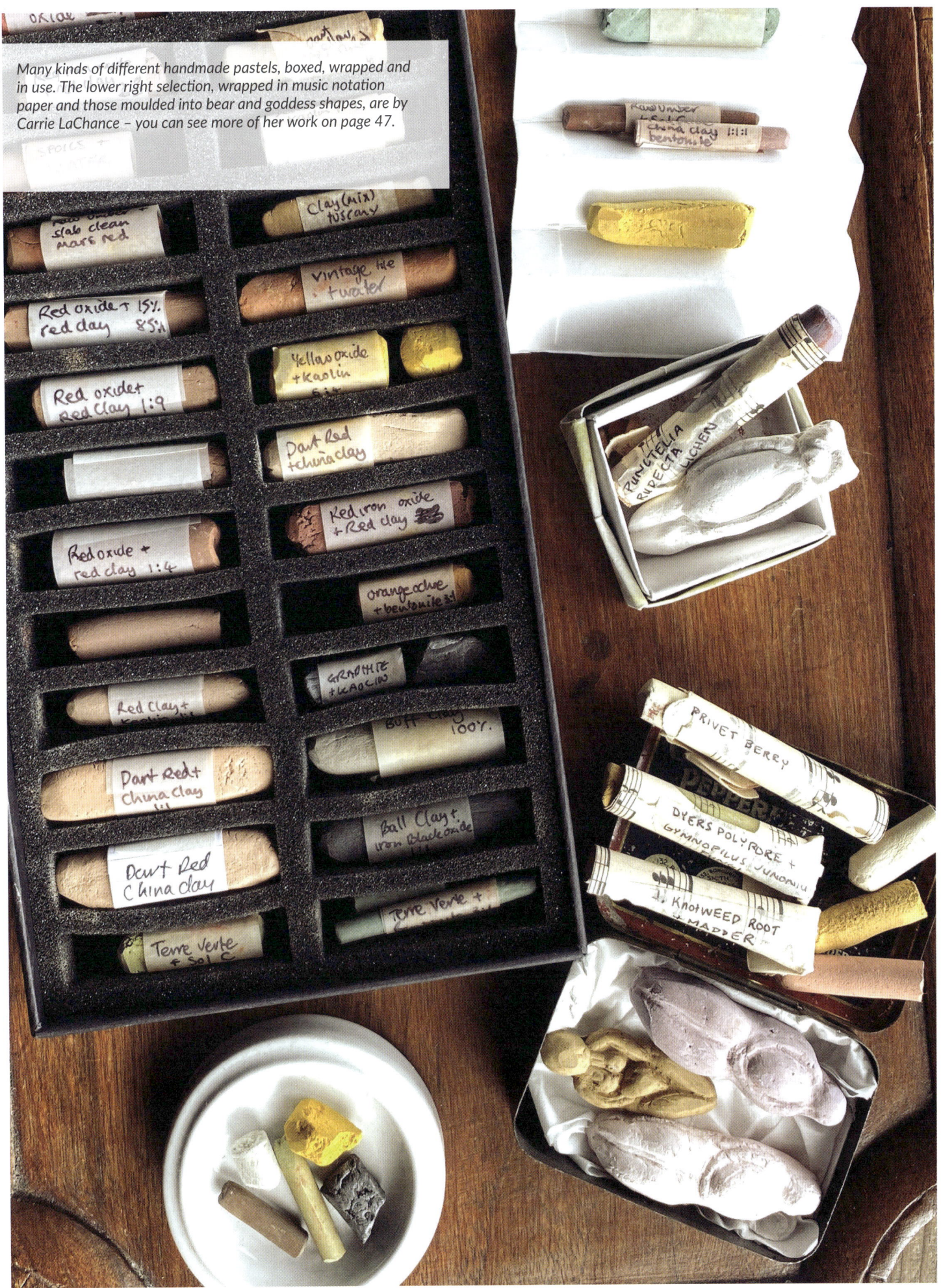

Many kinds of different handmade pastels, boxed, wrapped and in use. The lower right selection, wrapped in music notation paper and those moulded into bear and goddess shapes, are by Carrie LaChance – you can see more of her work on page 47.

Glair fixative

Glair comes from the French *clair*, meaning 'clear', and is a transparent, low-gloss paint medium made from egg whites. A versatile medium, it has been used for over fourteen centuries in Europe as one of the binders for pigments for illuminated manuscripts on parchment.

When my first Renaissance materials teacher Daniel Chatto mentioned that he wished there was an eco-friendly fixative for pastels that didn't involve aerosol cans and great expense, I took this as a personal challenge. I came back the following week with a solution: I found that glair medium can be used diluted as an excellent fixative for pastels. You can either lightly wet the whole sheet of paper before drawing with them, or use a blow diffuser or pump mister to spray the whole drawing lightly after it is finished. It doesn't discolour or smell, and is easy and non-toxic to use. All you need is an old spray bottle, such as used for some vitamins or cosmetics – just clean them out fully before use.

Tools needed

Large clean mixing bowl, electric whisk, (or a hand whisk if you have plenty of time and energy to spare), a spotless spray bottle, or jar and diffuser.

Useful extras:
A small funnel

Using glair as a fixative

In the large bowl, whisk an egg white to hard peaks, and set aside. Underneath the peaks you'll notice a liquid start to form. After half an hour, start to pour this off every so often into a clean jar (keep it in a cool place between each pouring). After a few hours, the peaks won't give any more liquid, and you can discard them. The liquid in the jar is glair. It will keep for a couple of weeks in the fridge.

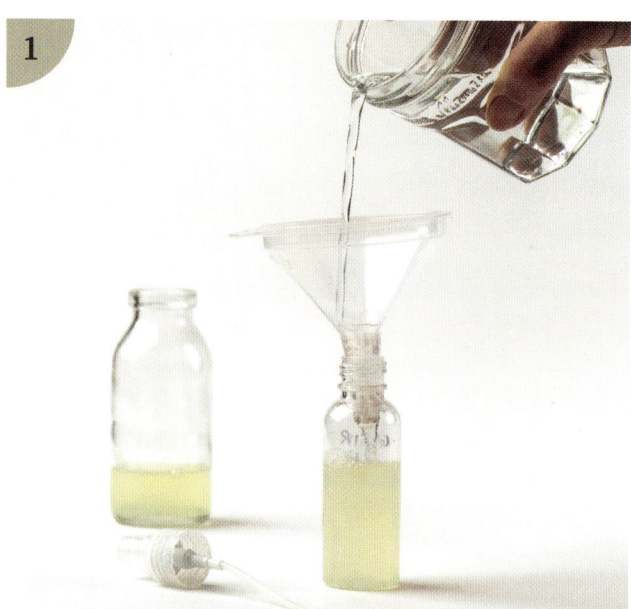

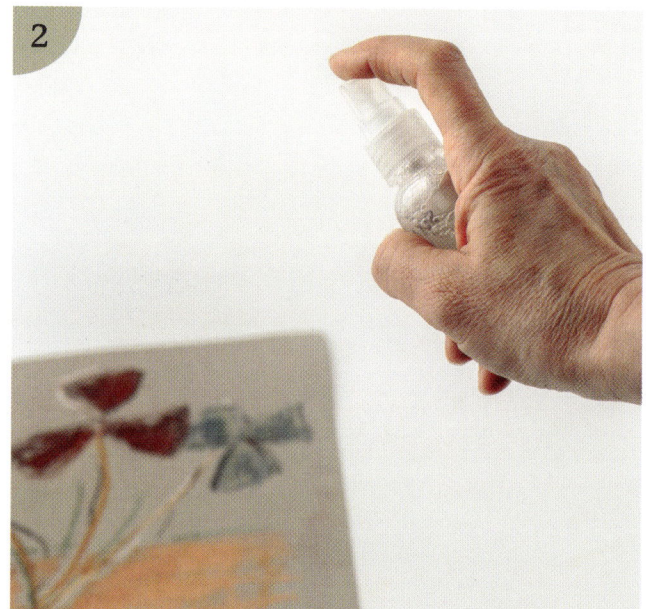

1 For use as a fixative, pour your glair into a spray bottle and dilute with at least the same amount of clean water. It can be diluted even further, for a lighter adhesive quality, or used more thickly to bind heavier particles to the paper.

2 Hold the spray bottle at least 30cm (12in) away from the painting and lightly mist the surface. Leave it to dry – depending on the temperature of the room, this may take anywhere from 15 minutes to an hour or so.

Vegan glair fixative (Veglair)

After creating a vegan medium for paints for my Found and Ground course, I have taught it to many students and asked them to test it for me in their own practice, which will differ from mine. I am happy to say that veglair works well as a fixative. It is not quite as adhesive as egg glair, and takes up to an hour or so to dry, rather than minutes, due to the linseed oil content.

You'll need a sieve, a can of white beans such as cannellini (the best), butter beans, or chickpeas, artist's linseed oil, a teaspoon, a storage jar and diffuser or a spray bottle.

Open a can of white beans and pour the liquid from the can through a sieve into a clean jar. If you don't have a fine sieve, you can just let it settle for an hour. Suspended particulates will drop to the bottom and you can pour the clear top layer into a new jar. Save the beans for your supper.

Use an electric whisk to add one or two teaspoonfuls of linseed oil to the bean water. It will stay in emulsion in a similar way to the oils in egg yolk. You can dilute the veglair with distilled or previously boiled and cooled water until it sprays smoothly and finely. Whether you brush the veglair on before drawing in pastels, or spray it on afterwards, leave the work to dry flat.

As veglair is still what I would call an experimental medium, rather than a traditional artist's medium, make sure you do plenty of tests with your work before offering drawings for sale, or ensure works are properly framed and glazed.

Veglair can be stored in the fridge or a cool place for a few months. As with egg glair, trust your nose as to whether you need to make a new batch!

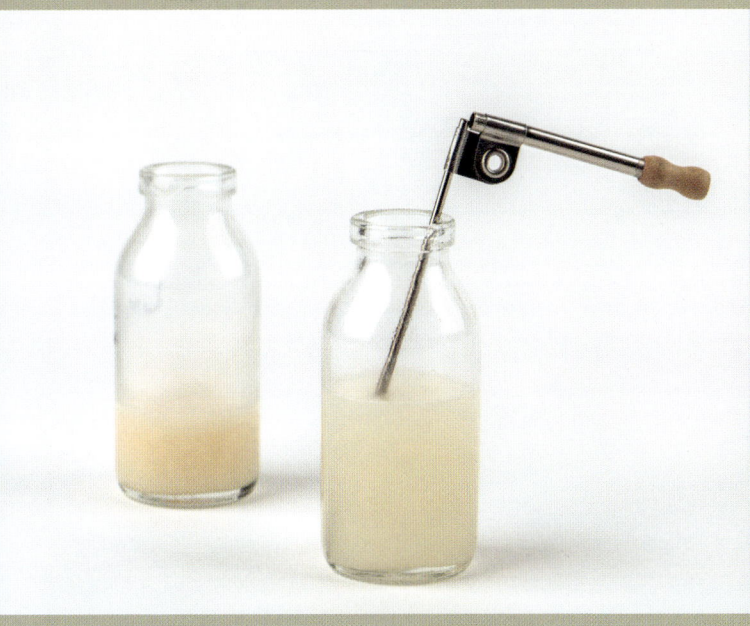

Veglair at full strength is shown on the left. Once diluted, it is ready to use. If you prefer a completely non-plastic practice, use a diffuser rather than a spray bottle.

How to use your pastels

Test your pastels on different kinds of papers and surfaces, making marks, drawings and experiments in blending and hatching. Try spraying glair on the paper first or afterwards, and compare the results. Unlike shop-bought supplies, handmade materials, especially natural or foraged ones, have not been standardized, so it can take a little time to become familiar with them. If you treat it as an adventure, you won't go wrong.

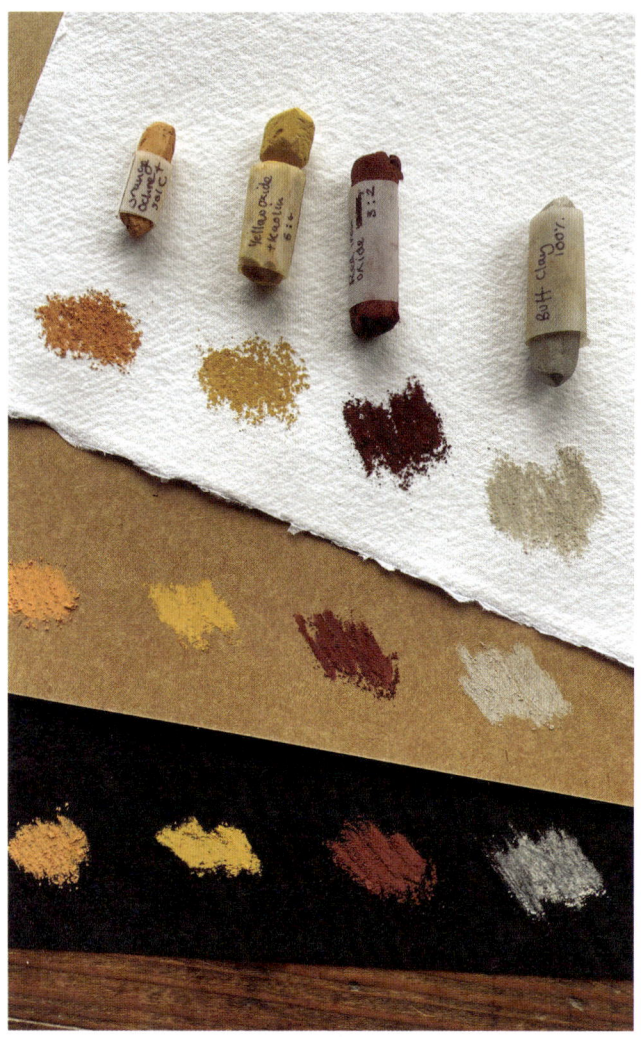

Test your dry, newly-made pastels on several papers of different colours and textures. What may seem a dull pastel on one surface will stand out on another. Slightly harder pastels may skid over smooth papers but work beautifully on textured papers with a bit of 'tooth' to them.

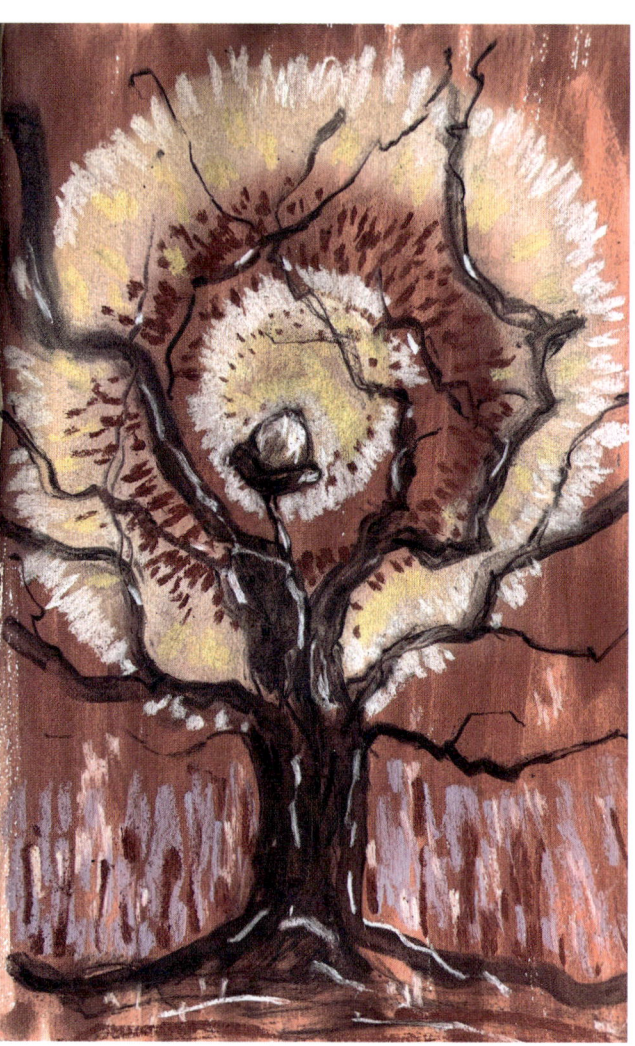

SAINT OAK THE ELDER   21 x 30cm (8¼ x 11¾in)
Handmade pastels, charcoal and chalk in sketchbook.

Carrie LaChance's approach

Carrie makes incredibly beautiful tools and materials while minimizing her environmental impact. Treating the landscapes from which they come with respect and care, she uses fallen bark, fungi, lichen and shells that are already dead or disturbed as her resources.

Clockwise from right:

Carved human figure mould made from fallen eastern cottonwood bark, and a sanguine clay pastel that was formed within it.

Carved bear mould made of fallen cottonwood bark and pastels/seed vessels made of fine clay gathered from a puddle in a dirt road.

A blend of eastern oyster (Crassostrea virginica) shell-derived calcium citrate and homegrown and processed Japanese indigo (Persicaria tinctoria) pigment being processed using a pestle and mortar.

A selection of calcium citrate pigments made from terrestrial and aquatic shells moulded using unmodified scallop shells. Carrie uses these as pastels, tailors' chalk, and for storing and transporting pigments easily.

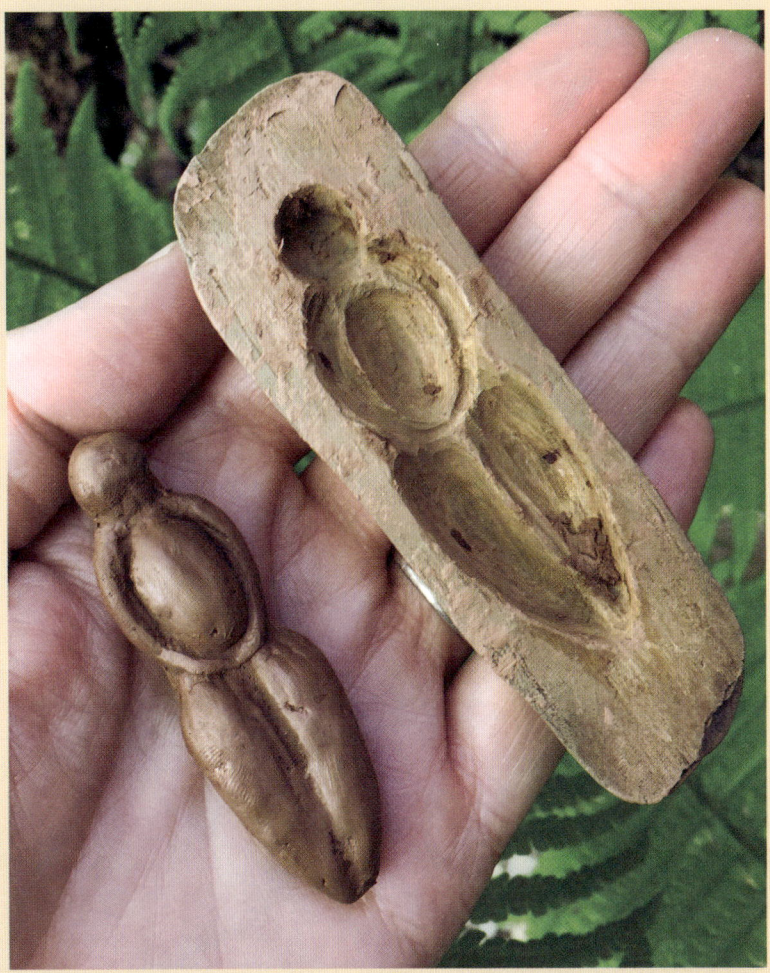

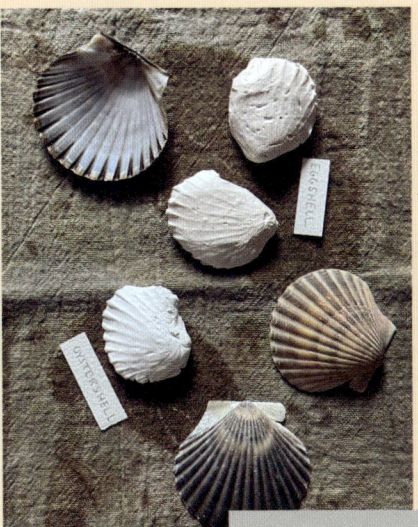

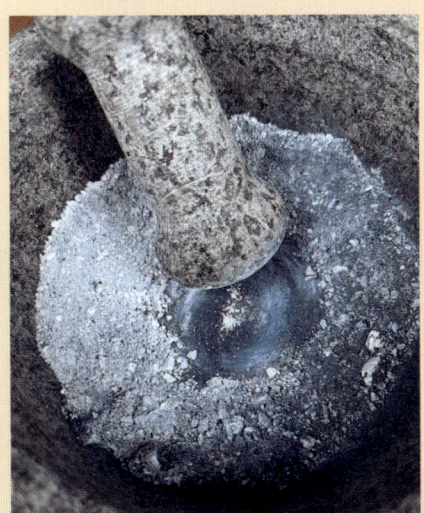

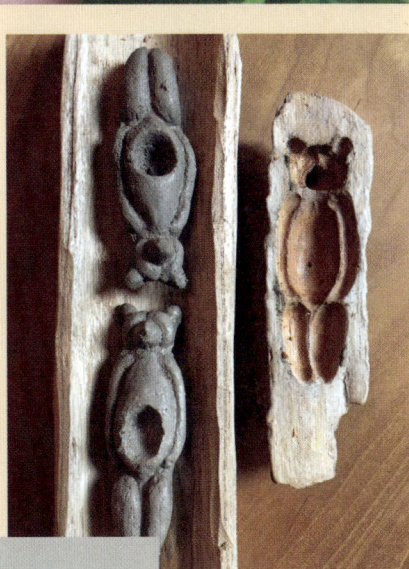

Carrie LaChance is a multimedia artist who has spent her entire life immersed in the northeastern forests of North America. Her work is a distillation of her day-to-day connections with this biome. She aims to be useful in increasing awareness about the importance of using material culture as a portal to reciprocity with the local ecologies of the land we find ourselves upon. You can follow her on this path via her Substack, 'A Little Lichen'.

CHARCOAL

"The very first drawing material?"

Even before mankind harnessed fire, we had charcoal to draw with from the remnants of natural fires caused by lightning or volcanoes (though sadly probably not dragons…). In cave art the world over, black charcoal marks join with those made with ochre to create images of the megafauna of those times.

Charcoal is still as important a drawing medium today as it was in prehistory. The go-to medium for sketching out a canvas before painting, making tonal studies, portrait drawings or abstract works, charcoal remains unbeaten for its versatility and ease of reworking.

Though not expensive to buy, nothing beats making your own charcoal from offcuts and clippings from your back garden or local trees. I'll be showing you a few harmless ways to gather raw materials – thin twigs of wood – and how to prepare them to make the best of your harvest. Then we'll look at how to safely and effectively turn these twigs into fine artist's charcoal.

Gather your secateurs and a basket; we're going on a stick hunt.

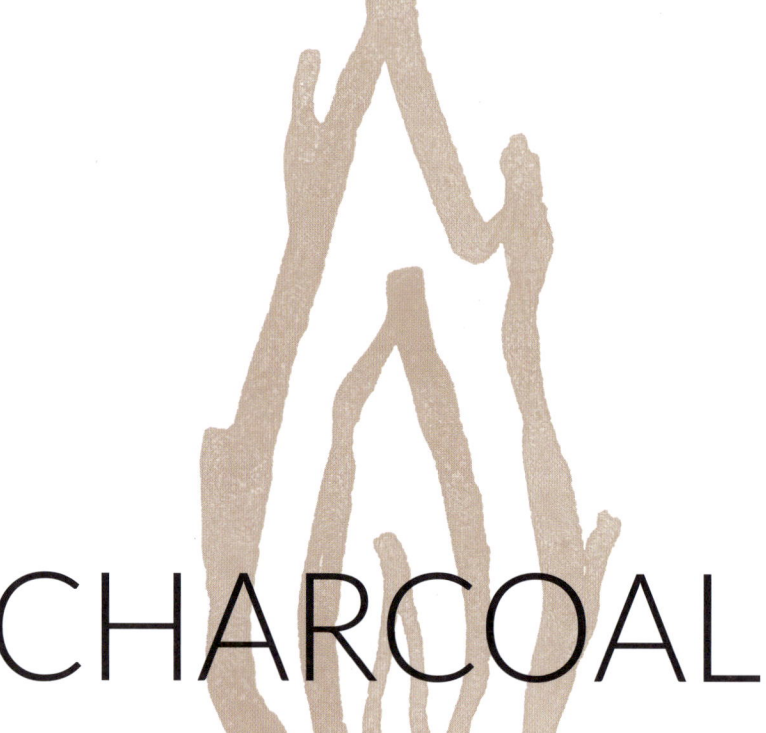

Some of the red ochre and charcoal drawings of wild horses in French caves are so accurately rendered that we can see the clear likeness of what we now call Przewalski's horse, the last extant truly wild horse.

Opposite:
It's easy to make a safe bonfire in a simple garden fire-pit.

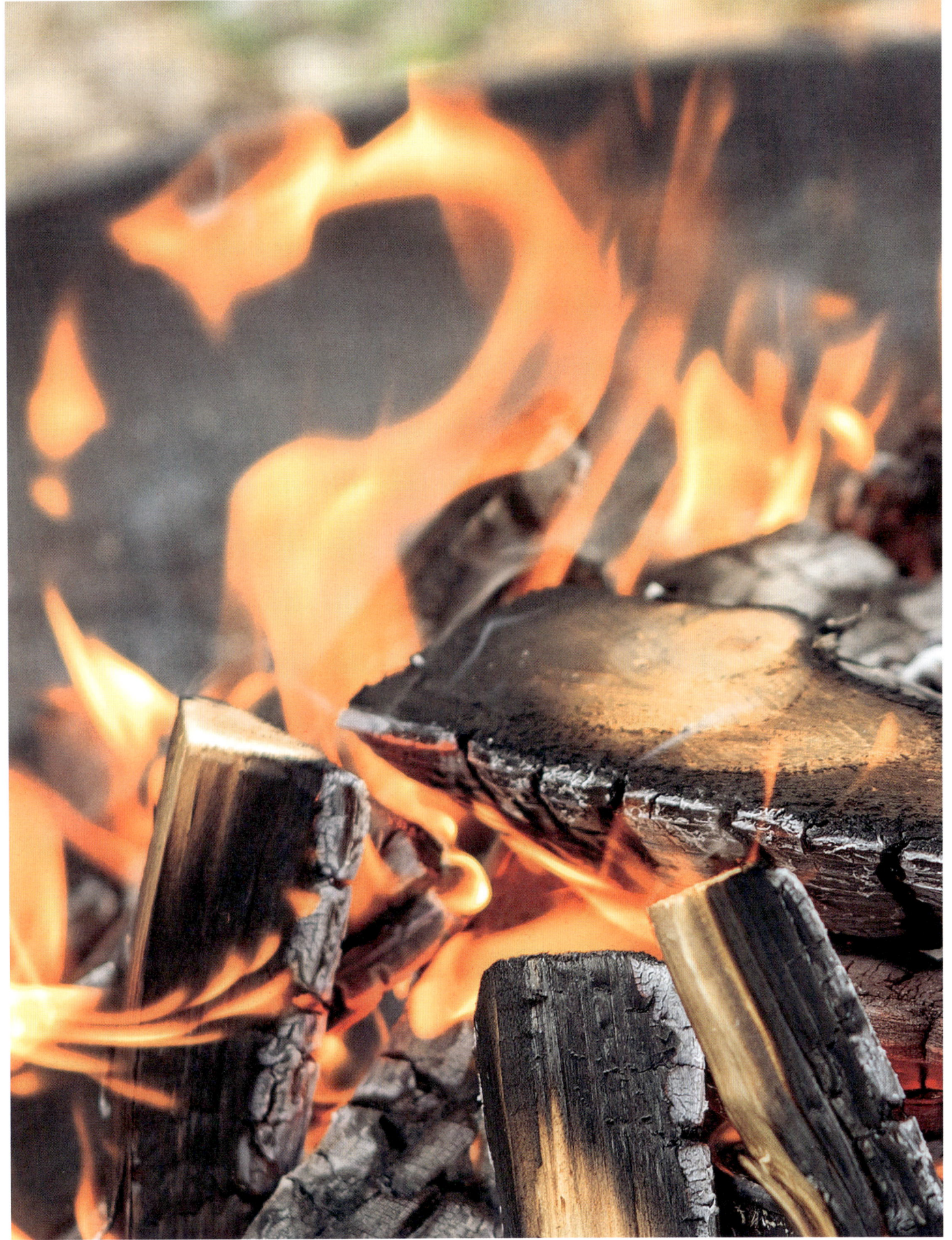

WOOD, VINE AND BONE

Once upon a time, before mining fossil fuels became widespread, what we now call coal was referred to as 'seacoal', as it was found washed up on beaches from seams that ran out by the shore. 'Coal' instead referred to what we now term charcoal. Charcoal burners were a familiar sight working at their kilns in the woods, turning coppiced wood into fuel for blacksmiths.

Charcoal was first used in the Paleolithic era, with the use of cold firebrands for cave art. The method has been somewhat refined over the centuries and today you can make a wonderful drawing material even when using a small-scale set up. You'll need evenly sized sticks; around pencil thickness is a good size for a first try. Vine clippings of a similar size are a good alternative.

Where to find wood

Almost any wood can be used to make charcoal. My friend, foraged food experimentalist and all-round crafter Fergus Drennan, tested 40 different woods for charcoal, all gathered within five minutes of his front door in Ashdown Forest, UK. Like me, he found most woods to be good, but chestnut, willow and vine particularly so.

If you have a garden or allotment, or neighbours whose trees and bushes dangle into your yard, then your usual winter woody trimmings will make good sticks for charcoal. If you live near woods or forests, then there will be an abundance of broken twigs just lying on the floor after any high winds or heavy rain storms and you can go and gather them as soon as conditions are safe to do so.

Where I live, non-native grey squirrels cause lots of damage to trees by biting off thin twigs, eating some of the inner bark and then dropping them to the ground. I collect these stitcks to use for both inner bark fibre from lime trees (*Tilia*) and charcoal sticks from chestnuts.

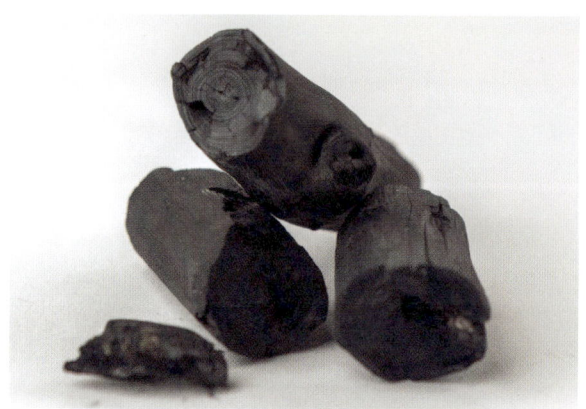

FIRE PIT CHARCOAL REMAINS

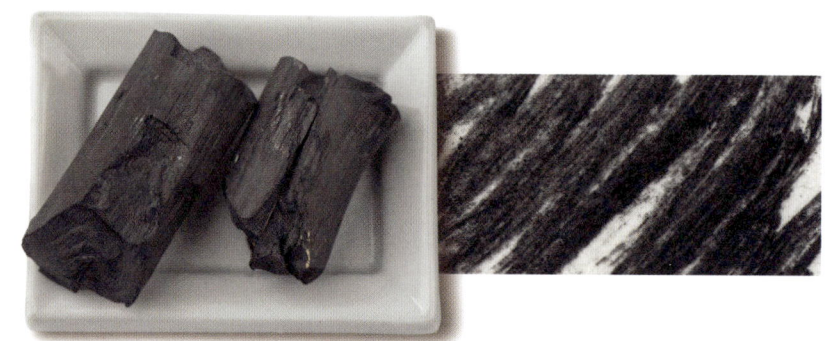

Materials to try

FORAGED MATERIAL	THE CHARCOAL	RESULTING MARK
WILLOW		
VINE		
CHESTNUT		
BONE		

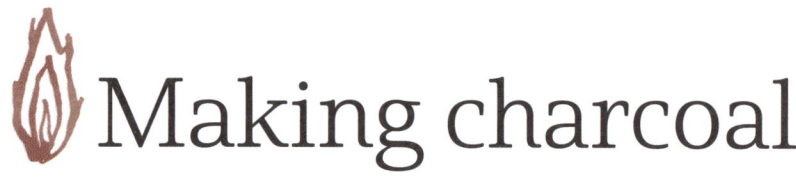

Making charcoal

Refining

The wood I'm using here is chestnut. Whatever sticks you choose, scraping off the bark beforehand will help to give the resulting charcoal a consistent texture. Scraping is optional, but recommended for the best results, and we can keep the bark shavings to make ink! You can strip older wood, but it's better to use freshly-cut green wood – it's easier and makes for better charcoal.

For control and safety, it's much better to move the wood than the knife when stripping bark. Hold the handle of the knife firmly in a punch grip as shown below – that is, balling your fist tightly, with the whole palm tight against the handle.

Tools needed

Sharp sturdy knife, suitable dry twigs or vine cuttings, metal tin or box with hole punched in the top, green (live) twigs, firepit, barbecue, outdoor grill or fireplace to safely make a fire, fire lighting materials, kindling, logs, fire safety materials such as heatproof gloves and fire tongs, bucket of water, secatueurs

Useful extras:

Hammer and nail or screwdriver to punch hole in top of tin

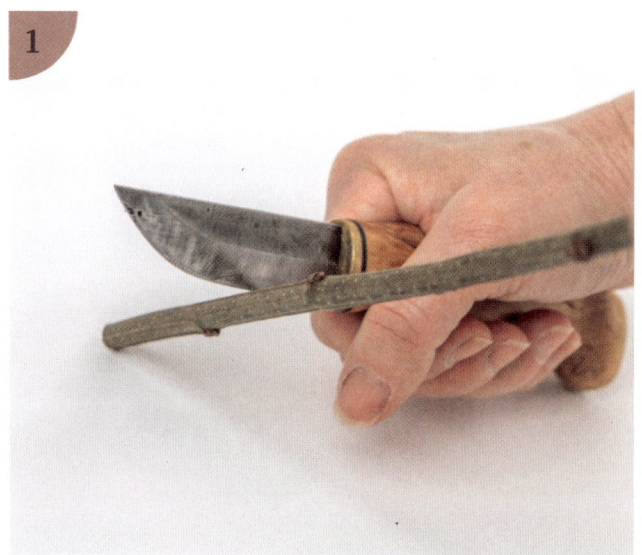

1 Select a length of wood – ideally as thick as a pencil, and no thicker than your little finger. Holding your knife in a punch grip (see above), brace your hand against a solid surface (the floor is ideal, as is a sturdy table top), and bring the wood up perpendicular to the blade as shown, around 15cm (6in) from the end.

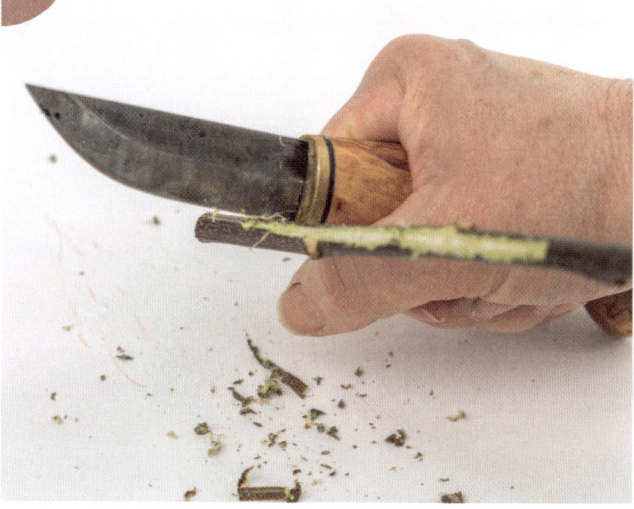

2 Holding the knife steady and firm against the wood, smoothly draw the length towards you to remove the outer and inner bark to reveal the wood underneath.

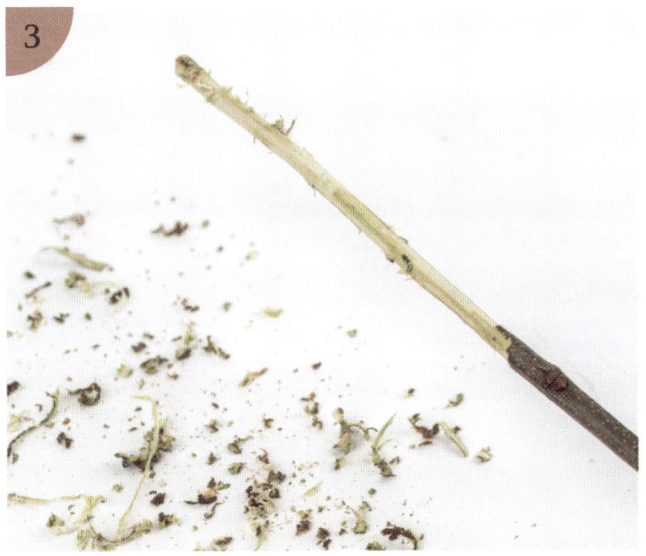

3 Work all the way around the wood.

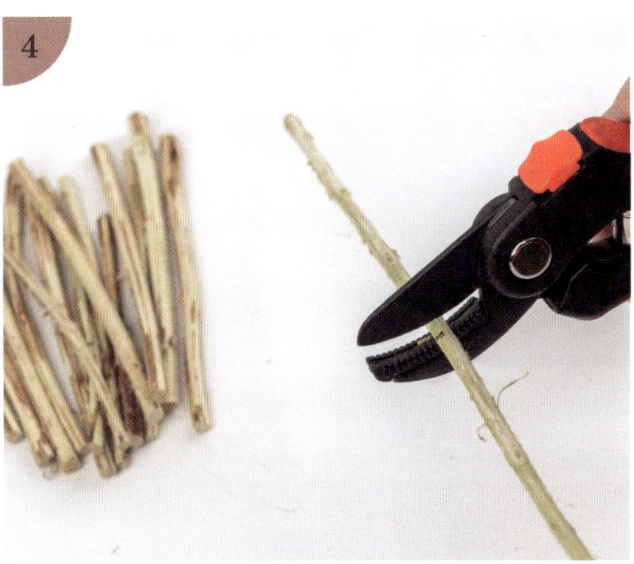

4 Repeat the process another 15cm (6in) further up, and again, until all the bark has been removed. You can now use secateurs to trim the wood to length to fit your box. Repeat until you have enough to fill your tin.

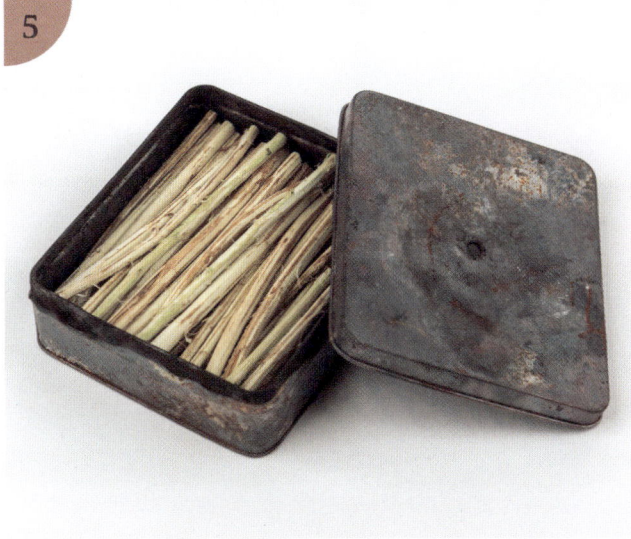

5 Leave the lengths of stripped wood on a warm windowsill for a couple of days until they feel dry to the touch. At this point, they're ready to be turned into charcoal. Pack them into a tin with a hole in the top. You can punch the hole with a screwdriver, or use a hammer and nail.

Burning

You can prepare a couple of tins at once, to make best use of the fuel. I use tins from gift boxes of teas, biscuits or sweets as well as the classic cylinder tins which contain syrup or treacle. Here I'm processing birch, chestnut and bone at the same time.

Conscientious burning

I always take great care when making charcoal and use a fire pit or designated fireplace, with water and safety equipment on hand. Always follow local fire guidance and extinguish your fire fully after use. Here you can see me using padded leather safety gloves in a designated stone surround fireplace on bare earth in a forest school site in managed woodlands.

Research what is appropriate and legal in your locale and season, as conditions vary considerably depending on where you are in the world, and the time of year.

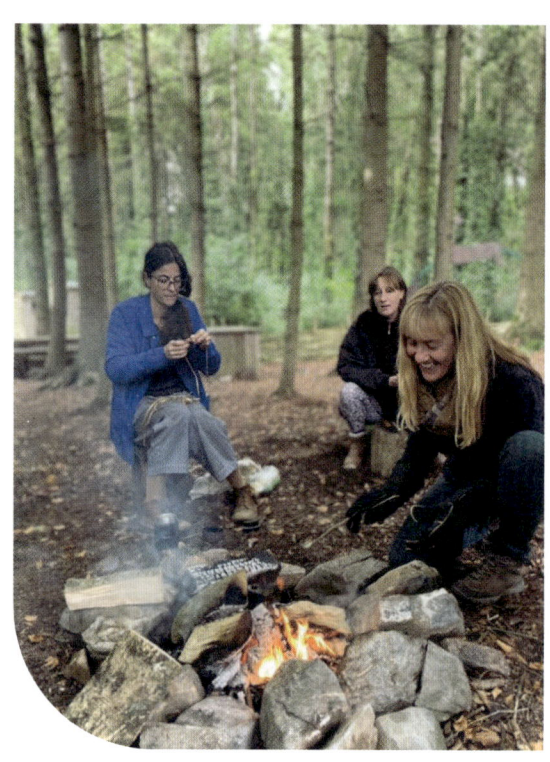

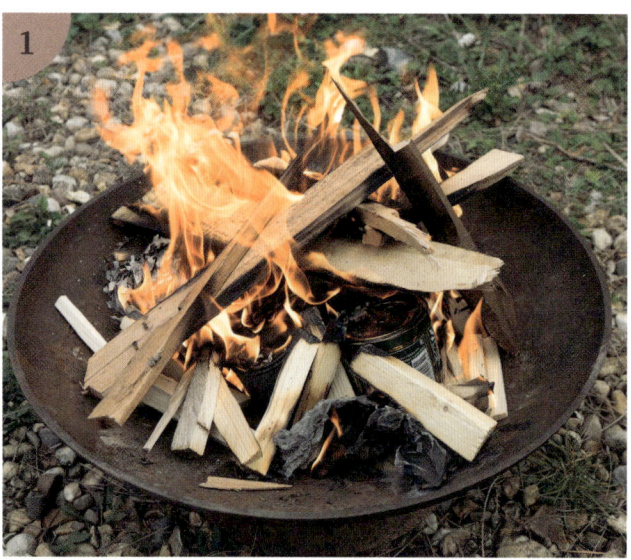

1 Place your tins of prepared wood in a fire-safe pit, and build a fire around them, covering and surrounding the tins. Light the fire and let it burn for around ten minutes.

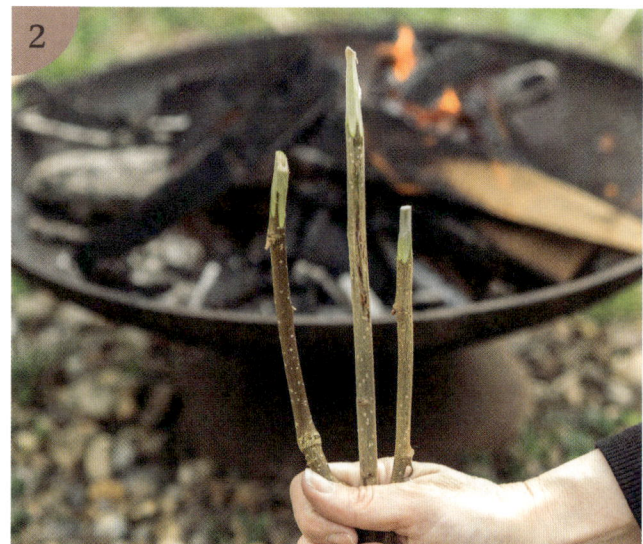

2 While the fire burns, cut some green wood and whittle it like pencil points. These will be used to fill the holes in the lids and stop oxygen getting in, so make sure they are the right size to plug the holes in the tins.

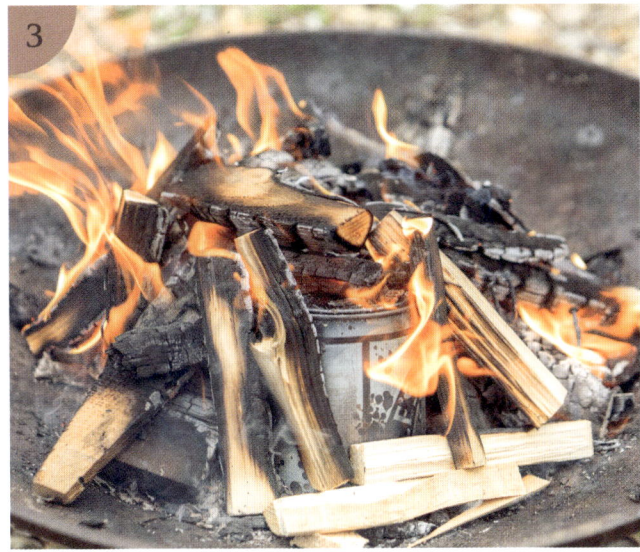

3 Tend the fire, adding more wood to keep the temperature consistent around the tins. Keep an eye on the holes in the tins – look for opaque smoke, which will indicate the wood is beginning to be reduced to charcoal.

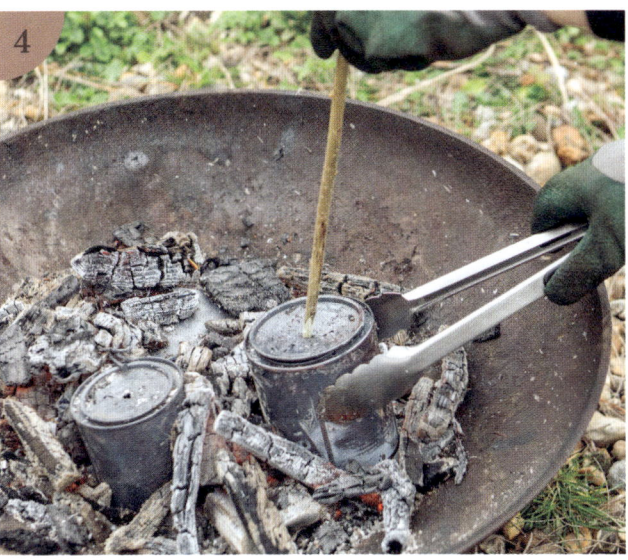

4 After twenty minutes or so, when there is no more opaque, cloudy smoke (you may see outgassing, and a flame coming from the hole), the charcoal is ready. Use tongs to remove the tins from the fire, push the green wood into the lids to stop the burn, and place them on a fireproof surface.

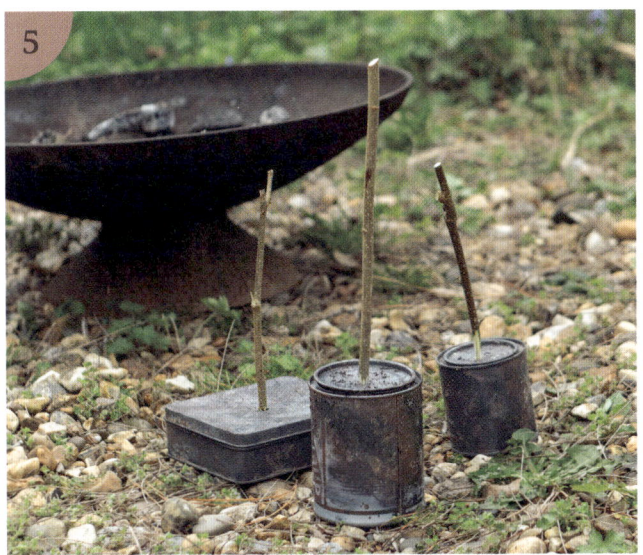

5 Allow the tins to cool, leaving them for five to ten minutes to ensure they are cool to the touch.

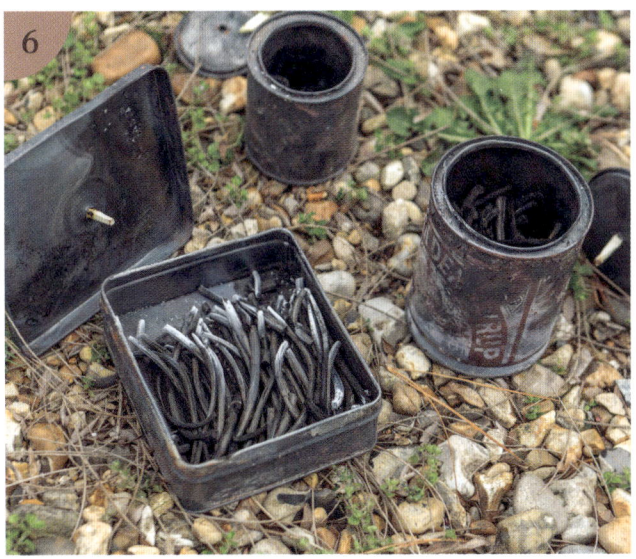

6 Remove the lids to reveal your completed charcoal. Sometimes, a few pieces of leftover burned wood from the fire itself can also make big, lovely lumps of charcoal. That's a bonus!

How to use your charcoal

Using charcoal is simple and intuitive – at its most basic, just pick it up and apply it to paper to draw dark, sinuous lines. There are many other approaches to try including putting down a ground first. This is done by covering the whole paper with charcoal and rubbing it in to create a mid-tone. You can then work back into it with the charcoal for darker areas, or with a putty rubber for highlights. The light and shade create the sense of depth, and this is how classical artists have worked from the life model or from sculptures for many hundreds of years – it is the nearest you can get to sculpting in two dimensions.

Alternatively, pick up a big chunk of your charcoal and draw bold lines. Try doing a drawing without taking the stick from the surface. Work from life, from photographs, or imagination; there is no correct way. Charcoal is utterly adaptable; you can rub it out, or in, with the side of your palm or a rag. Make tonal studies from your favourite paintings.

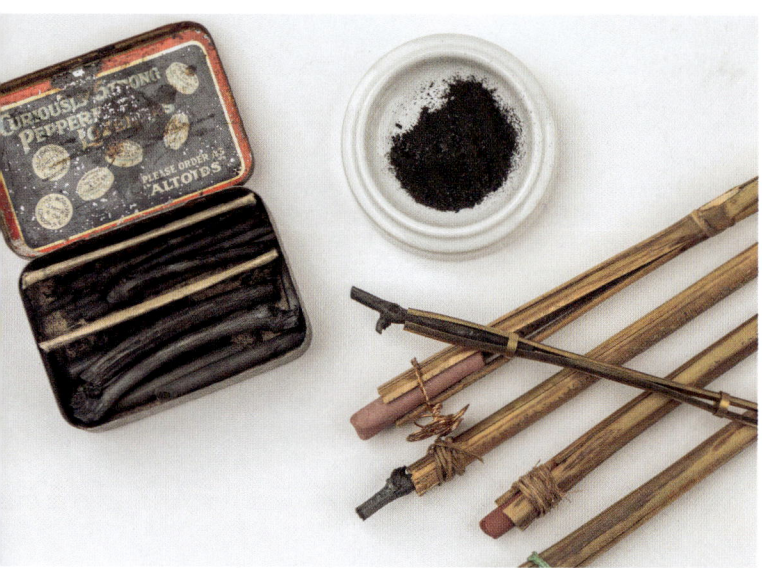

Charcoal or pastel holder

If you prefer a little less dust and to have your hand further back from the paper, you can fit the charcoal stick into a holder improvised from a bit of bamboo cane or a hollow twig, such as elder. Porte-crayons like the antique brass example above (a gift from Italian friends) have been popular for centuries, but you needn't splash out: a cane and some string, or an elastic band, will do just fine.

Storage

Keep your different types of charcoal in separate labelled boxes or tins, so that you can really get to know how they handle. I like to use little vintage metal tins, into which I place folded paper to grade the stick thicknesses. You can use the dust collected at the bottom to tone your papers by rubbing it in, or use it to make watercolour paint.

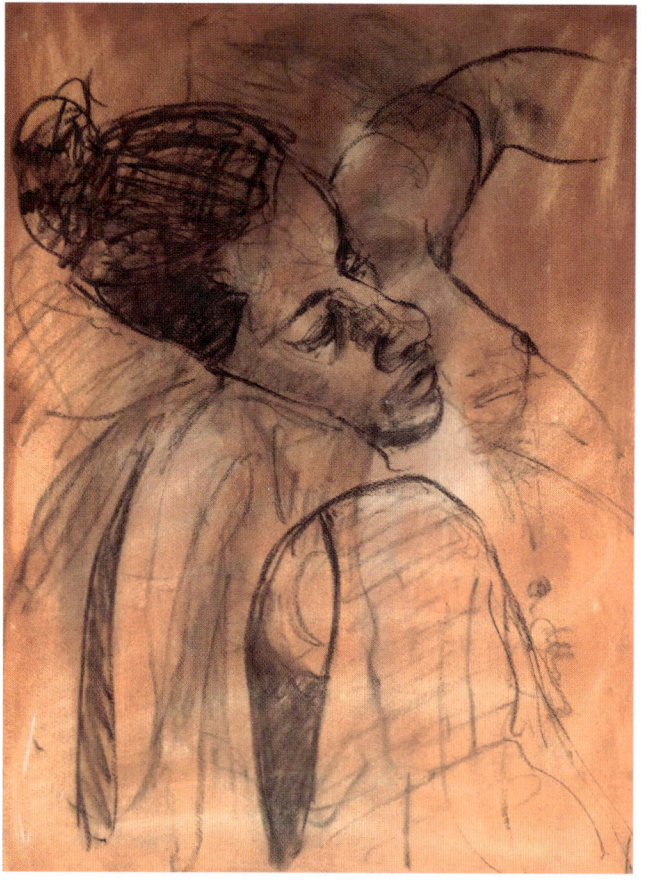

RECLINING MODEL   30 x 42cm (11¾ x 16¾in)
Charcoal on ground prepared with ochre wash.

Martyn Cross' approach

Martyn brings knowledge of traditional materials and working methods into his contemporary art practice of painting and drawing.

Weaving recognizable elements such as limbs, eyes and clouds together, his paintings often appear as fantastical landscapes imbued with a deeply uncanny mood. 'Folk' motifs such as the sun, iconic trees or Wayland's Smithy (an ancient barrow in England) appear in his ambiguous drawings and paintings, which I appreciate for their colourful strangeness. To me they are windows into a timeless zone, at once earthy and celestial, where both gods and mortals are at the whims of sentient clouds and fiery forests.

I sent Martyn a short film on how to make artist's charcoal and he made a batch with which he created a series of new drawings, shown here.

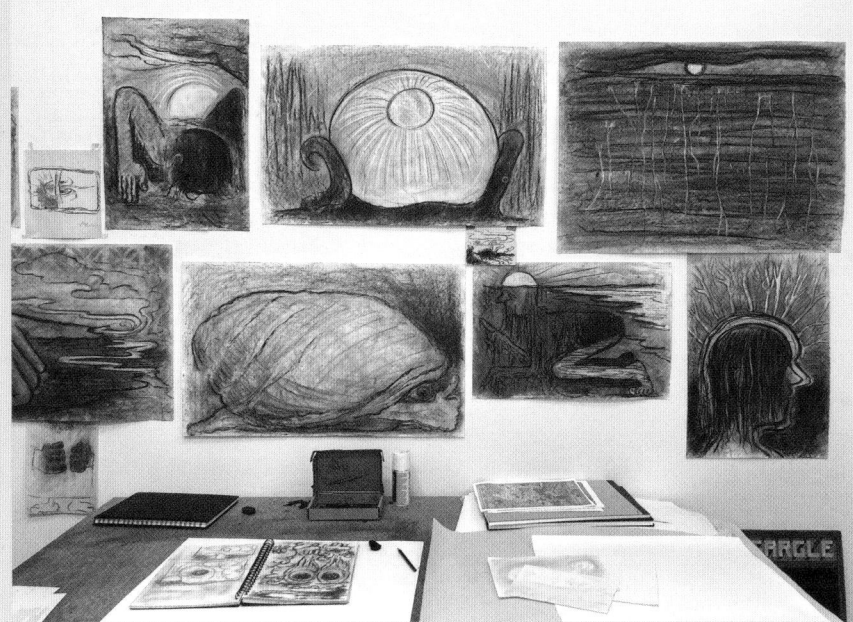

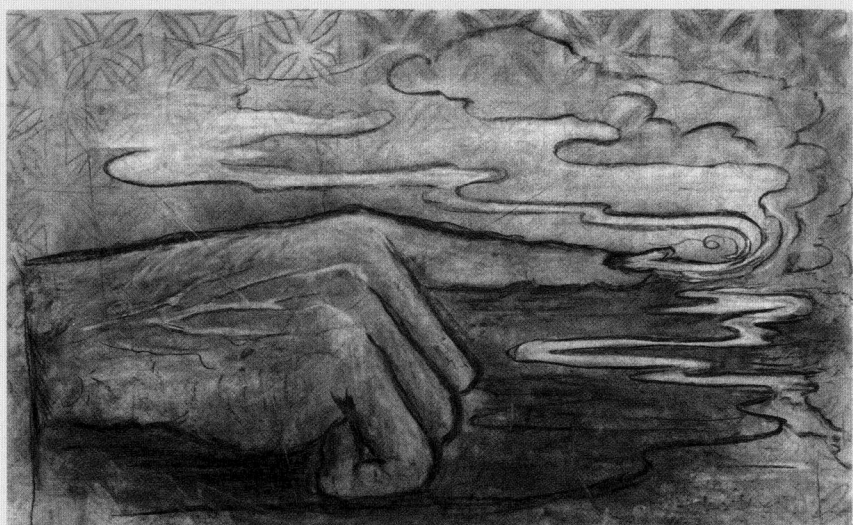

TEETH LENGTHEN   84.2 x 59.5cm (33 x 23½in)
Bristol willow charcoal on found paper.

Martyn Cross is a British painter with a deep interest in drawing, history and mediaeval murals. He lives in Bristol, England.

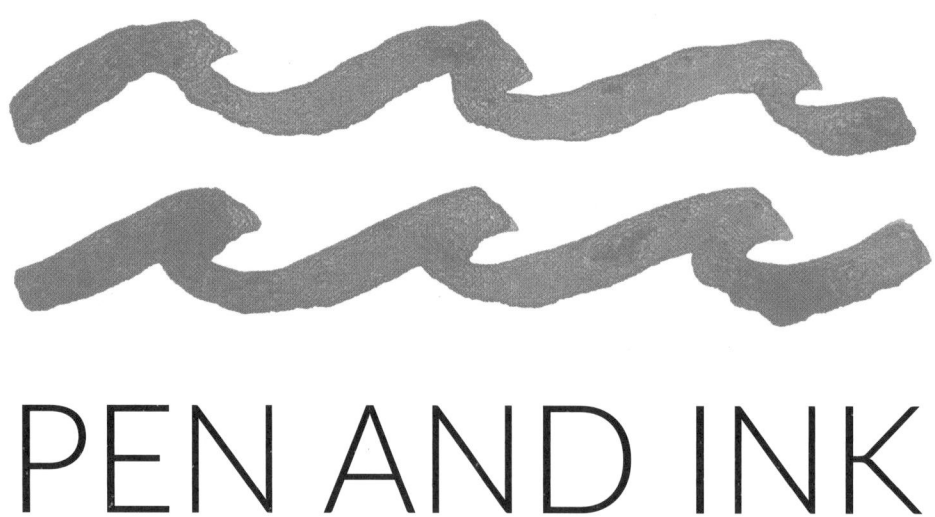

PEN AND INK

"...That in black ink my love may still shine bright."

From Sonnet 65 *by William Shakespeare*

For me nothing compares to the drawing experience of using quill pen and ink that I have made myself. I love hearing the ancient sounds of a freshly cut pen nib lightly scraping across the surface and leaving behind the flowing line. Unlike the standardized marks left by factory-made pens, these are punctuated by an ebb and flow, like a tide or a breath: the newly dipped stroke is minutely thicker and darker. To look closely at something written this way is to somehow sense the rhythm of the hand that made it, and the mind of the scribe behind it. The pen will be just the right length, the ink can be the perfect black. Even an inadvertent blot can become something beautiful, the start of a drawing.

I first made a dip pen from a wooden chopstick many decades ago and dipped it in fountain pen ink, after seeing an Elizabethan-style glass dip pen in a gift shop. My pocket money did not stretch that far, so I improvised with my penknife. Over time, I taught myself how to cut quills in the manner of those used

for over a thousand years for lettering and drawing illuminated manuscripts such as the *Book of Kells*, or for writing documents such as the Magna Carta, or the Declaration of Independence.

Elsewhere in the world, as far apart as Ireland and Egypt, the go-to pens were often reeds, and these beautiful common plants can still be harvested to create wonderful pens that take seconds to make. Similarly, bamboo and other common or invasive cane species can make wonderful drawing and writing tools, traditional or experimental, with only a few strokes of a knife.

Inks come in so many forms, from the fine solid blocks of the carbon blacks of the Far East, to bottles of iron gall ink of Europe. Whether for writing or drawing, careful calligraphy or impromptu sketching, pen and ink remain the perfect combination of medium and tool.

Opposite:
Iron gall ink.

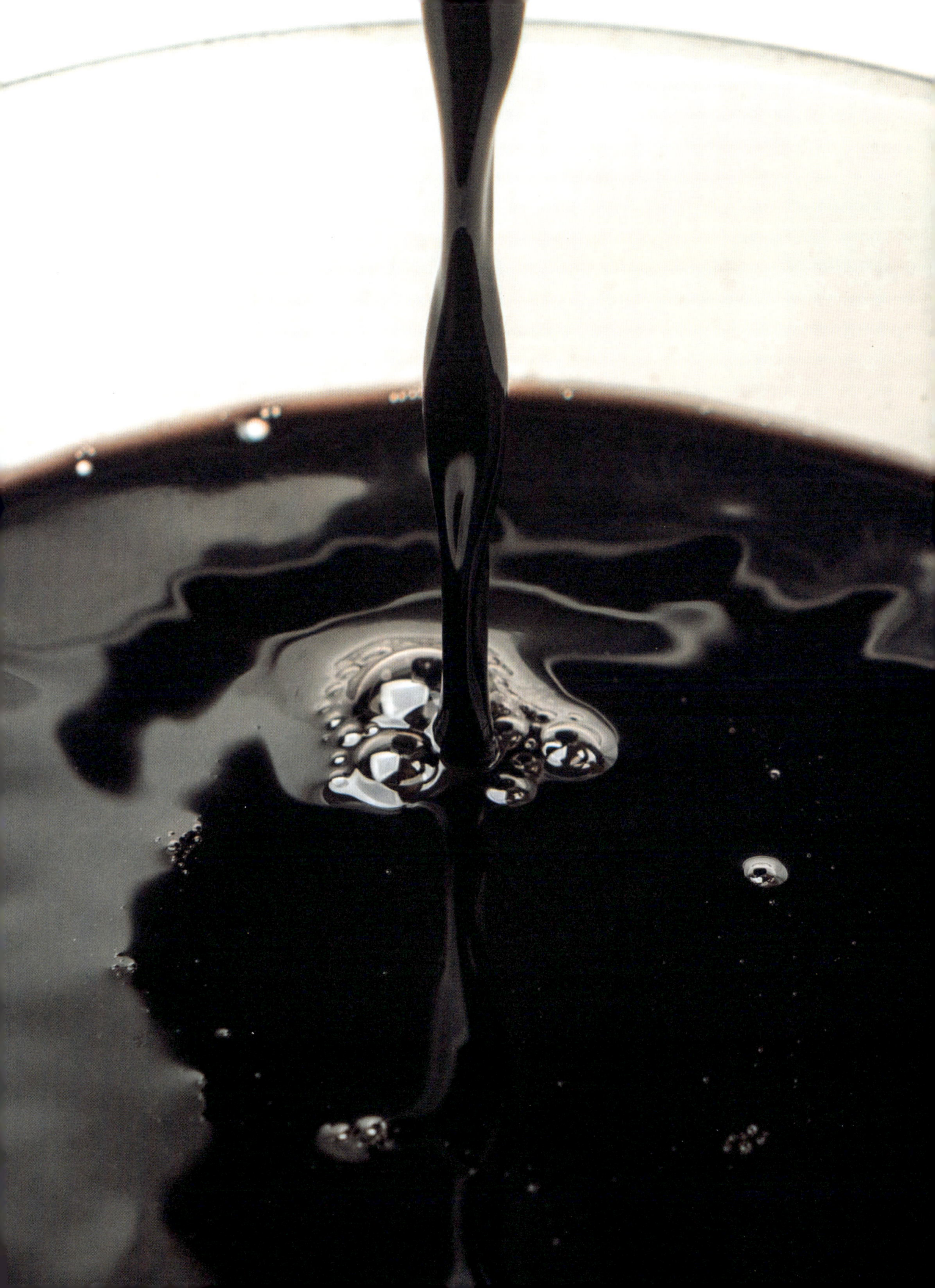

DRAWN TO THE DARK

Prized for flavour, colour and medicinal properties, tannins are polyphenols, chemicals produced by plants to keep them safe from insect attack, grazing or disease. These compounds make the plant somewhat distasteful to predators, but often very useful to humans. They have been used for many thousands of years in the production of medicines, dyes, poisons, flavourings, preservatives and more. We'll be using a variety of plant sources for our inks, some of which are also used in the traditional tanning of leather.

When simmered, many tannin-rich plant materials yield beautiful colours on their own. Onion skins produce warm browns, willow bark can yield spicy russet, bay and rosemary leaves create a surprising gold ochre colour, and ornamental purple cherry tree leaves give a mysterious maroon. These are often pretty good lightfast inks. If, however, you want deep tones or true black, then you need to add iron in the form of rust or iron salts, such as dyer's mordant (iron II sulphate), known by early European ink makers as 'copperas'.

Where to find tannin sources

Some common sources for tannins are:

- Acorn shells (not the nut meat)
- Horse chestnut shells
- Alder cones and other woody tree seed pods
- Trimmings from woody hedges
- Miscellaneous bark from the bottom of your log basket or from discarded christmas trees is ideal, so keep an eye out in the winter
- Stripped bark from preparing basketry weavers from willow or hazel
- Fruit and vegetable peels such as pomegranate rinds, onion skins, chestnut shells
- Dark leaves, such as purple ornamental cherry tree leaves, also make a great mahogany-coloured ink which combines tannins with other colour-bearing compounds. Gather these leaves in early autumn, just before they all fall and get washed out by rain.

Abundant in September, round oak galls are easily found within oak hedgerows in Suffolk, UK.

Here you can see the holes where the gall wasps have escaped to fly away and continue their life cycle.

Fridge contents of inks 26.5.22

PAGE OF INK TESTS

From time to time I take an inventory of all the inks I have in my studio. It helps me know what I need to make more of and shows me how the inks change over time.

Don't worry, the fridge top shelf is labelled 'Ink – Not Drink!' so my housemate Duncan and our guests are kept perfectly safe.

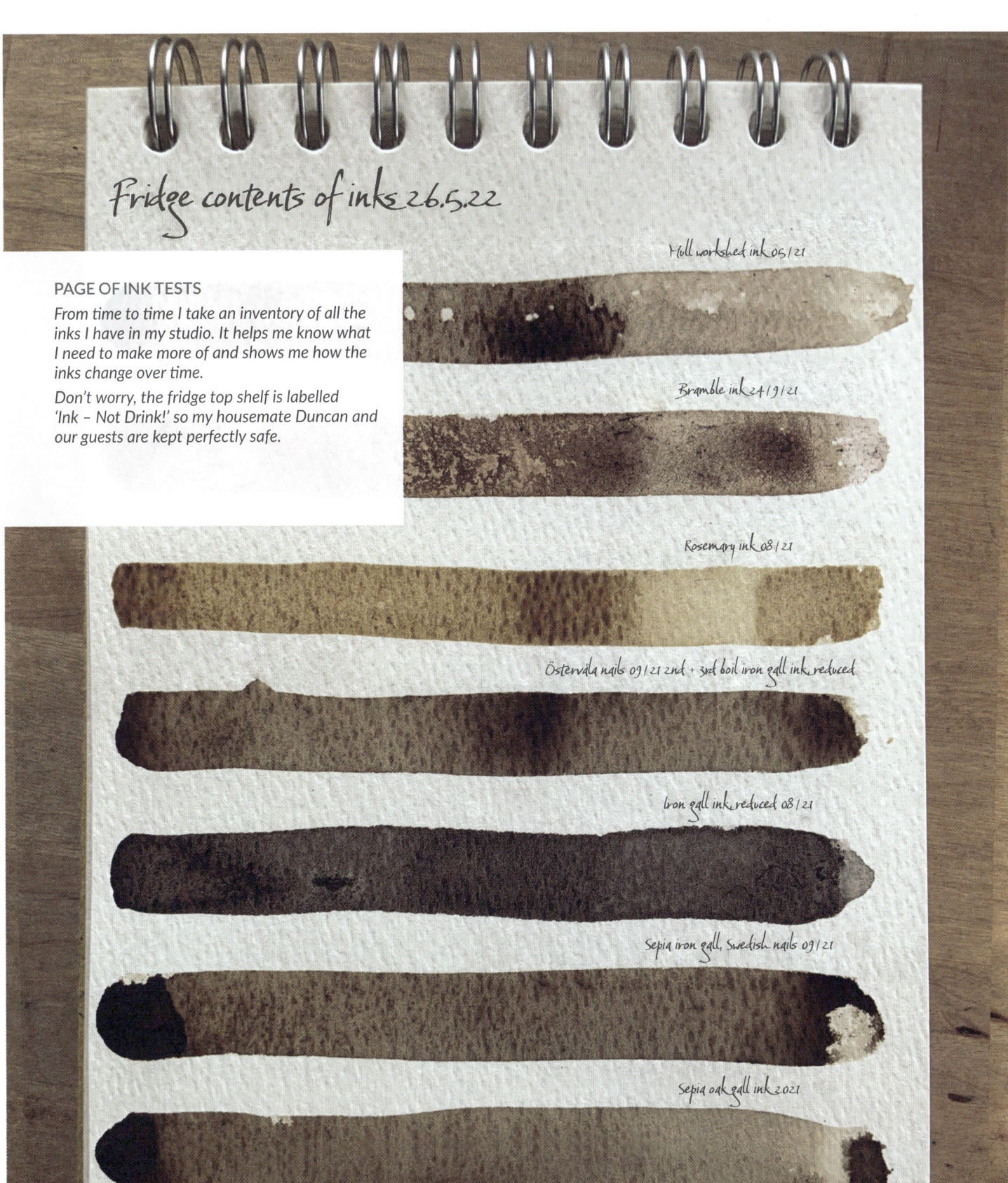

Mull workshed ink 05/21

Bramble ink 24/9/21

Rosemary ink 08/21

Östervåla nails 09/21 2nd + 3rd boil iron gall ink reduced

Iron gall ink reduced 08/21

Sepia iron gall, Swedish nails 09/21

Sepia oak gall ink 2021

Round gall iron gall

Themazi gall powder

26/5/22

Tannin-bearing media to try

Once you start looking, you'll find tannins everywhere: in these inks, in your tea, even in your glass of full-bodied red wine. Depending on where you live, these sources may be more common or scarce, so any bark or abundant woody seed pod is worth a try.

FORAGED OBJECT	THE RESULTING INK	RESULTING INK MARKS

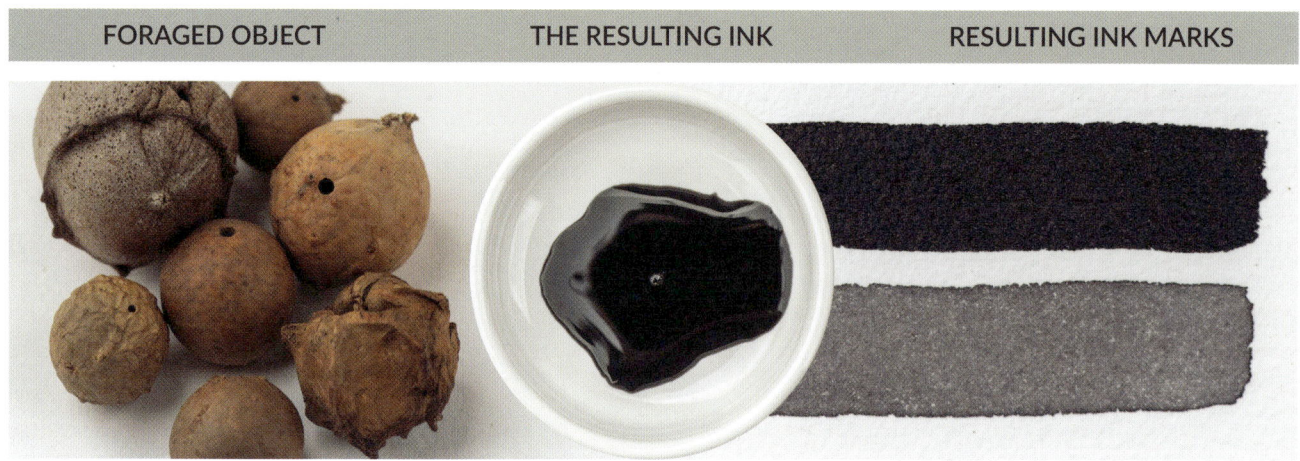

OAK GALLS

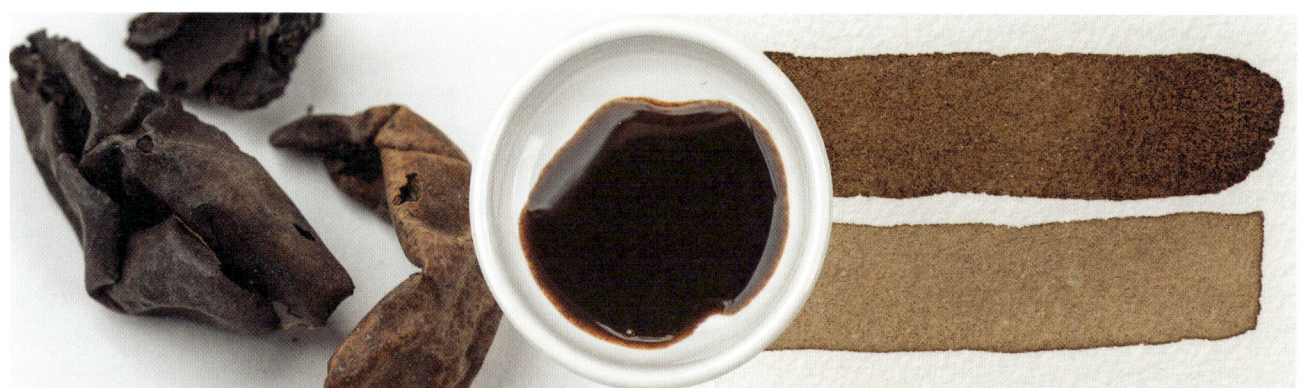

WALNUT HUSKS

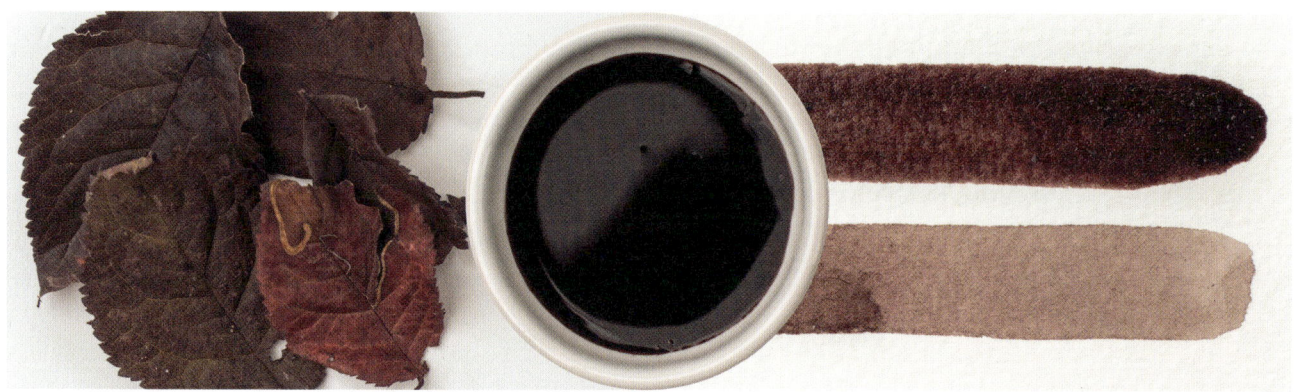

PRUNUS LEAVES

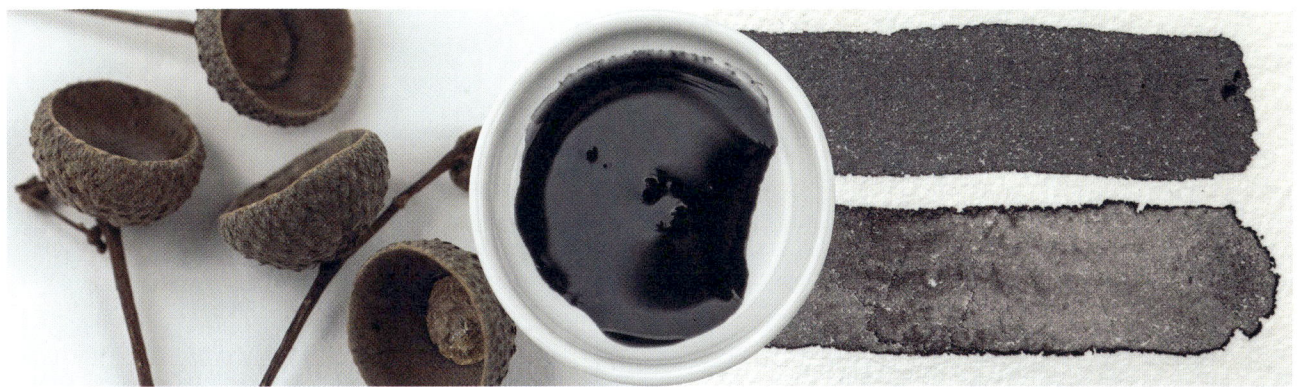

ACORN CAPS

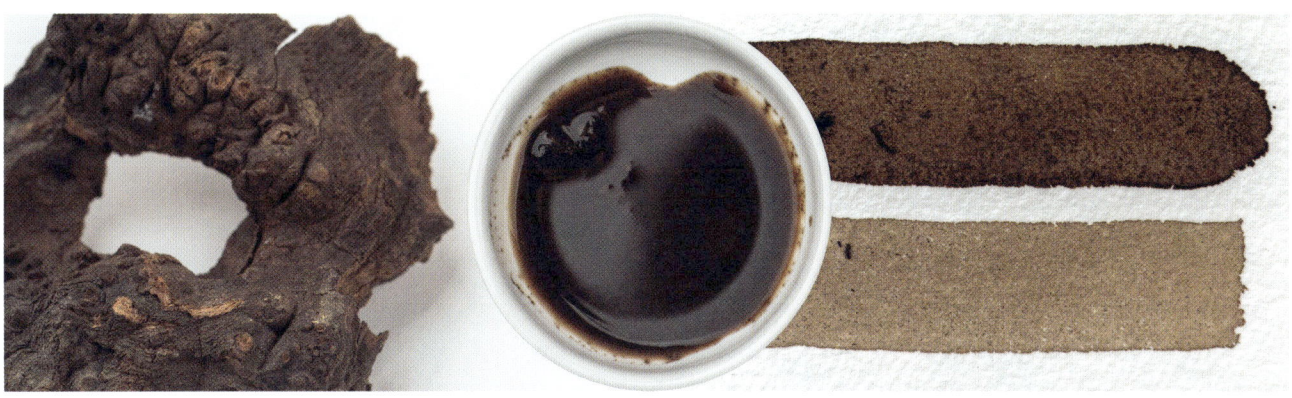

TREE BARK

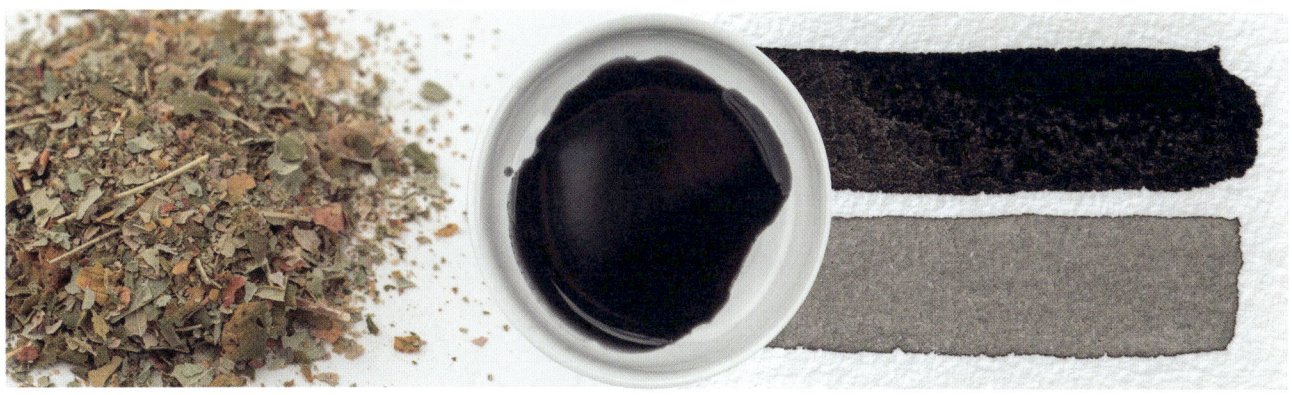

SUMAC LEAVES

INKS

We'll be looking at ways to make a few wonderful traditional inks as well as a method to get you experimenting with what's abundant near you.

Making tannin inks

Tools needed

Tannin source, cloth bag, rolling pin, water pans, stove, non-metallic spoon, sieve, heatproof jug, test paper strips, iron source

Useful extras:
Funnel

With this method you can produce traditional European-style black iron gall ink, (also known as oak gall ink), as well as equally traditional oak bark ink, as used in ancient manuscripts.

You can make a pure ink by using just one type of tannin source, such as one kind of oak gall, or – as here – you can combine different sources, which is useful if you only have a little of each. For this 'forest floor ink' I'm using a mix of English round oak galls, large oak galls from Italy and holm oak caps from Dorset clifftop. You'll also need some rusty nails or other rusty iron, as we have some chemistry to do.

Creating the liquor

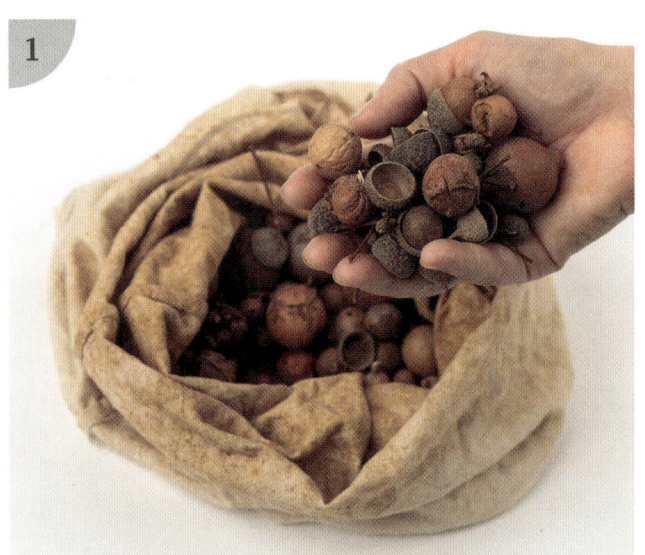

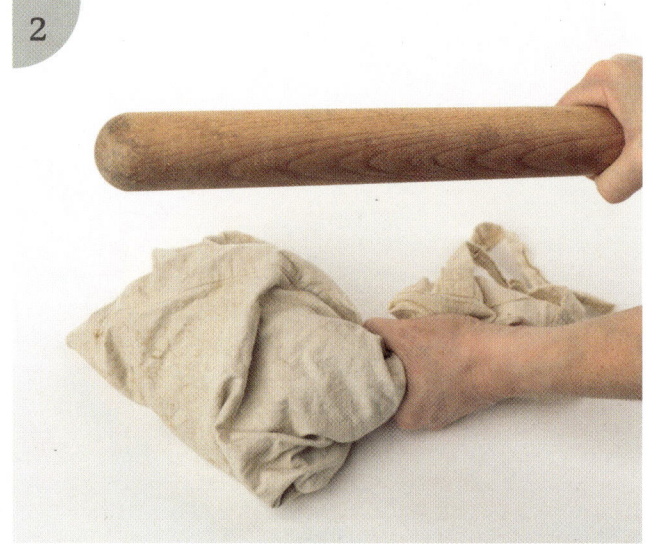

1 If bulky, like galls or acorn caps, place at least two large handfuls of your tannin source into a cloth bag and smash them, the finer the better. If using bark or woody cones, you may need to chop up the material on a stump using an axe. Lighter materials, such as leaves, can be crumbled by hand.

2 Close the bag and use a rolling pin to smash the tannin source – breaking them down into pieces the size of breadcrumbs is ideal. This is best done outside.

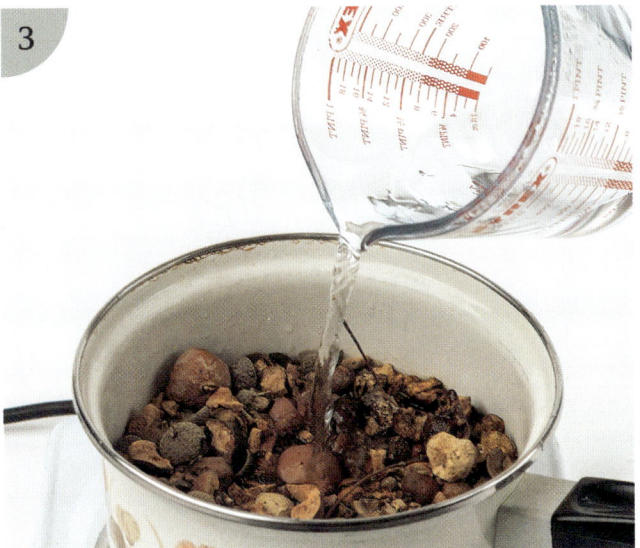

3 Place the smashed tannin source into a saucepan, and cover with at least twice as much water. Bring to a boil, then turn down to a simmer. Stir occasionally to keep the galls submerged.

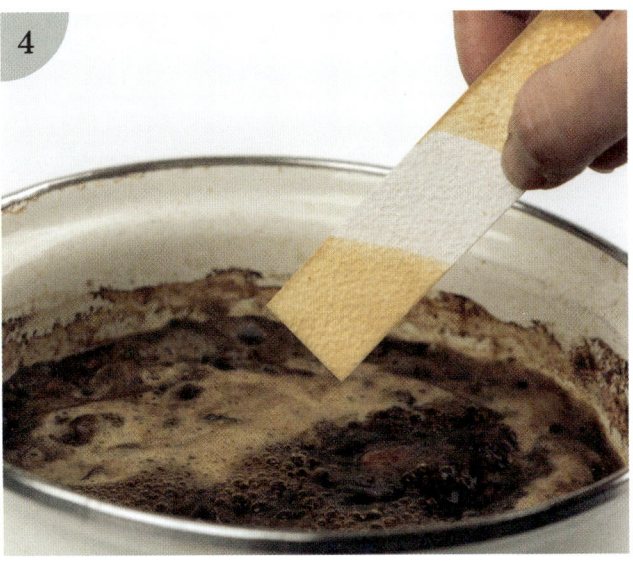

4 Simmer very gently for around half an hour. If you wish, you can dip a strip of paper in to see the colour that is developing. Depending on what you're using as your tannin source, you may end up with a rich brown liquor – but equally many tannins, such as sumac leaves or Aleppo galls, give a paler liquor. Don't worry; both coloured and colourless tannin liquor will make a strong black when combined with iron.

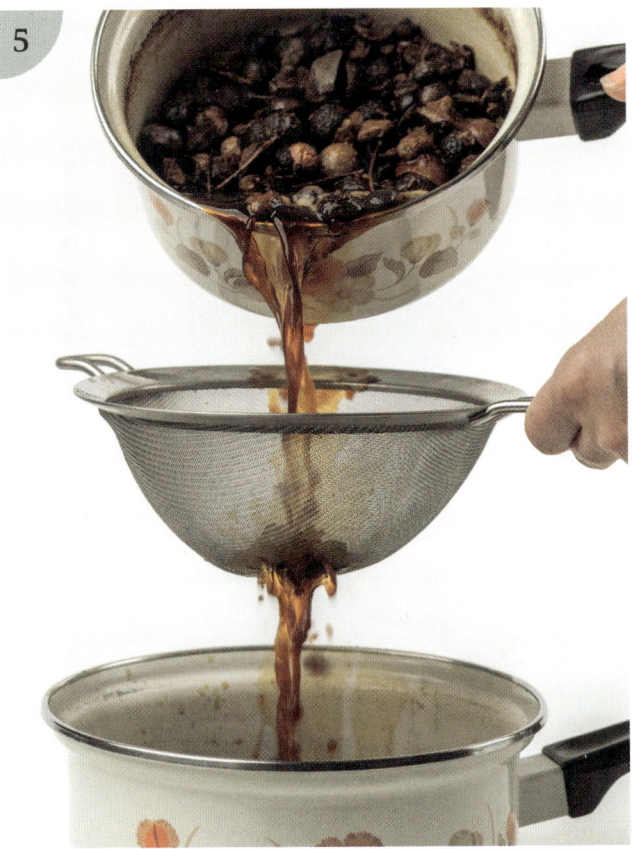

5 After 20–30 minutes of simmering, take the pan off the heat and pour the liquid through a sieve into a heatproof jug. This is your liquor. The tannin source can be re-used several times, so set it aside, or freeze it for later use.

Tip

At this point, the liquor can be used straight away as a brown ink. Walnut husks, purple prunus leaves, alder cones, willow bark and many more tannin sources give wonderful rich colours without iron. Bottle a little with up to 10% added gum Arabic for a range of harmonizing inks before modifying the rest with iron to darken it.

Iron gall ink: turning the liquor black

The term for the process of turning the liquor darker (up to and including black) is 'modifying' the ink.

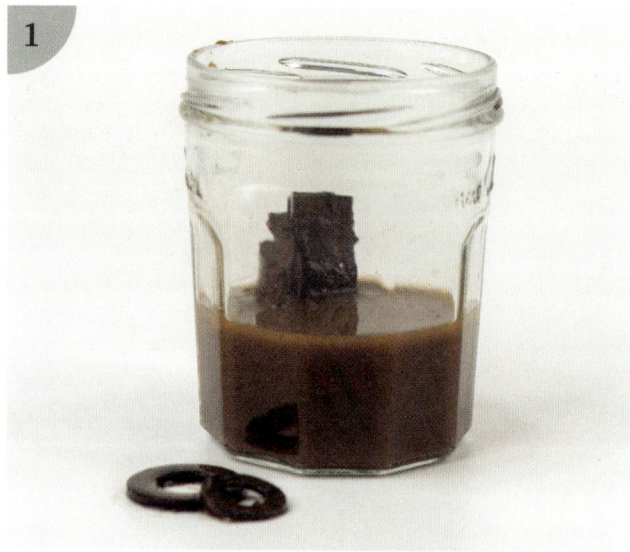

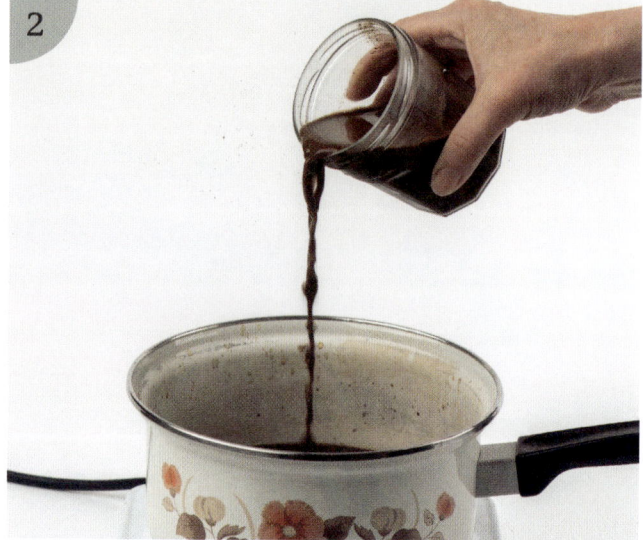

1 Make a rust plant. This is very simple, but takes some time. All you need to do is place a few rusty items in a glass or plastic container. Add just enough water to mostly cover them, leaving some exposed to the air. Leave the container open to the air in a sheltered place for a few weeks until you get rust sediment forming. The liquid is rust water.

2 Pour a large splash of rust water into your prepared ink liquor – the proportions are not critical. The liquor will instantly start to darken.

Rust plant

Rust is just oxidized iron. You can use anything iron for your rust plant: nails, bolts or other scrap iron; or even flakes of rust. Optionally, you can add a splash of vinegar to help oxidize the iron.

Top up your rust plant from time to time as you use it. Keep your rust plant away from pets and children and wash your hands if you spill any rust on them. Alternatives to rust are dyer's iron mordant (copperas) or crushed iron sulphate food supplement tablets.

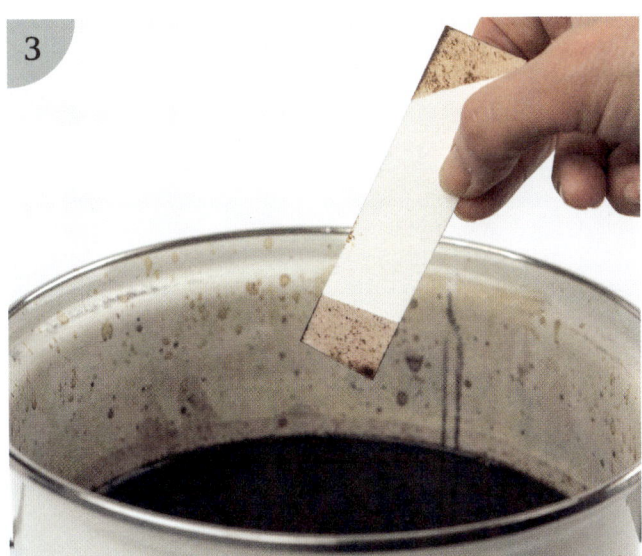

3 Use a strip of paper to test the colour – wait for three or four minutes, as the test strip oxidises and darkens. If the result is not dark enough, you can add more rust water.

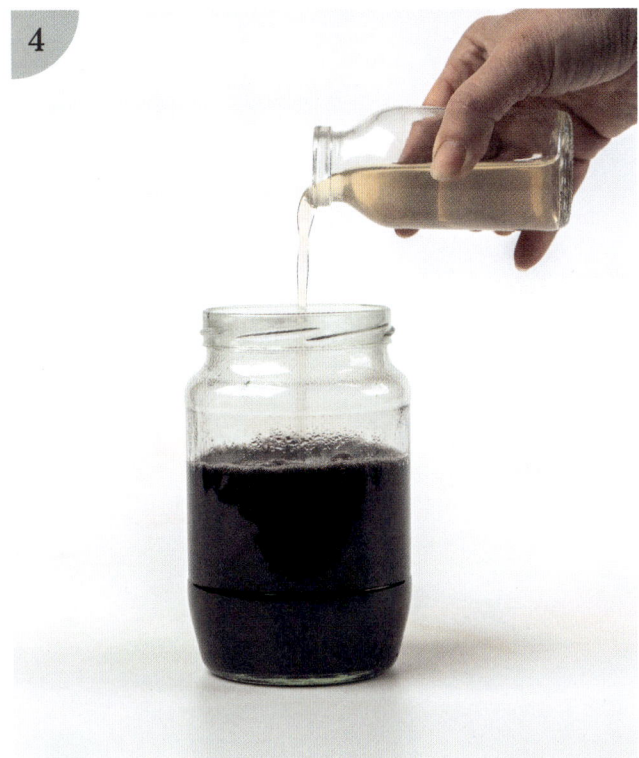

4 Simmer the ink for a few minutes to reduce and thicken it. When it is as dark as you want your ink, pour it into a container. Add liquid gum Arabic to the ink to give it adhesion and fluidity – the proportions should be around nine parts ink to one part gum Arabic. After a quick shake, the ink is now ready to use.

How to use your iron gall ink

Some of my favourite drawings of all time are those of wheat fields by Vincent van Gogh (see right). Created with wide reed pen, slimmer quill pen and metal nibbed pens in dark brown ink, they are full of every kind of mark making – lines, curves, hatching, dots. Some of the most evocative of these drawings formed parts of letters to his brother and are surrounded by words, little details and diagrams and colour notes.

Good black ink encourages us to make a bold mark. I was commissioned to draw from Norse mythology and drew Yggdrasil, the World Tree (see below). On top of some wild improvised feather brush strokes and splatters I continued with a quill pen until the drawing felt alive, the tree had roots and the blots had become crows.

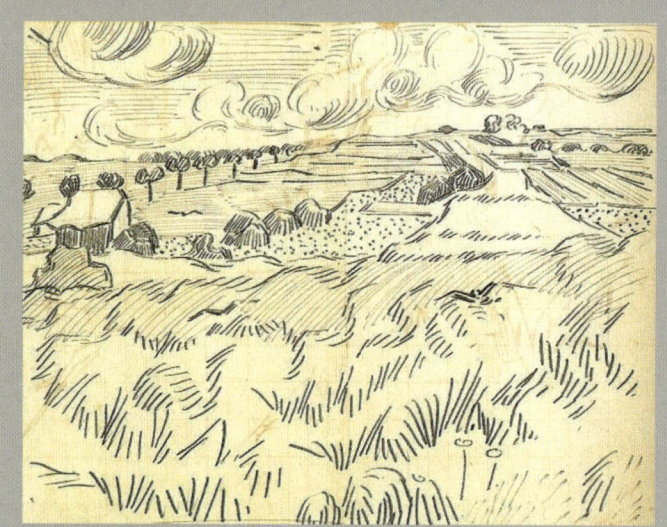

SKETCH OF WHEAT FIELDS 21.7 x 17cm (8½ x 6¾in)
Artist: Vincent van Gogh (1853–1890)
Reverse of a page from a letter to Theo van Gogh, Vincent's brother, showing the wheat fields of Auvers-sur-Oise, France. In the collection of the Van Gogh Museum, Amsterdam (Vincent van Gogh Foundation).

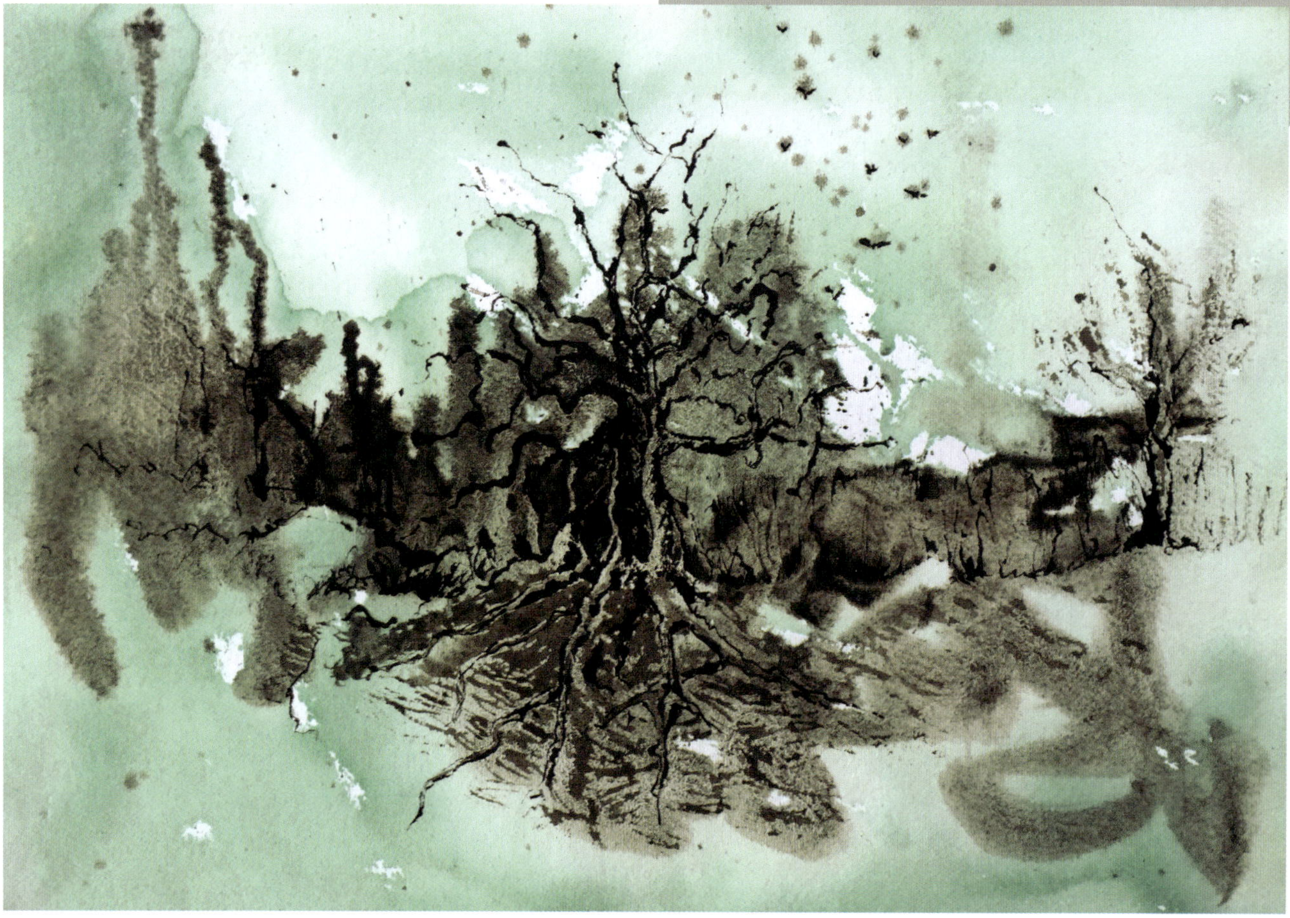

YGGDRASIL 42 x 30cm (16½ x 11¾in)
Iron gall and copper oxide inks on paper. In the collection of Anna Bjorkman.

Candace Jensen's approach

Candace creates exciting drawings through her expressive use of pen and ink line, highlighted with rich colour. This makes even her tiny works vibrate with a mythic atmosphere.

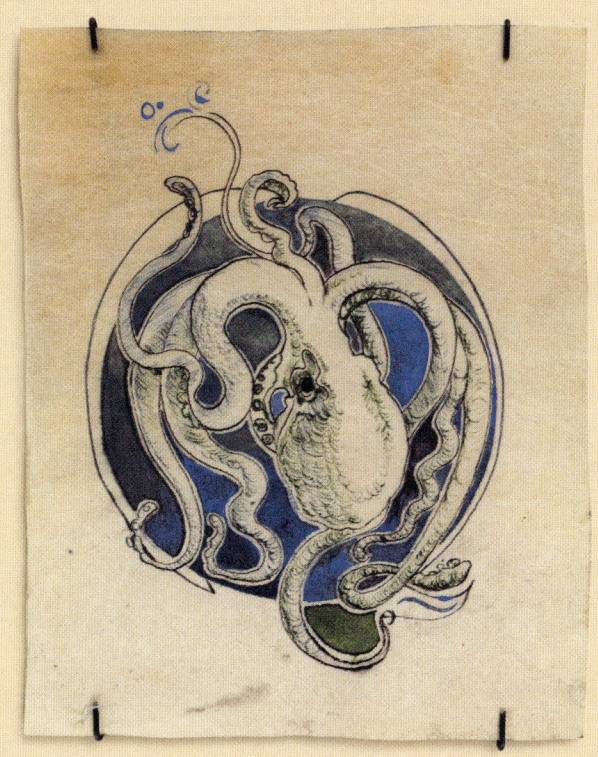

'M' OCTOPUS 7.5 x 12.5cm (3 x 5in)

Ink, homemade indigo ink, watercolour and graphite on goat skin parchment. From the 'Beasts of Sound Made Flesh' series, Recalling the Chimæra.

Candace Jensen Committed to realizing a culture profoundly informed by deep ecology, Candace is an interdisciplinary visual artist, activist, rewilding hype-woman and woods witch. She lives and works in Southern Vermont, part of unceded traditional lands of the Western Abenaki Peoples, or *Elnu Abenaki*.

Jesse Ajilore's approach

Jesse's approach to drawing inspires me with its juxtaposition of the everyday and the lyrical. Elements from the digital world mix with sinuous lines and carefully-drawn textures. I love their hybrid energy.

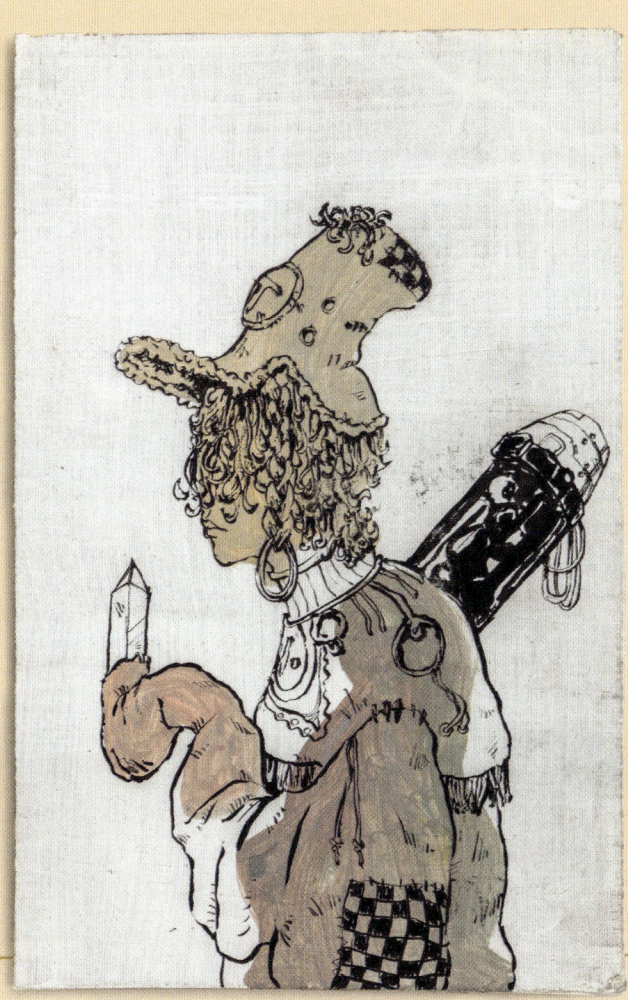

JUSTICE 10 x 15cm (4 x 6in)
Acrylics and ink on cardboard.

Jesse Ajilore Born in London, UK, in 1999, Jesse has a PGDip from the Royal Drawing School. His work blends drawing from memory, observation and imagination, using these to explore how the mind's conscious and subconscious imagery informs our perception.

Modifying your iron gall ink

There are several ways to change the consistency of your inks for interesting drawing and painting effects. Ink can be thickened by fermentation, evaporation or boiling. Simmering the ink is a quick and easy way to thicken it and is a great way to use ink that has had a little mould growing on top. Just pick it off and discard it, then boil.

Thickened ink can be used to make simple block prints with the addition of a little extra gum Arabic liquid.

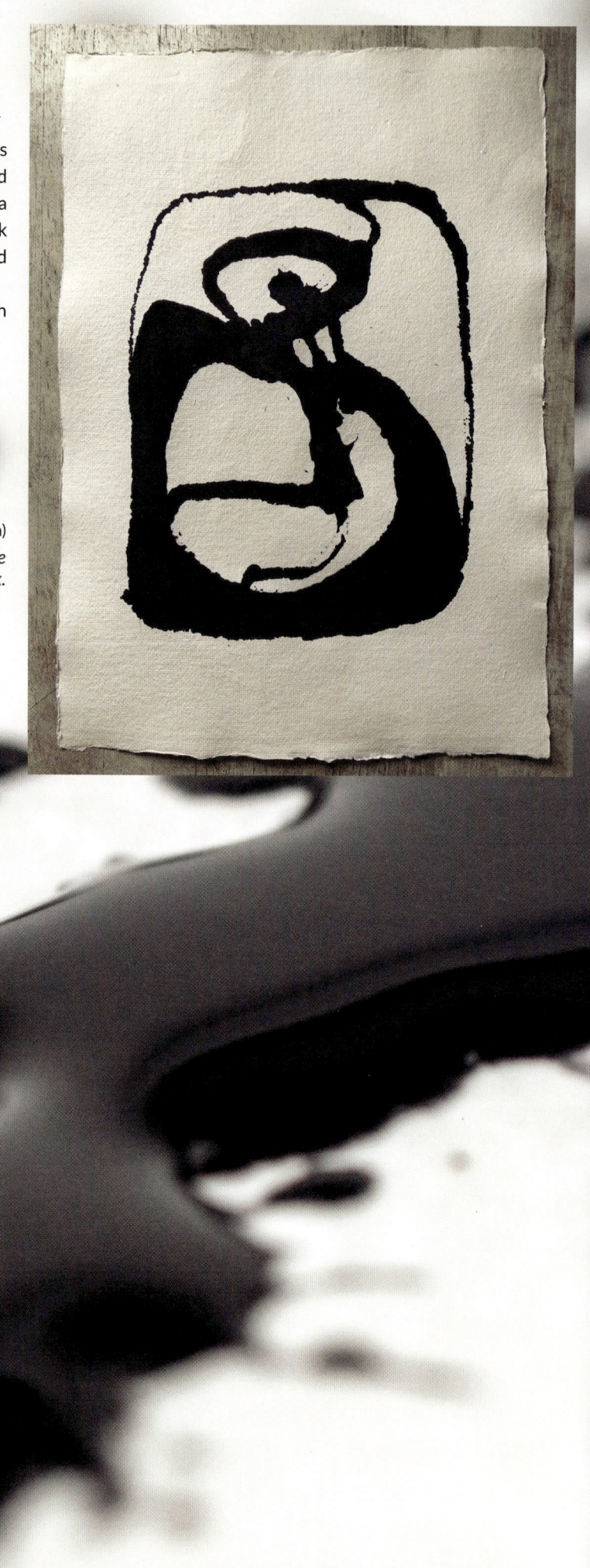

UNTITLED   30 x 42cm (11¾ x 16½in)
Iron gall ink on khadi paper. In the collection of Marcel Theroux.

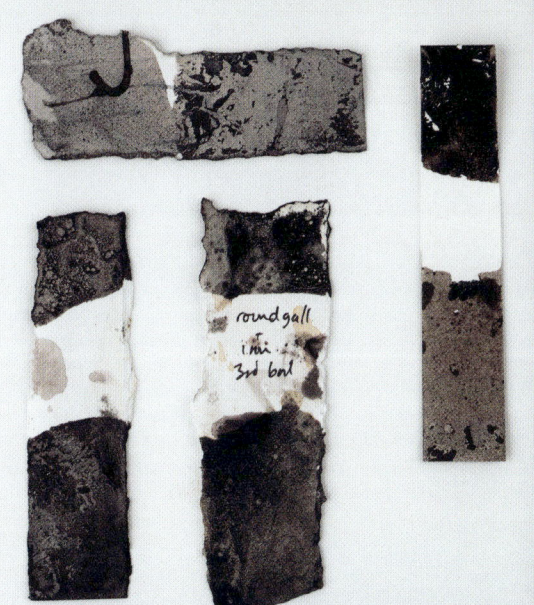

INK TEST STRIPS

Granulating and particulates

Once you know how to make a fine smoothly flowing ink, it's fun to go back and make an ink with more texture, like the example test strips shown to the left. This is easily achieved by using a wider gauge sieve when straining the original boiled tannin source, thereby allowing slightly coarser particles of gall, wood or leaves to come through. As long as you have a good amount of gum Arabic in the final ink, these particulates should adhere to the paper.

I like to use these characterful inks for abstract and landscape drawings. Sometimes I drop salt onto the brush marks, to draw up some of the water and to change the texture of the finished drawings. Use good quality watercolour paper for these heavier inks and techniques so that they don't buckle or bend.

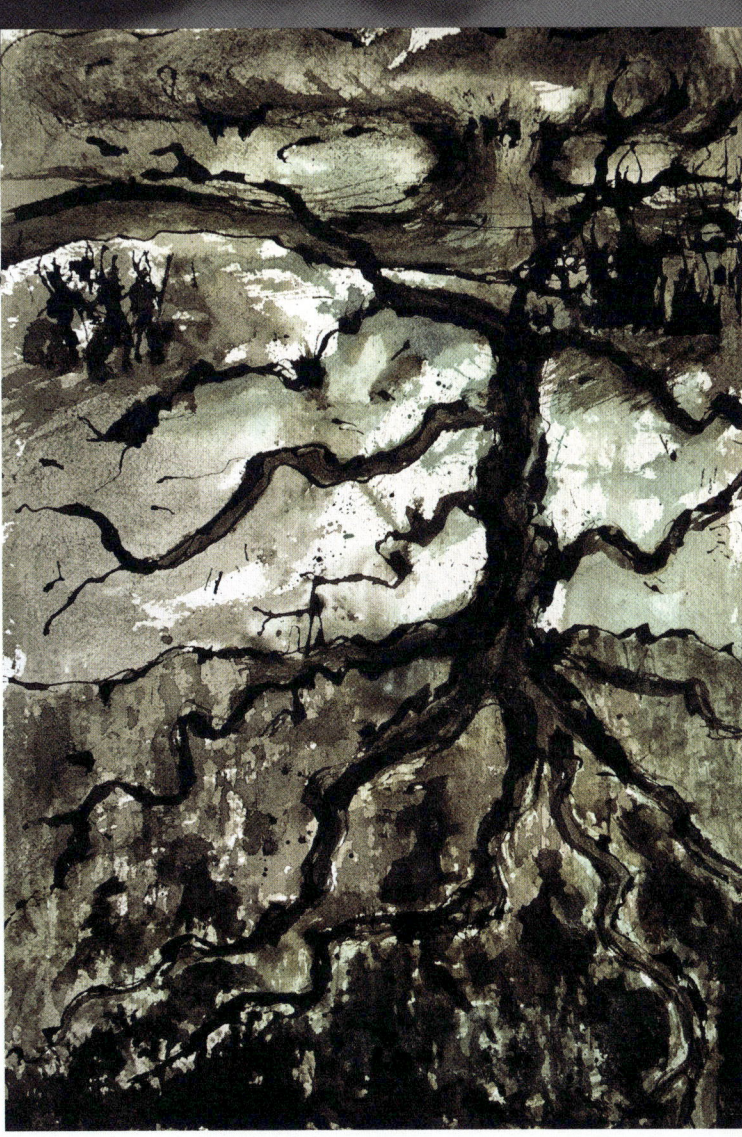

RAGNAROK 30 x 42cm (11¾ x 16½in)
Iron gall and copper acetate inks on khadi paper.

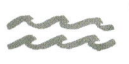 # Making botanical inks

Now you have made sepia and black inks, it's time to experiment with colour. I use tannin inks almost exclusively for my ink artworks, as they have good lightfastness. However, there is much fun to be had making inks that are colourful, even if they are prone to fading after a while. If you take a good photograph of your artwork when it is freshly made, you will see how it changes over time by placing the test in a sunny place, or do two similar tests and keep one in a dark drawer, one in the light. That way, you'll get to know your own ink palette.

You can make inks from a host of botanicals, giving you a way to try out whatever you have a glut of in your home, garden or locale. Ephemeral inks like these are great for making with kids and for greetings cards, which don't have to stand the test of time. There are countless ways to make inks; this is one of the simplest.

1 Place your botanicals (see opposite and overleaf for some suggestions) in a saucepan and cover with hot water.

2 Simmer very gently, and use strips of acid-free watercolour paper (this is because botanicals are often pH sensitive) to test the colour every five minutes or so until the desired colour is reached.

3 Strain the liquid through a sieve (paper coffee filters can be useful for straining particularly gritty sources), and add ten per cent gum Arabic. Pour the resulting ink into a spotless jar or bottle to prevent fermentation.

Tools needed

Pan, sieve, jug, spoon, water, crushed or powdered botanical source for colour, gum Arabic or cherry tree gum liquid, spotless storage bottle or jar, label and pen

Useful extras:

Paper coffee filters

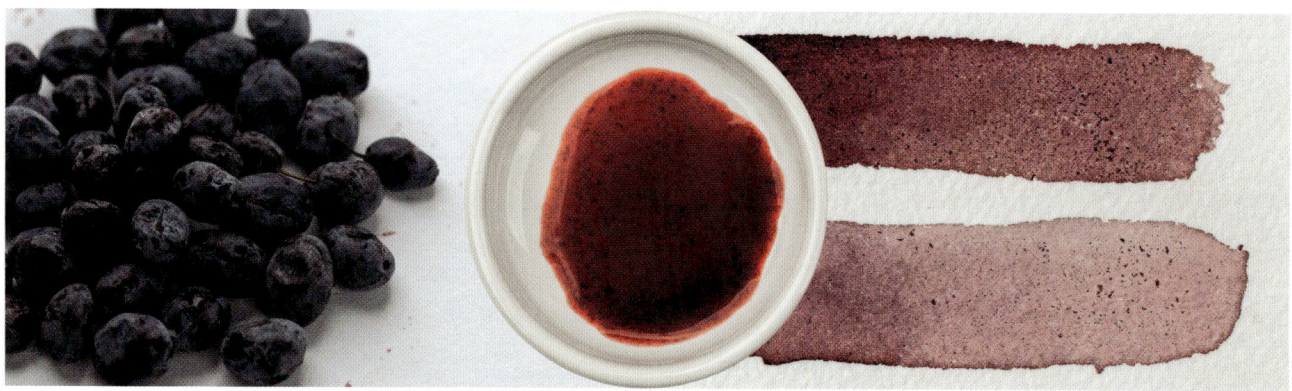

MAHONIA BERRIES

A range of colours

Mahonia berries – or 'Oregon grape' – is a common non-native bush in the UK where I live. Planted for ground cover and park edging, they have spiky leaves and early fragrant yellow flowers in February. The berries produce a ruby red.

Also shown here are elderberries for violet ink; daffodil heads for yellow ink; bay leaves for golden ochre ink and marigolds for orange ink.

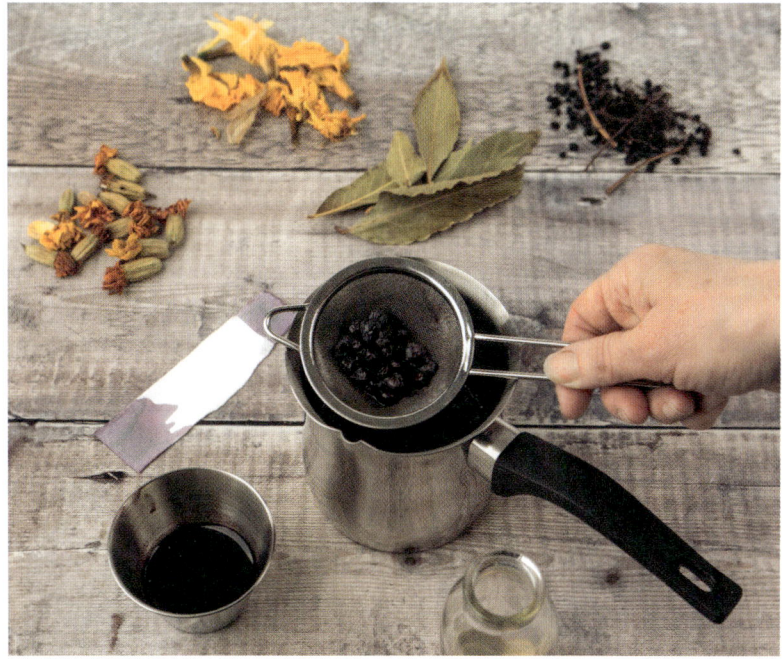

INTO THE MOUNTAINS   28 x 42cm (11 x 16½in)
Mahonia berry, bay leaf and iron gall inks on khadi paper.

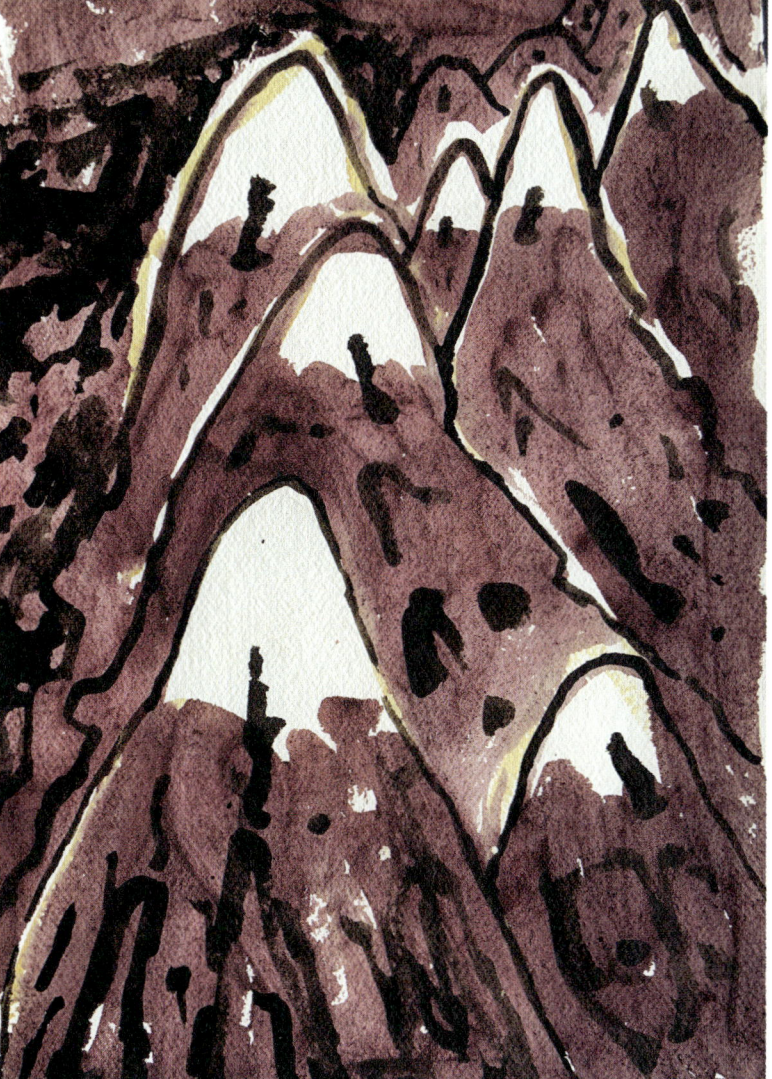

Colour from everyday life

I've lost count of the botanical inks I've made using household waste or garden cuttings from around my neighbourhood, and though none of them is as permanent as walnut, oak gall or iron gall inks, all were a pleasure to swatch and draw with.

You can also experiment with darkening the inks with iron, like we do with the tannin inks. Botanical inks and dyes are both wonderful worlds to explore. See my recommended reading on page 126 for more information.

Flowers from bouquets or the garden Even once they are wilting, flowers are a great no-cost source of colour. Save and dry the petals to make small batches of bright inks. You don't need to have a dedicated dye garden, as many common garden flowers such as marigold or coreopsis are excellent for inks.

Bay leaves Boiled and thickened, these give a wonderful gold.

Blackberries, elderberries, damson These will produce a purple hue. You can add lemon juice to make it lean more red-purple, or bicarbonate of soda to make it more blue-purple.

Lingonberries A good red will result from these.

Rice/bean water Water left over after cooking red rice, black rice and black beans will result in interesting coloured inks when strained and thickened, and are completely free!

Privet berries, ivy berries These are toxic to eat but safe to handle carefully; label any bottle very well. The ink colours you can get from them will depend on the pH of the paper and modifiers you use, and can range from golden yellow to dark grey, via green.

Buckthorn berries This is the original souce for the commercially-available colour 'sap green', but they can give anything from yellow to purple, depending on the pH.

Gorse flowers, or daffodil heads Dried out after the flower wilts, these will make a good yellow ink.

Avocado skins and pips These will produce a rose-coloured ink.

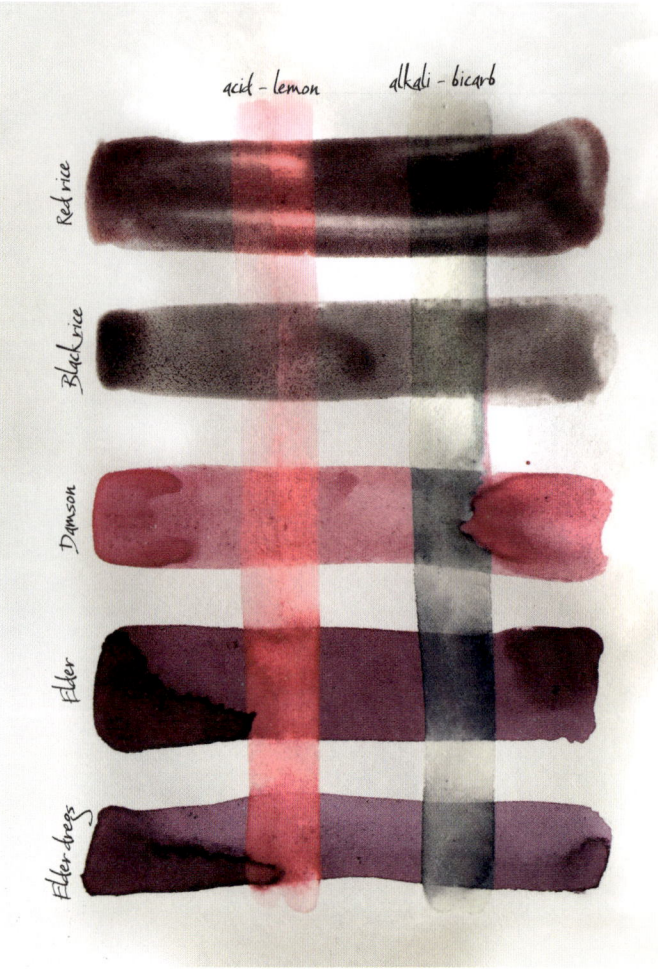

EXPLORING FURTHER

To play, you can add a drop of lemon juice or a little baking soda in water to modify the colours on the paper by changing the acidity (pH). This image shows the effect of adding lemon juice (acidic) and bicarbonate of soda (alkali) to botanical inks.

Thomas Little's approach

Through the transformation of firearms into pigments and inks, Thomas creates art and materials from a deeply ethical source. Removing guns from circulation and dissolving them in acid, Thomas creates high quality pigments and inks for his own and other artists' use. The iron-rich Mars black, red and yellow pigments he creates may be familiar to you in paints already nestling in your palette.

I find Thomas' inks a delight to use with a fine quill pen, whether already liquid, or reconstituted from more easily transported dried powder. His materials and artworks speak to me of alchemy and transformation, completely separate from the mundane trappings of contemporary life. Mythic labyrinths, arcane glyphs and inscrutable ciphers interweave with filigree, shadows and Rorschach blots to create his uniquely arresting graphic art.

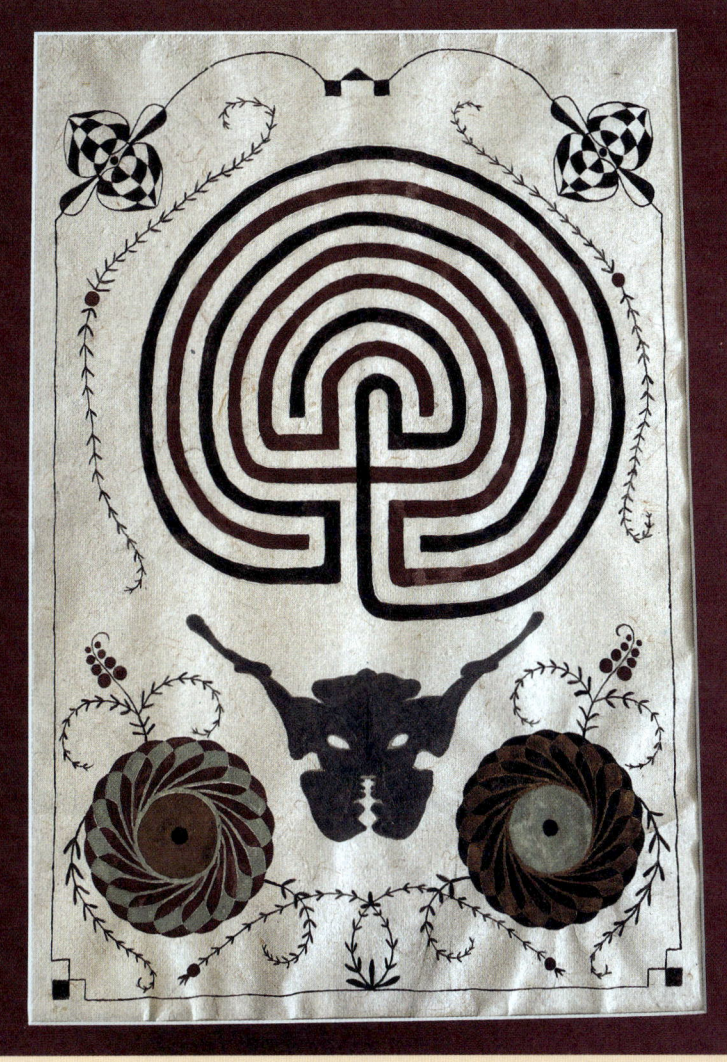

LABYRINTH 42 x 60cm (16½ x 23½in)
Inks made from dissolved guns on paper. In the collection of Caroline Ross.

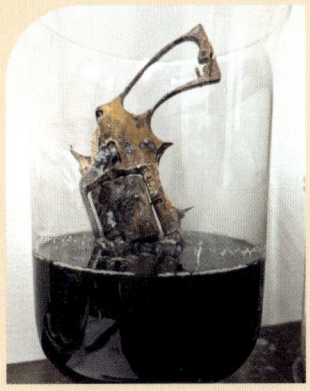
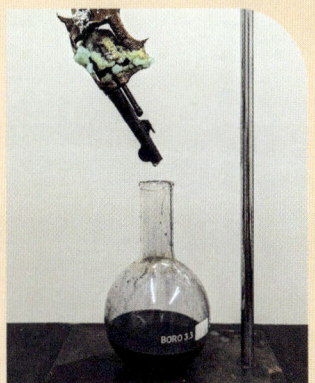
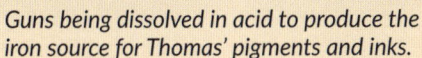

Guns being dissolved in acid to produce the iron source for Thomas' pigments and inks.

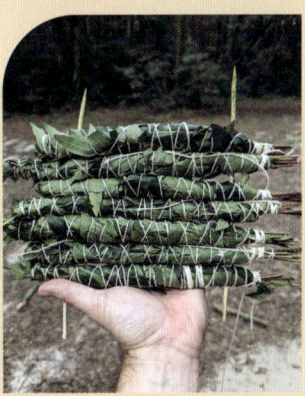
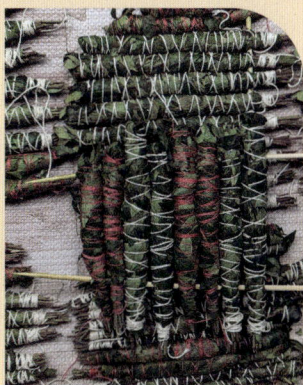
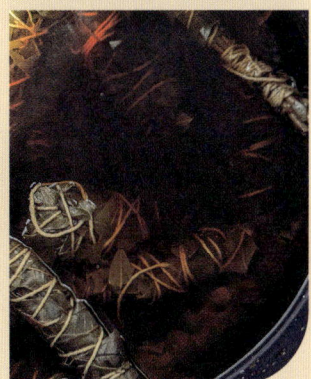

Sumac leaves provide Thomas with the tannin source for his inks. Clockwise from above, they are shown fresh, drying and in use.

Thomas Little was born in 1981, in Sampson County, North Carolina, USA. He still works there.

PENS AND BRUSHES

Quill pens

Quill pens are my favourite drawing tools. For almost a decade I lived aboard boats on the River Thames with a herd of swans as neighbours. Each year during early summer, they and the local geese would moult their long flight feathers, which would come floating downstream on the current. Usually I would pick them up on the shingle beach overlooking Hampton Court Palace. If a particularly good feather was floating past, I'd lean over with a fishing net and pluck it from the water.

Nowadays I collect feathers in a local estuary and harbour, along the beach, and on the clifftop. I use herring gull feathers too, and have successfully used huge feathers from peacocks, pheasants and even one from a black swan.

If you cannot find large feathers, you can easily buy them from shops that supply calligraphers and illuminators, or from online craft or millinery suppliers. Bought feathers will have the advantage of being ready cleaned, sorted and graded for quality.

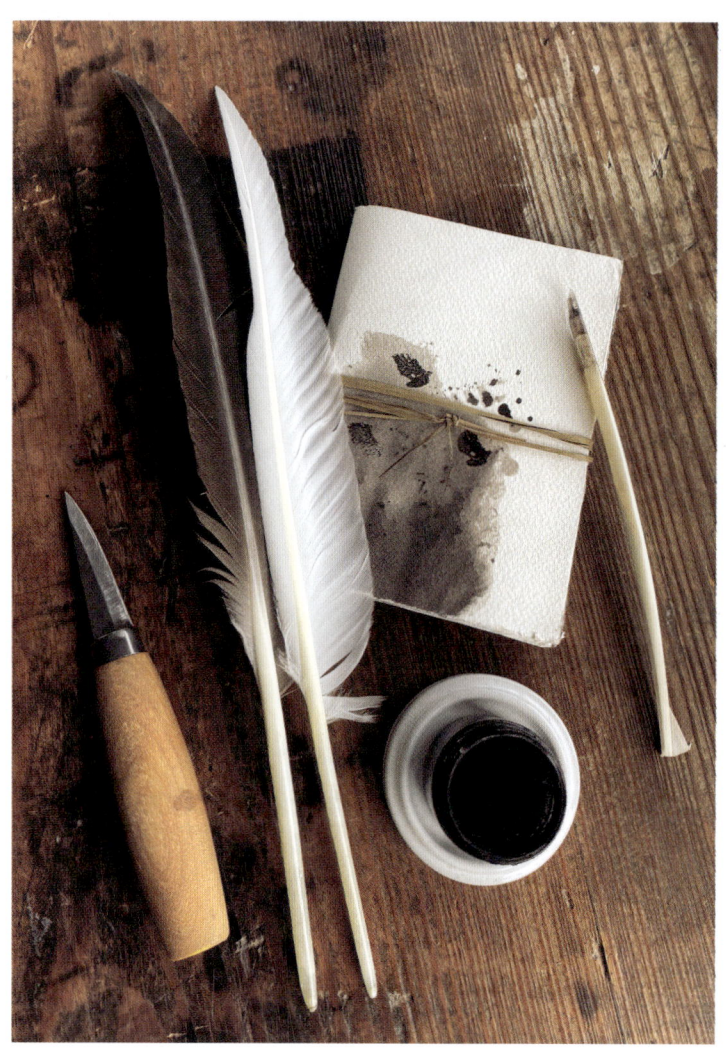

A finished quill pen alongside fresh feathers, ink and a notebook.

Preparation and safety

Bird feathers must always be washed as they can harbour mites which can destroy leather or fur belongings. They can also carry bird flu, so don't bring them home unwashed if you have birds at home. Always wash your hands after touching foraged feathers and discard any that are broken or split.

I bring all feathers home to give them a good wash in the bath using a little dishwashing liquid and a small capful of bleach. Wearing gloves, I wash them thoroughly with an old nailbrush saved for the purpose, then rinse them using the shower. I shake them hard then hang them up to dry. Only when they are bone dry do I store them, usually in earthenware jugs, as they look so beautiful.

Penknives

The first cut is indeed the deepest when it comes to making your pens. Until mass-produced metal nibbed pens became the norm, a penknife was an essential piece of everyday kit, carried by anyone who could read or write. Sharp enough to cut a quill or resharpen the nib as it wore down, the penknife could come in many shapes, some with rounded leaf-shaped blades, others with a gentle curve. These everyday quill cutting tools gave us the term 'penknife' for pocketknife in British English, still in use today for any handy little knife we carry.

For this technique, we use a sharp knife – the sort of thing you might use for whittling wood – for the initial cuts. It needs to be strong, very sharp, and have a slight curve. We also need a sharper scalpel-like blade for the shaping. A dead straight scalpel or knife is not ideal, although you can use it to sharpen a pen once it is cut.

To the right you can see a selection of the knives that I use to cut feather and reed pens. One day I would like an historically accurate leaf blade penknife, but for now this selection is perfect for the job.

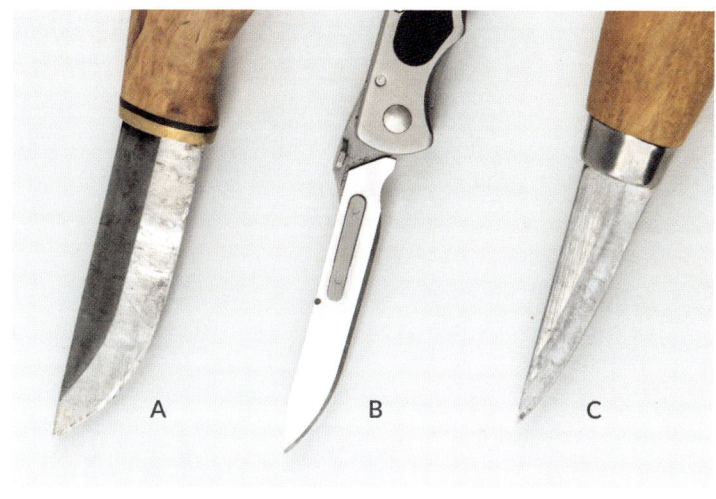

SELECTION OF KNIVES
A – *Small bushcraft-style knife*
B – *Rounded scalpel-style craft knife*
C – *Small whittling knife*

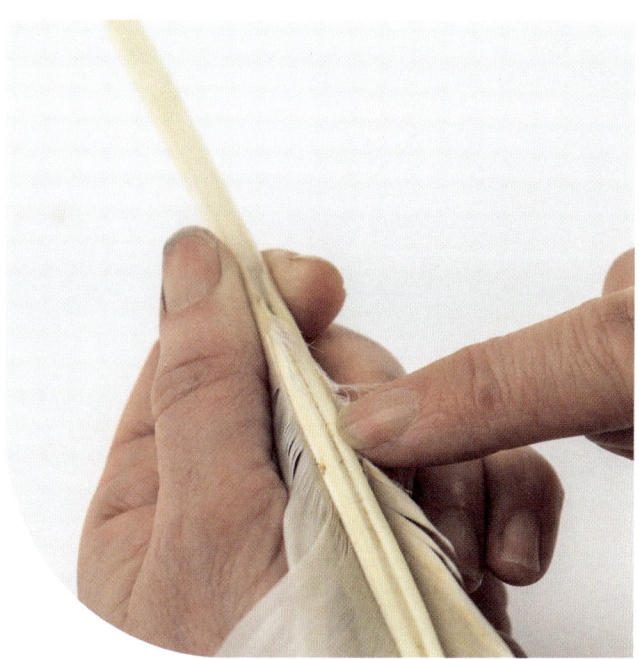

Feathers have a groove that runs along the bottom of the feather's shaft, all the way to the tip. While making a quill pen, we always keep this groove facing upwards.

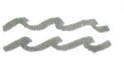
Making a quill pen

Although it is not a long or complicated process, like many craft skills, quill making can take a little while to master. The trick is not to rush, and to check that your feather is in the alignment you need for each cut, especially having the groove facing straight up to start with. Have a few practice goes with a less than perfect feather before committing to that huge one you were saving for best.

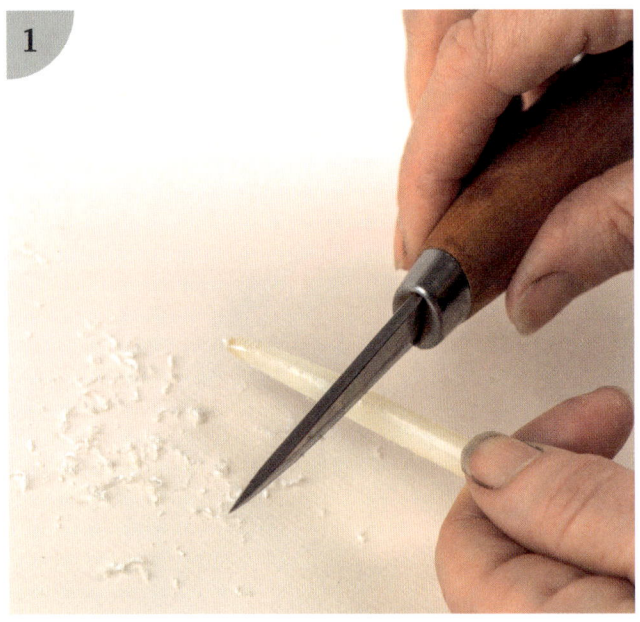

1 The shaft of the feather has a plastic-feeling surface that we need to remove. Use the knife to scrape the film off the first 6cm (2¾in) from the tip of the feather.

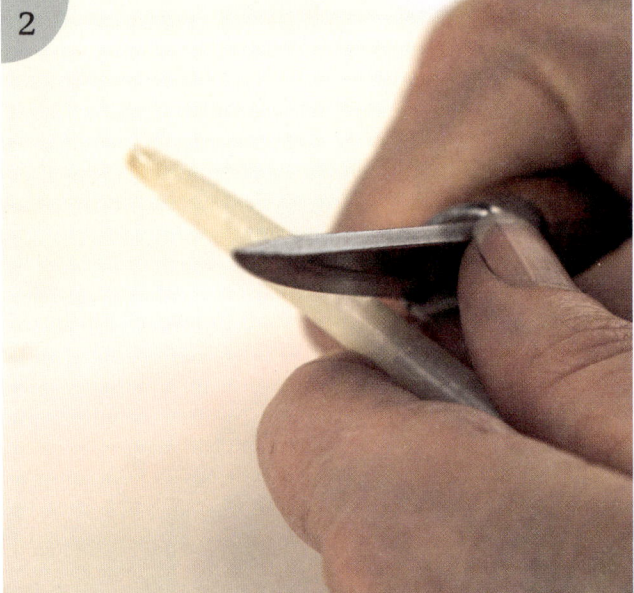

2 Holding the feather firmly with the groove facing upwards, place your knife around 4cm (1¾in) from the tip, at a 60-degree angle.

Safety

Use a sharp knife. Dull blades can cause injuries as we tend to be less accurate when we use force to make the cut.

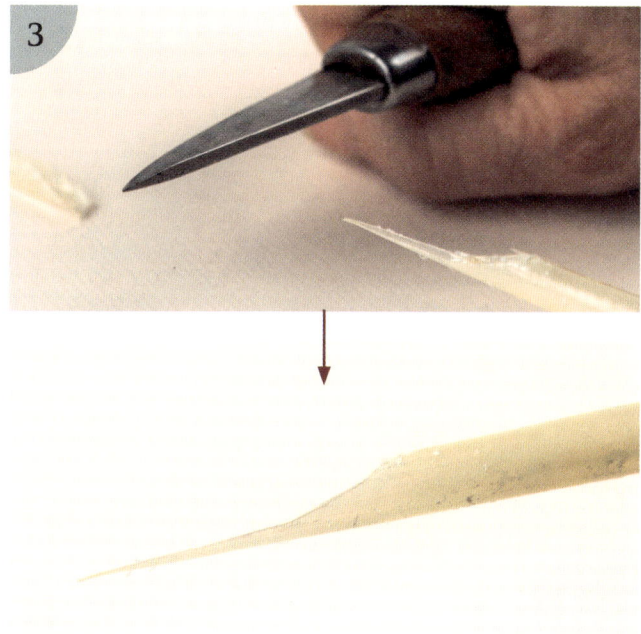

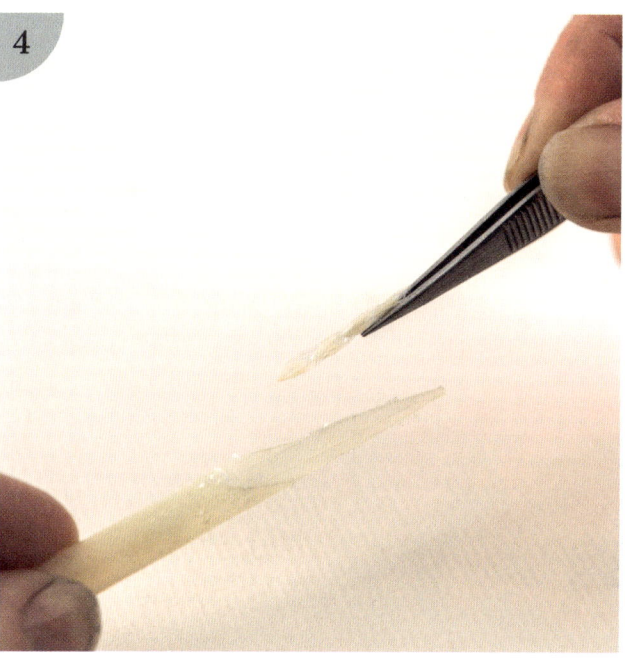

3 Using a curved, scooping action, make a firm cut to take off the end, leaving a curved tip as shown.

4 Use a pair of fine tweezers to reach inside the shaft and firmly grasp the filament (the remnants of the feather's blood vessel) and pull it out.

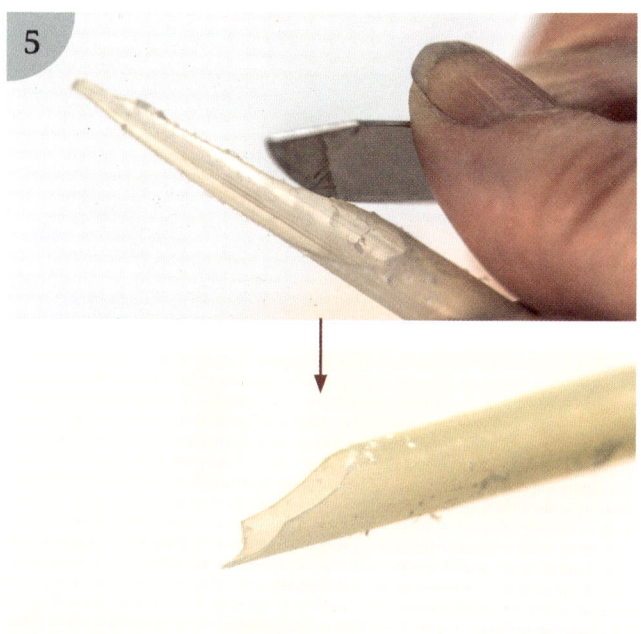

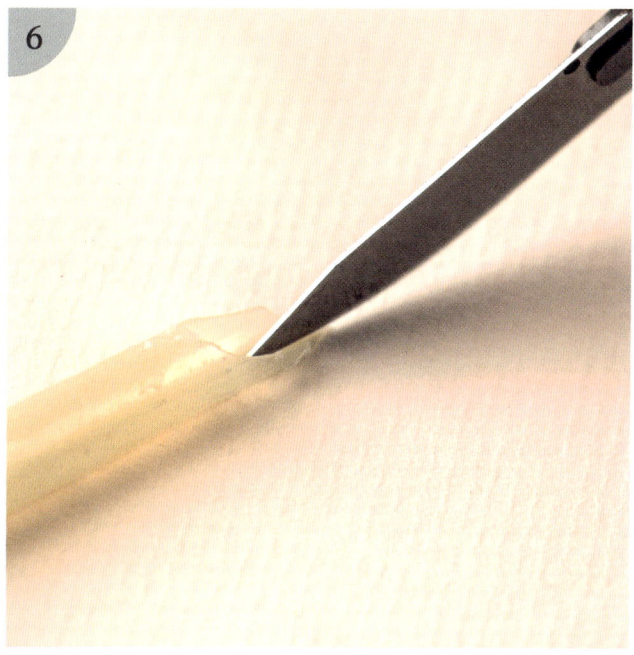

5 Swap to a scalpel to shape the nib. Make two curved cuts as shown, one on either side of the tip.

6 Place the pen on the mat, and use the scalpel to gently score the inside of the tip, by pulling the feather while holding the knife in place. Scoring helps the ink to flow towards the tip. You don't have to cut all the way through – but if you do, that's fine.

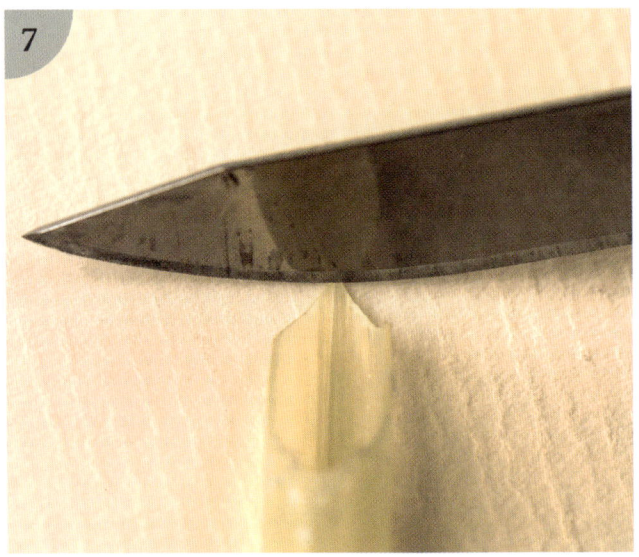

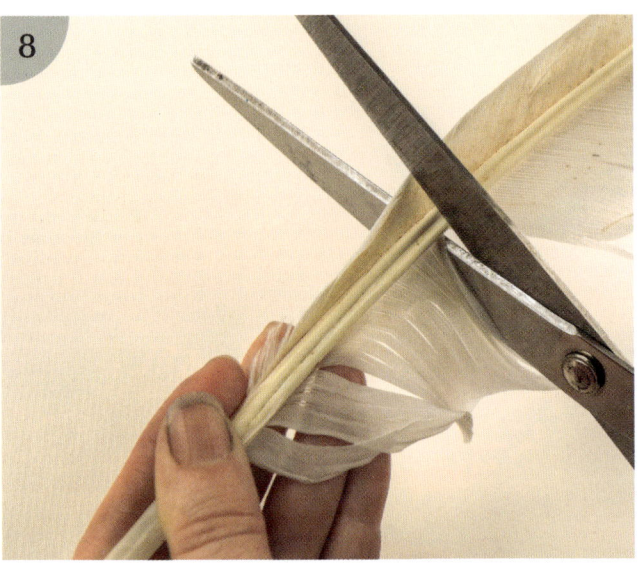

7 You can now reach inside with the knife to gently scrape away the plastic-feeling sheath from the inside of the pen. With that complete, carefully cut away the tip – the resulting tip will give you the width of line the pen will make.

8 Using strong scissors, cut the feather to pen length – around 20cm (8in) from the tip.

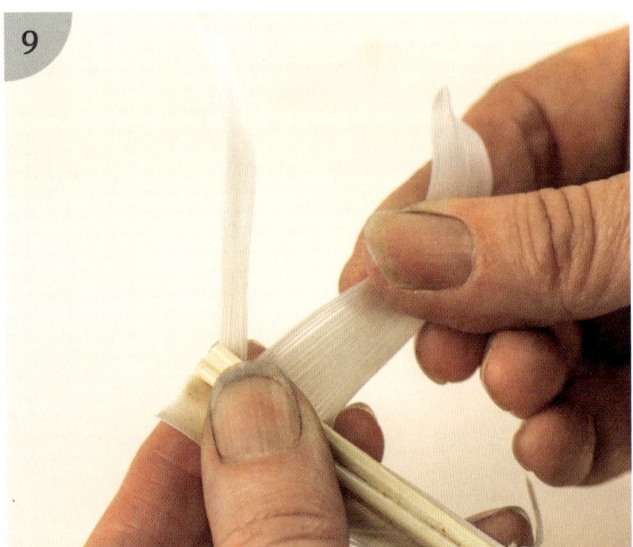

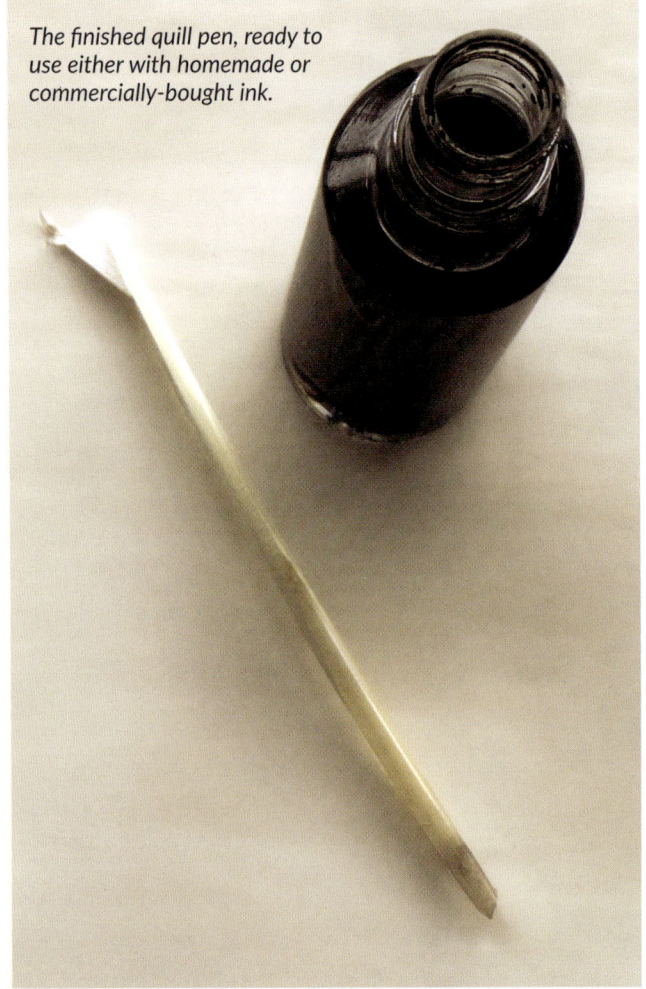

The finished quill pen, ready to use either with homemade or commercially-bought ink.

9 To finish, de-barb the feather – that is, remove the soft feathery parts by pulling or cutting them off – to finish your quill pen.

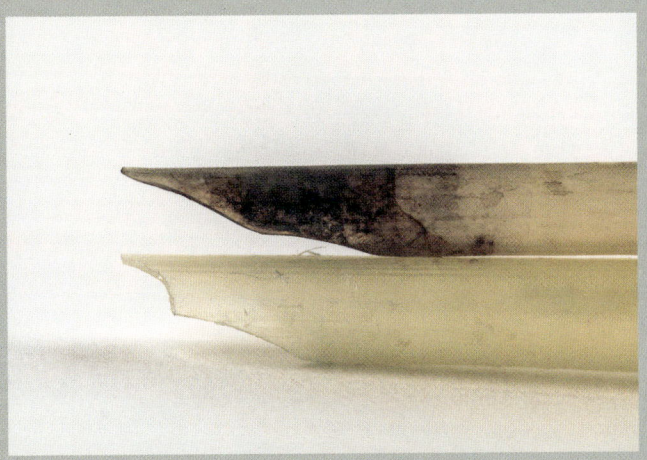

Different shapes of nib

The shape of modern metal fountain pen nibs is based on the type of quill pen we have made. On both modern and feather pens, back from the tip, we have the 'shoulders'. We don't usually want these to drag on the paper as we write, so after you have cut a quill, test it with ink to see if the line it makes is good at the angle you hold your pen. If the shoulders scrape on the page, it can double or triple the mark, which might be great for an expressive drawing, but ruin some careful calligraphy.

It is easy to pare back the shoulders a little at a time using a sharp scalpel or craft knife. In the picture above, the top quill has unobtrusive shoulders, which do not touch the paper when I draw with it. The newly-cut white quill below it will need its pointy shoulders paring back somewhat. By experimenting, find what shape works best for you.

Tempering quill pens

Quills used for calligraphy are usually tempered by plunging them for about 15 seconds into a pan of hot sand. This gives a tougher, longer-lasting nib, better suited to writing – but less suitable for expressive drawing lines.

To temper your nib, cut the end off your feather and pull out the filament using fine-nosed tweezers. Soak the shaft of the feather in a glass of water overnight. Next day, heat clean sand in a small pan until it spits if you flick water on it, then submerge the first 5cm (2in) of the feather into the sand, being careful not to let it touch the pan sides. Check every so often until the clear shaft has gone somewhat opaque or white, and repeat if necessary.

Compare tempered and un-tempered quills for cutting and drawing, and see what works best for you. You can get a similar effect to tempering by leaving the feathers to cure for up to a year in a warm dry place. I used to hang mine high in a corner above my wood stove for at least six months, after which time they were perfect for use. They always looked rather beautiful.

If you want a more decorative pen, then you can leave the feather at its full length. This is historically inaccurate and nose-ticklingly impractical – but looks suitably dramatic.

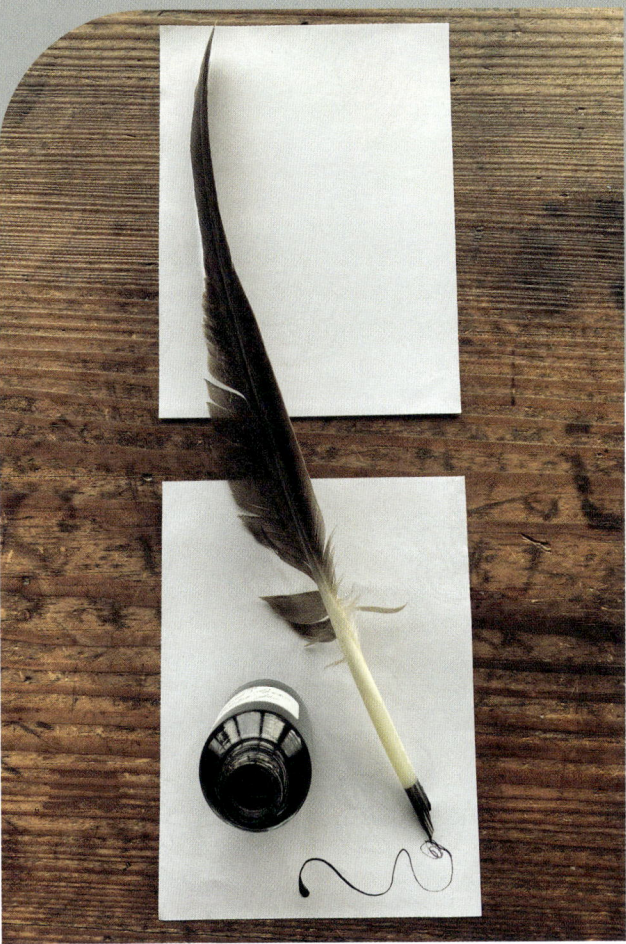

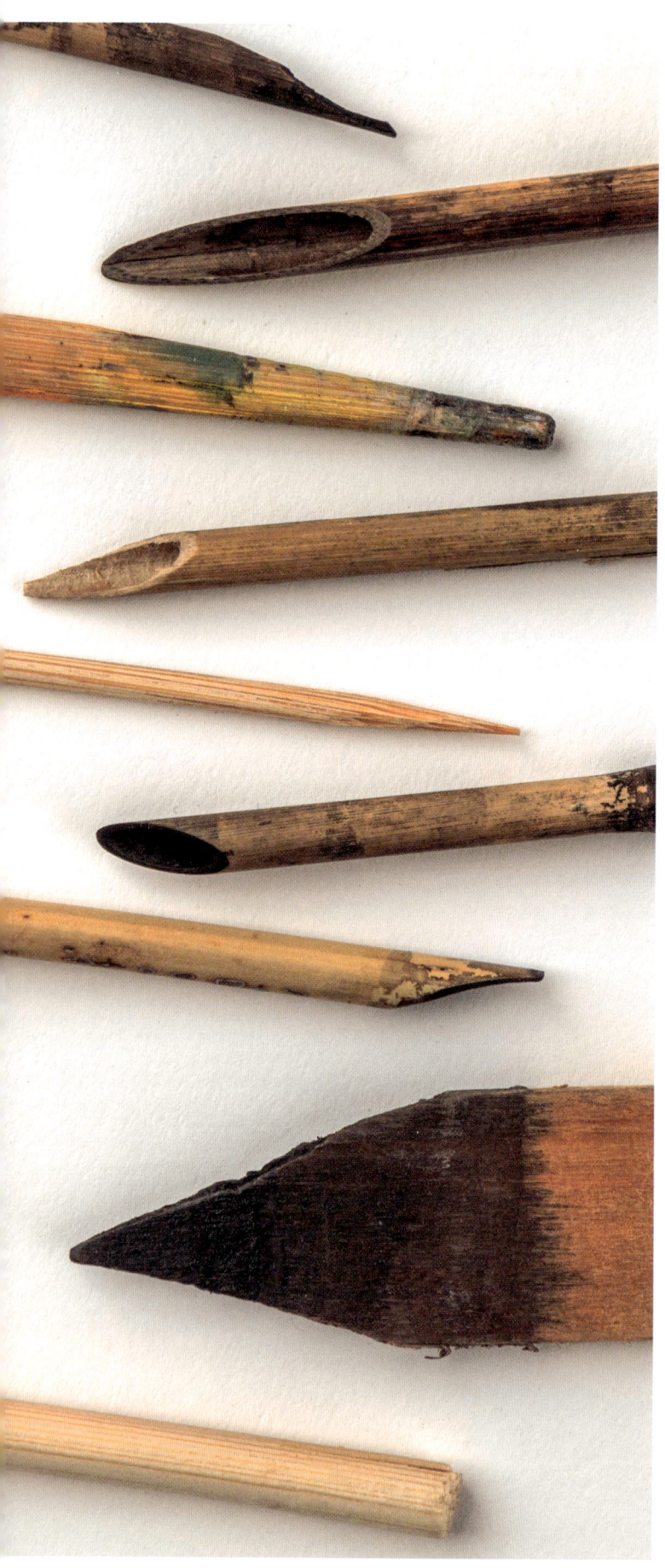

Reed pens

Reed pens are still the calligrapher's choice in the Arab world as the broad chiselled tip possible on reeds and cane are ideal for the long sinuous strokes of Arabic script. For countries using Roman script, reed pens were also used widely before the quill became popular from the sixth century onwards.

If they are soaked overnight, reeds (phragmites) and other canes can be cut with a good sharp knife. You can cut bamboo in exactly the same way, but it should be well-soaked so that it doesn't split when being cut.

Other good sources of raw materials are any strong hollow stems of plants, such as elder sticks, hogweed stems or discarded garden canes, which can be shaped in a similar way. If you find likely looking sticks on your travels, bring them home and have a go cutting them – any that split can be used to make a holder for charcoal or pastel (see page 56).

Re-use

Besides these options for raw materials, explore the possibilities offered by the waste stream. One of my all time favourite dip pens, shown to the left, second from bottom, is made from a piece of wood from a packing crate.

Chopsticks, old support sticks from potted orchids, broken leaded pencils, ice cream sticks, bamboo skewers and more can be fashioned into the most expressive of pens. You'll be bolder trying angles out on the nibs when you know the materials were headed to the waste bin anyway.

Some of my most frequently used pens are made from chopsticks, reeds, skewers and packing crate wood. Every now and then I retouch the points using a penknife, but otherwise they are maintenance-free.

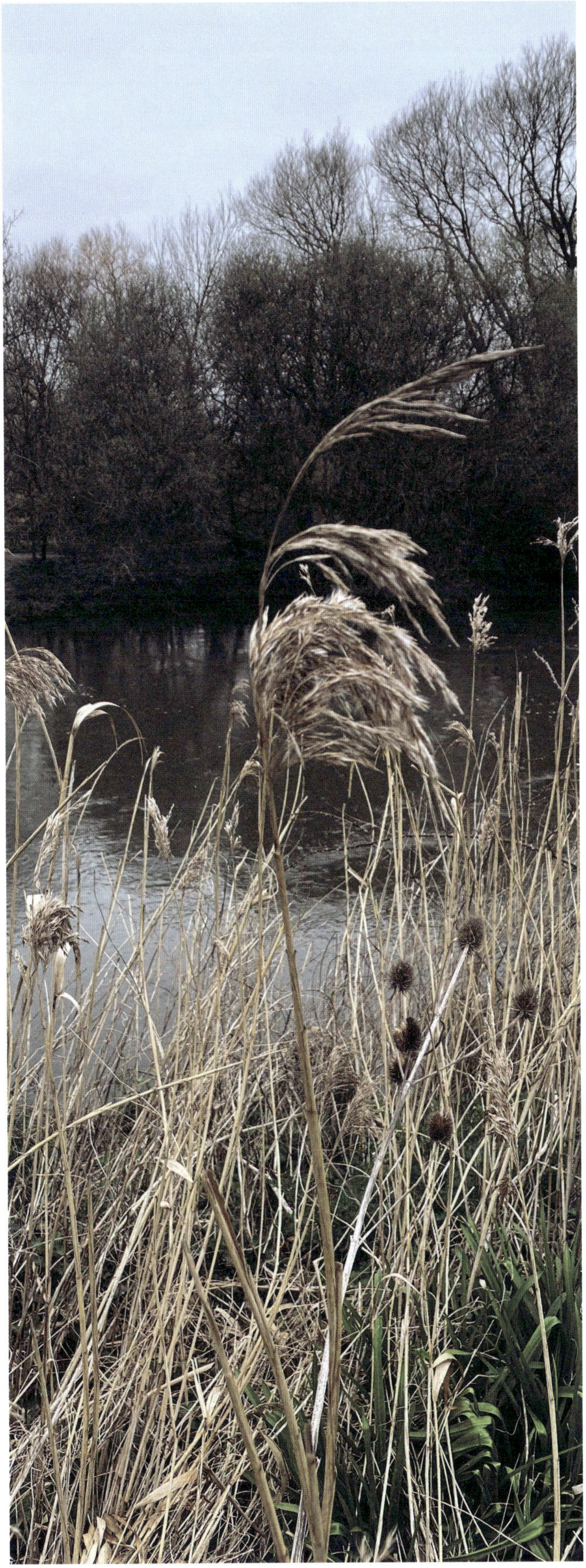

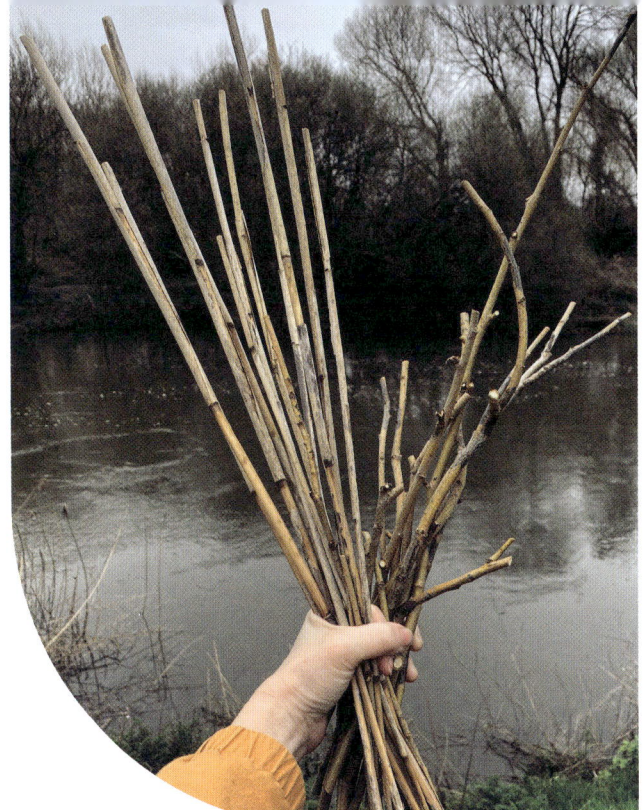

Foraging reeds

You can forage reeds in winter from where they grow abundantly along river estuaries, canals, lakes and ponds. Take care not to lean and fall in. I use secateurs and gather only a handful at a time from any one place. Cut near the base and keep the lower half of the stem. You can leave the top and head with all the other bent and broken stems that abound in any reedbed. Never collect reeds from protected landscapes, nor during the spring nesting season, so as not to disturb waterfowl.

Other ideal sources are ornamental bamboo and canes from gardens, which need regular cutting back as they grow and propagate extremely quickly. Your neighbours will probably be very happy for you to call round in the autumn and take some of their cuttings away to make pens.

Joumana Medlej's approach

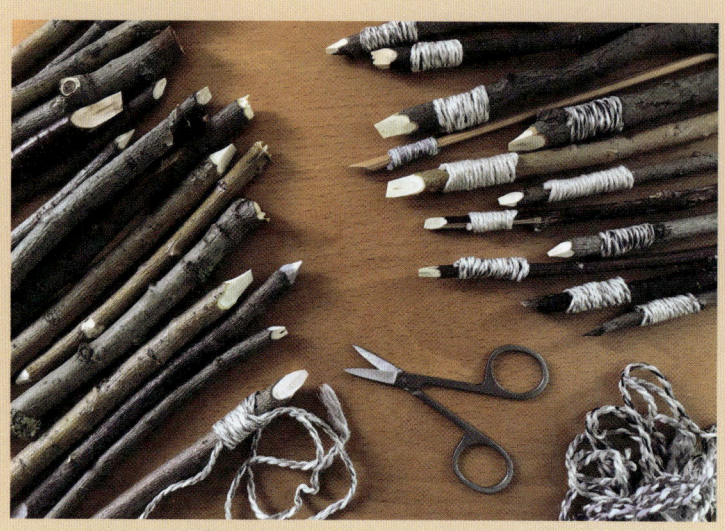

I first encountered Joumana's work online and was struck by the beauty and clarity of her ink drawings and calligraphy from a tradition from different to my own. I was entranced by her highly decorated 'treasure boxes', full of pigments made from semi-precious stones, which contrasted with her sometimes restrained and geometrically complex large drawings, many of which I have now seen in the flesh.

By using traditional tools and inks, Joumana shows how historic cultural practices can be woven into making resonant, completely contemporary work. Her ongoing research and deep knowledge of traditional Middle Eastern art materials and methods is inspiring and much of it can be found in her excellent books and online writing (see page 126).

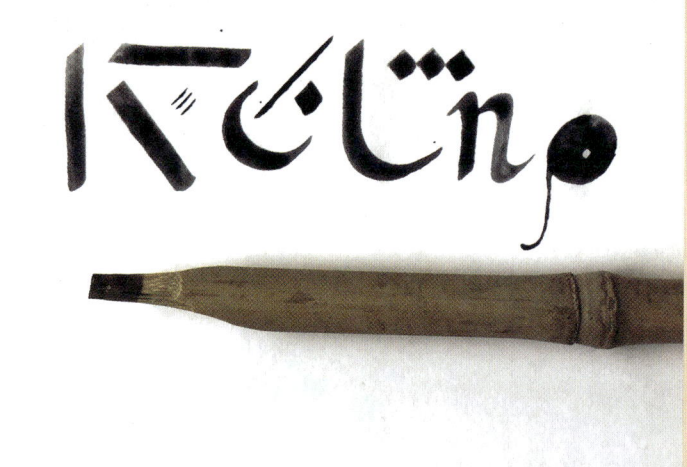

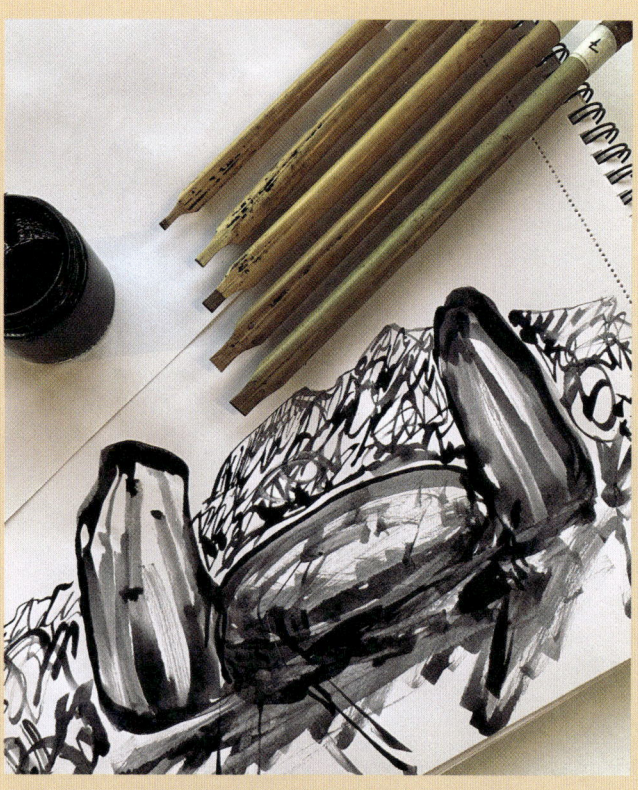

EASTER AQUHORTHIES STONE CIRCLE, ABERDEENSHIRE   28 x 18cm (11 x 7in)

Ink on paper; by the author, with pens made by Joumana Medlej.

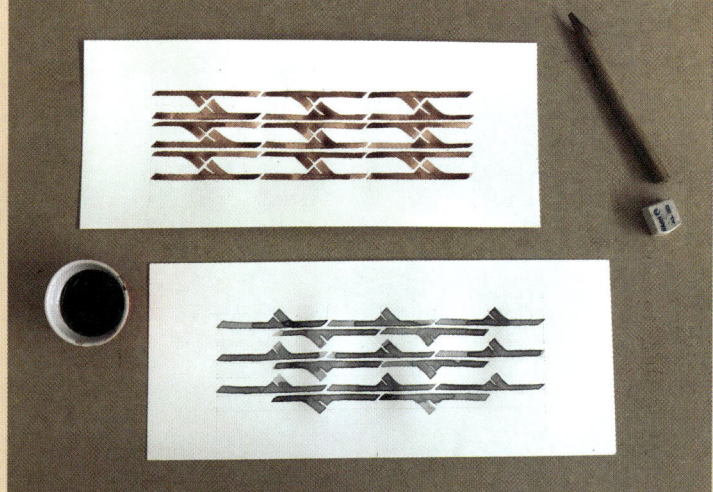

Top to bottom:

Various pens cut from fallen twigs: short-lived but handy, these will produce a variety of mark-making experiences depending on how hard or pliable the wood is.

Reed pen for calligraphy cut from cured bamboo.

Studies for a larger calligraphic piece, in avocado and oak gall inks.

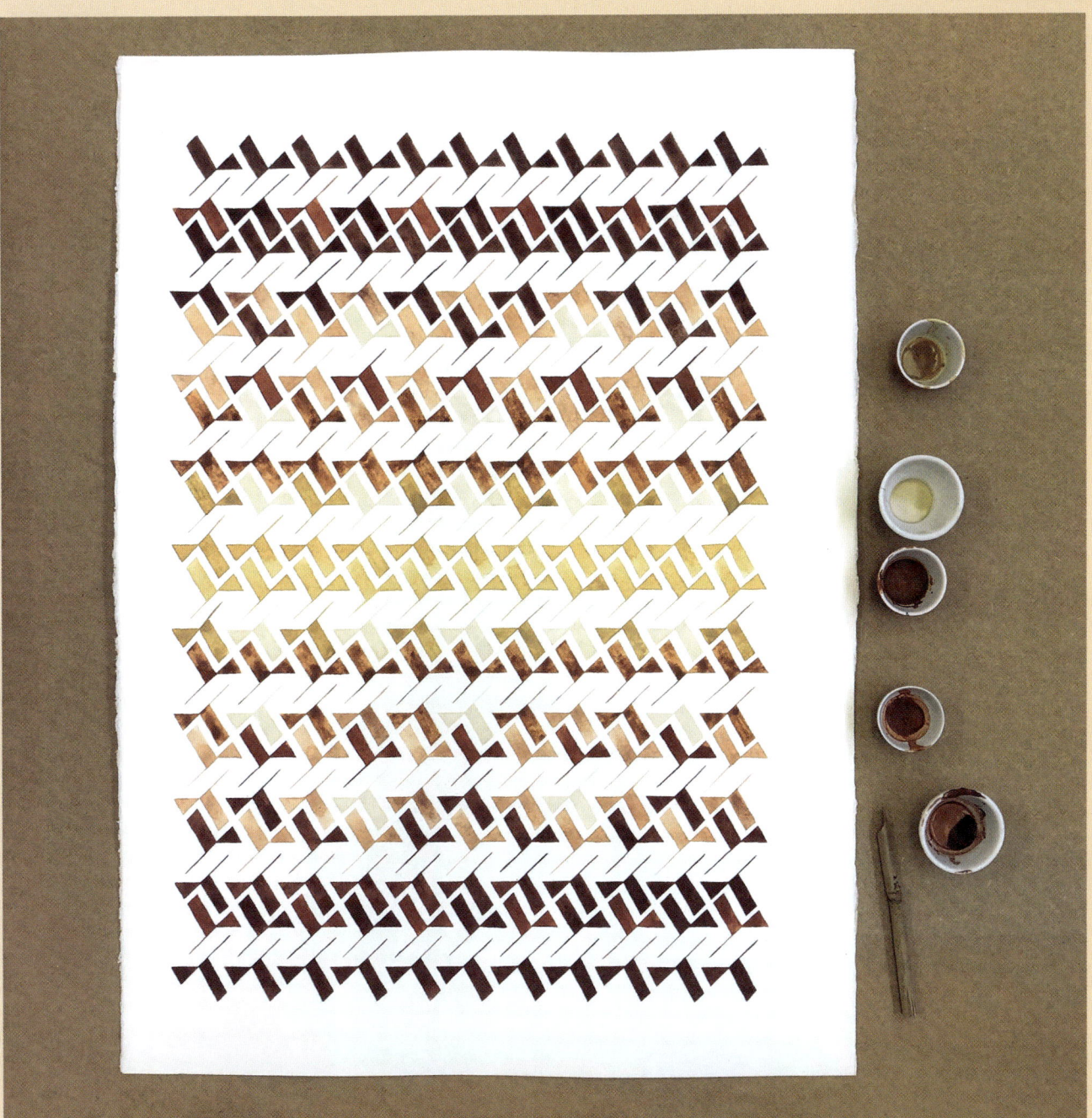

OUT OF THE UNTAMED LAND   56 x 76cm (22 x 30in)

Earth pigments in gum Arabic on paper. This piece can be called 'single origin' because it was made with six earth pigments all gathered in the same place, on the same day, in the mountains of Lebanon. The composition was inspired by this bountiful palette, and the word barr, which denotes the land, the earth, the wilderness. Its adjective, barri, meaning untamed, feral, wild – while at the same time, the same word pronounced 'birr' means great love, devotion and reverence.

Joumana Medlej teaches Kufi calligraphy at the Arab British Centre and her work is in collections worldwide. She is the author of *Inks & Paints of the Middle East*; *Wild Inks & Paints*, and *Stories of Abjad*. Born in Beirut, Joumana is now based in East London.

Making brushes

By now you will have gathered that taking a pinch of history, a peck of something no longer wanted, a handful of what's wild, and a smidgen of experimentation will get us a very long way towards having everything we need to make our art under almost any circumstances. That's my plan. But what is an artist without a brush?

The first kind of brushes we'll look at is the traditional feather brush, as used for mediaeval illuminated manuscripts. These can make extraordinarily fine lines, and complement quill pens beautifully.

Tools needed

Feather, stick, scissors, craft knife

Useful extras:

A spare feather or two to make the perfect ferrule

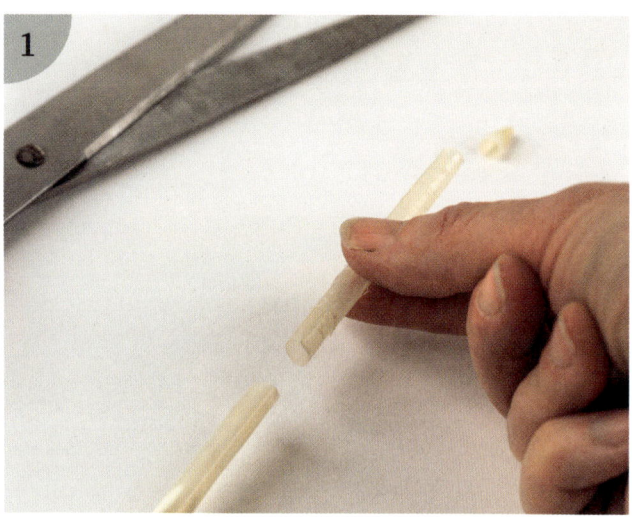

1 Use strong scissors to make two flat cuts in a feather shaft, as shown, to make a ferrule.

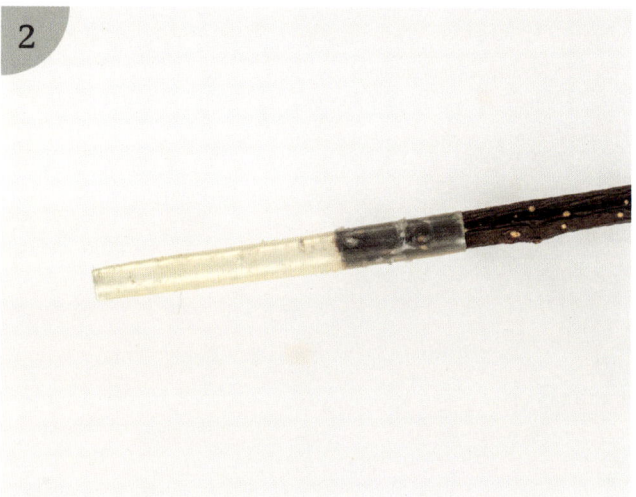

2 Find a stick that fits snugly into the wider end of the ferrule. You can cut a stick to fit; this can be a foraged stick, or you can recycle something like a takeaway chopstick.

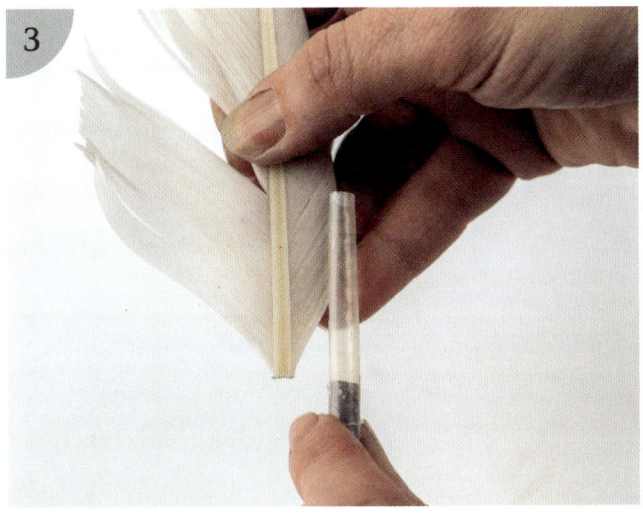

3 Hold the trimmed offcut up to the brush to work out the length, then part the barbs where the shaft will fit inside the ferrule.

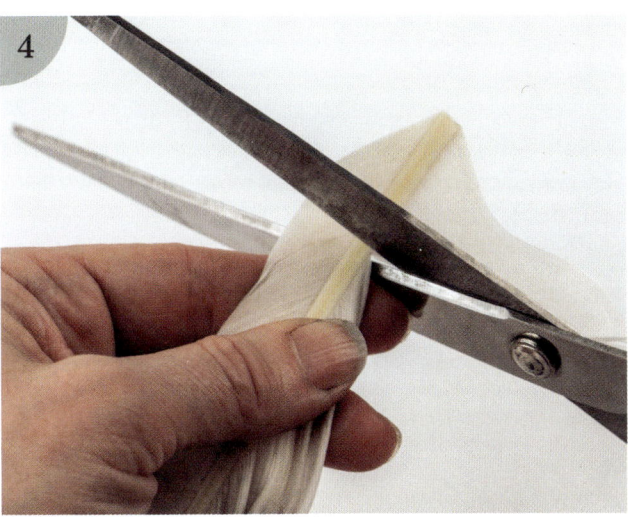

4 Take the feather offcut, and trim it down so the shaft will fit snugly into the narrow end of the ferrule.

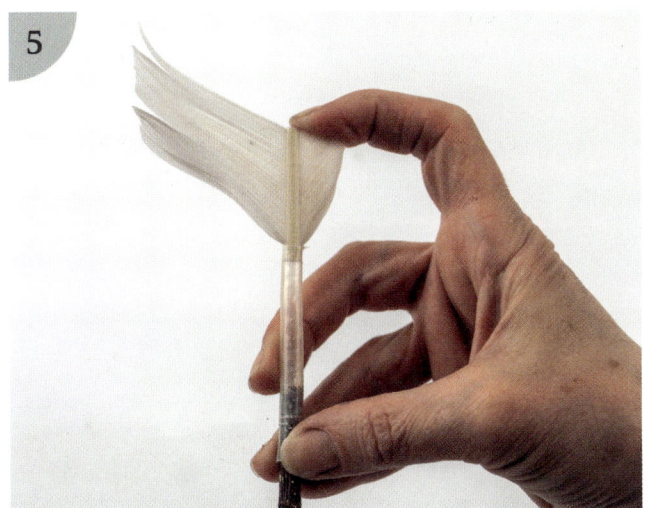

5 Slide it into the ferrule to finish the brush.

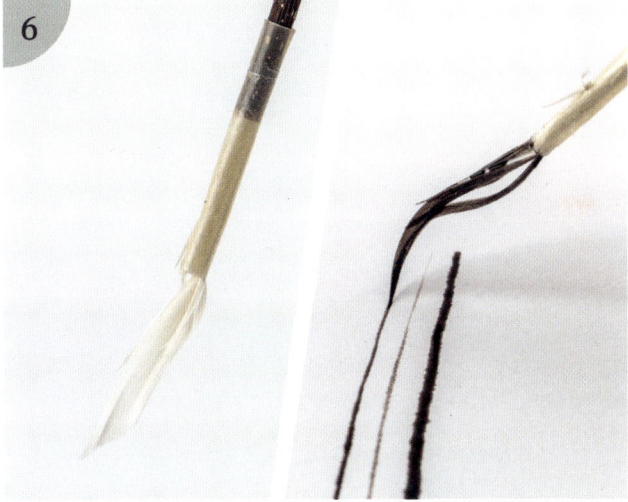

6 As the feather offcut slides in, the barbs will gather into a tip, as shown. The brush is now ready for you to load with ink or paint and use – here you can see me making a few lines with the new brush.

Wild and feral brushes

Now let's look at brushes made from plant matter and animal or human hair. These are great for experimental drawings, expressive, textural lines and unique mark-making with ink. We can also make broad pen-like brushes and stippling tools from wool, leather and fabric. These can be used almost like a broad pen, great for bold lines or filling in large spaces.

Whatever sort of brush you make will need a handle, so gather straight sticks, canes, hollow stems from the winter garden or the bonfire pile, or even some hollow bones. For the tuft or bristles, there are lots of options: look around your house, garage and garden for scraps of felt, chamois, leather, wool fabric, fleece or yarn. Retrieve some hair from your hairbrush (or from around your vacuum cleaner brush bar!). You can even keep a lock of your pet's long winter hair, next time they get a trim or have a moult.

Making wild brushes from materials like these is refreshingly simple but you can refine it as much as you'd like. Use ferrules made from drinking straws or feathers and fit them with cut feathers, tufts of thistledown or a little mop of bound hair or yarn. Using garden canes, bamboo or hollow plant stalks from the garden in winter, twist a handful of hedge-plucked sheep's wool, or cotton wool to make the best stippling brushes. Gather fallen pine needles and stick them firmly into a hollow elder twig, or bind them to a stick using reused string or strips of willow bark that you have peeled off sticks that will become charcoal...

The advantage of homemade brushes over standardized ones is that they immediately make fresh, expressive marks. The disadvantage is, if you get very attached to a particularly characterful brush and use it until it wears out, you may not be able to make exactly the same one again!

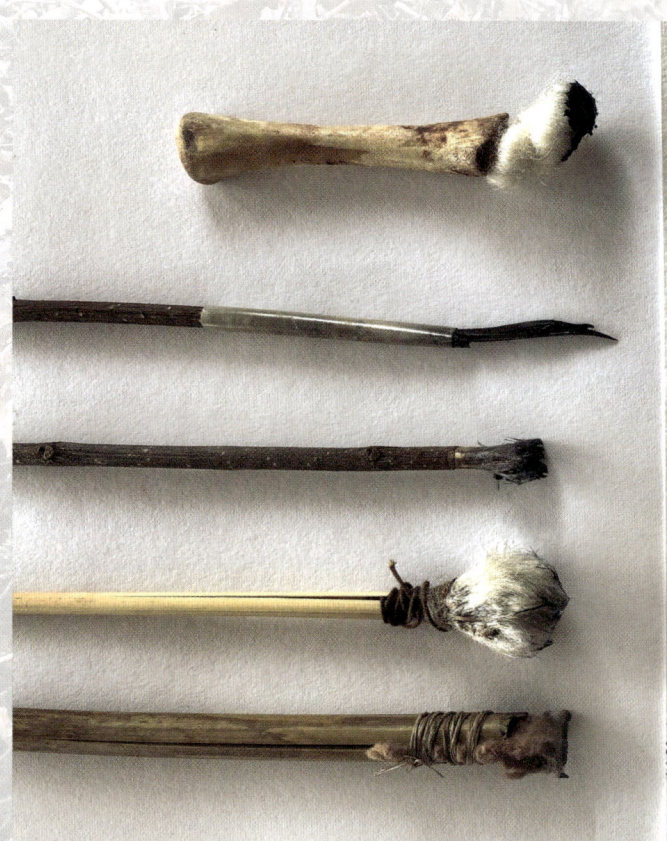
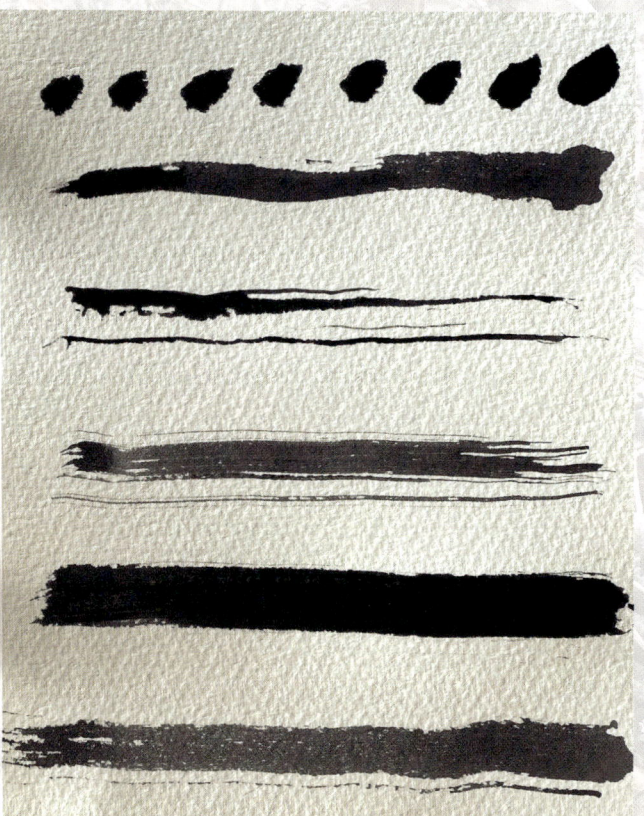

BRUSHES AND BRUSHMARKS
From top to bottom: twisted wool fleece in hollow bone; feather brush (you can make one of these following the instructions on pages 86–87); chewed pruned chestnut shoot; thistledown in a reed; wool felt fabric in bamboo.

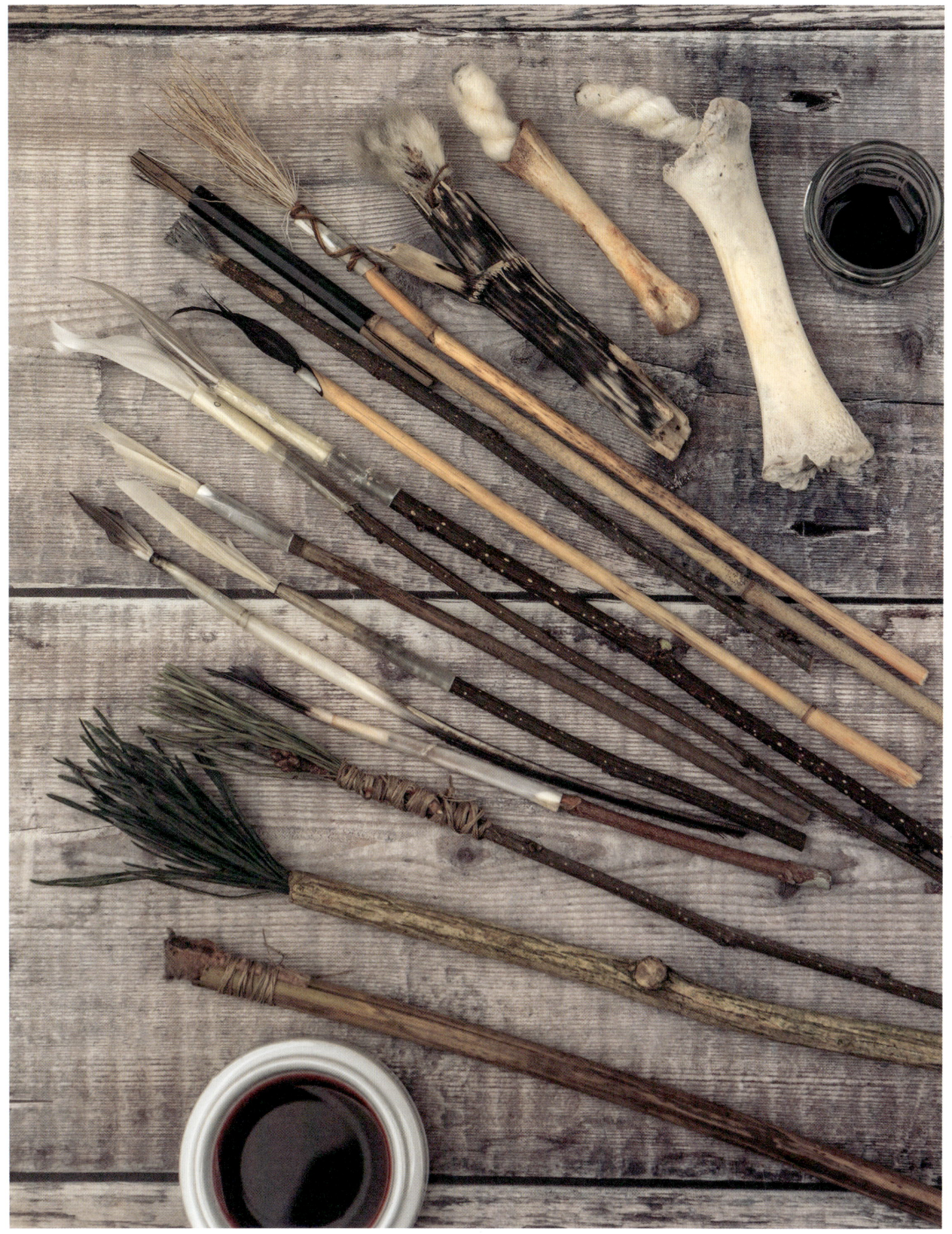

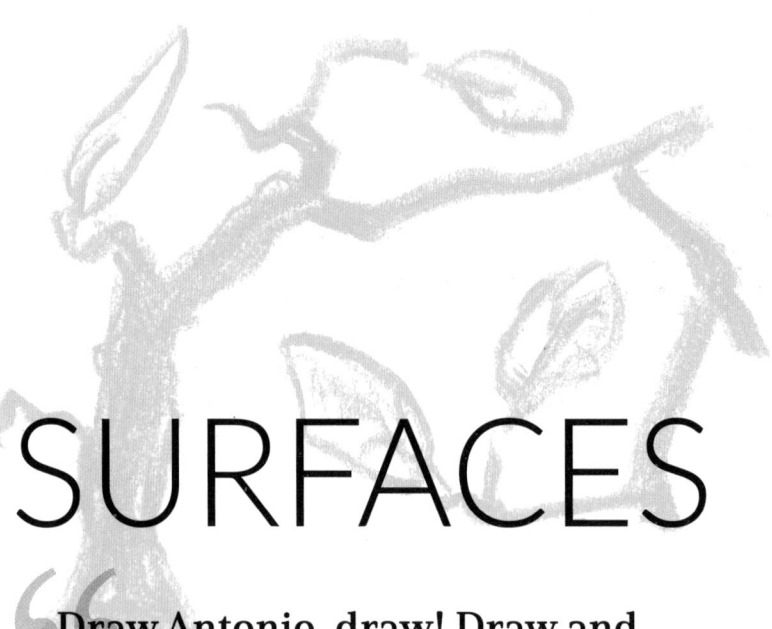

SURFACES

**Draw Antonio, draw! Draw and
do not waste time!**

So wrote Michaelangelo in red chalk on a study by his student Antonio Mini. You can go and see the drawing and the inscription in the British Museum. I repeat this here to inspire you to pick up drawing tools at any and all times. I would add, draw on everything! Scrap paper, envelopes, out-of-date road maps, waste cardboard, packing boxes, food cartons, discarded leather, suede or canvas items, pebbles, unloved furniture, in diaries, on love letters, in thank-you cards…

One way to ensure you always have the opportunity to draw is to make a little sketchbook to carry around. I make two kinds for myself: the first type from my favourite post-consumer cotton rag paper from Khadi, the second from all the old envelopes, packing paper and scrap paper that I deliberately save. I have several artist friends who also make their own sketchbooks; some include pockets, ingenious fold-out pages and beautiful handmade endpapers. I will show you how to make a simple sketchbook from what you might easily find, including sewing it with found fibres, either natural or manmade.

Drawing is akin to thinking aloud. It enlivens the mind, can solve problems, unleashes creativity and can even relax a brain tired of overthinking in words (a common side effect of contemporary screen-based life). All you need is a surface on which to practise. Let's start by looking at surfaces besides paper on which to try our materials.

Opposite:
*Improvised sketchbook made
from recycled papers.*

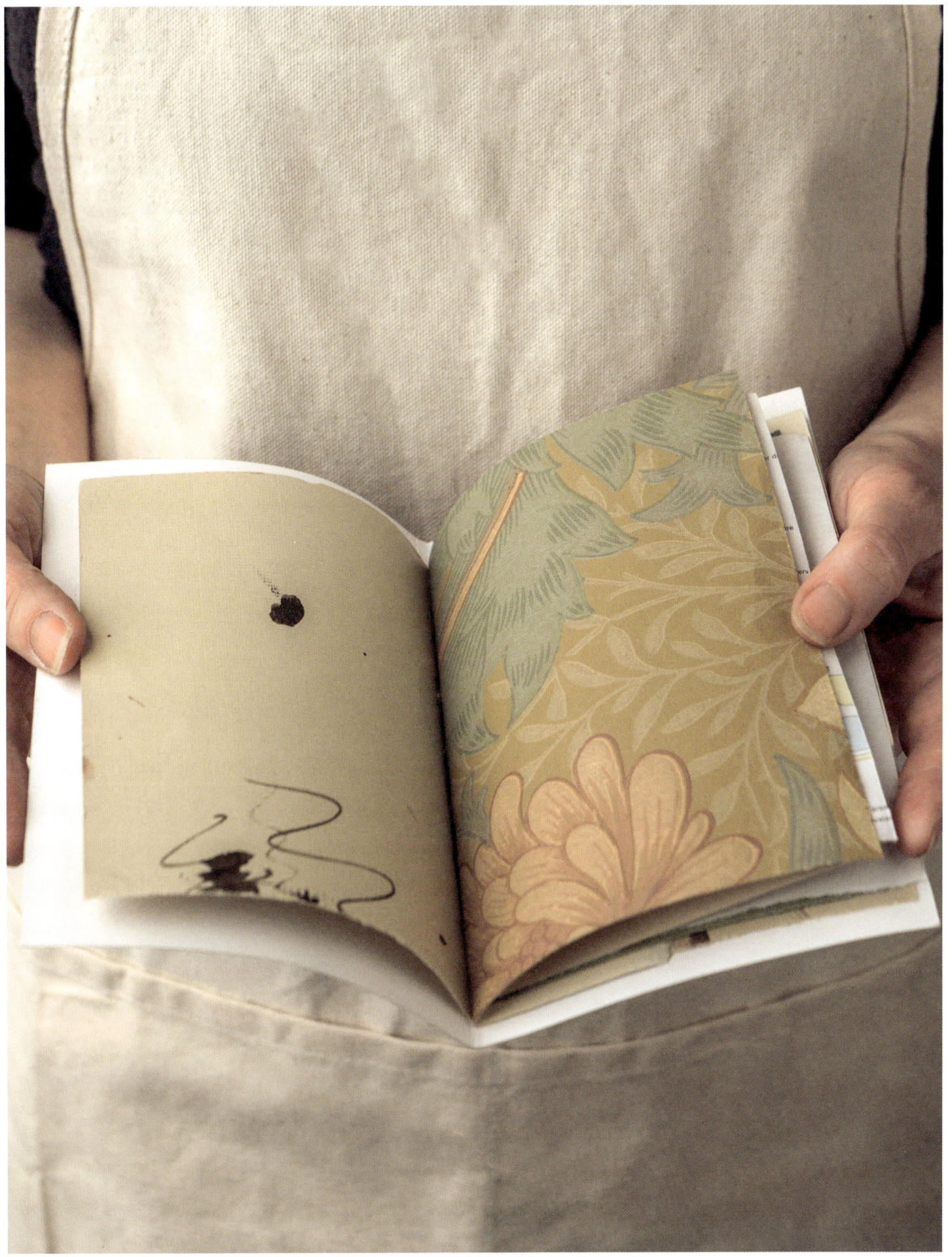

BARK, LEAVES AND MORE

Adornment is universal. Even during the Reformation in Northern Europe, when stained glass windows, statues and paintings were destroyed, and 'fripperies' were frowned upon, artisans still made the most exquisite – albeit monochrome – lace to frame their black Puritan garments. I hold that the urge to make things beautiful is as essential as fine art, poetry, music or dancing.

Folk arts are the carriers of each time and place's unique aesthetic heritage (so are often the first to be banned by authoritarian regimes). I like to subvert contemporary pale flatpack sameness with beauty, which for me means drawing on almost anything and taking inspiration from the world around me.

Where to find surfaces

Developing your forager's eye means looking in unusual places and always having a bag with you, or big pockets to stash things in. This doesn't mean we have to become hoarders! A discerning eye, and the ability to pass something on if it's not going to be used fairly soon are important (unless you have a very big garage or attic to store things in).

I find lots in charity stores, the recycling box in my flat, car-boot and garage sales or from friends who know to ask me before they throw anything interesting away. Outdoors, I find chunky bark or papery birch bark from fallen trees in the woods, sun-bleached driftwood and large shells on the beach, and interesting bits of metal or wooden board in the streets where I live.

Materials to try

You don't need anything special or expensive to get started. Surfaces to experiment with include the inside of almost any cardboard packaging, balsa wood cigar or cheese boxes, old canvas and leather bags and accessories, birch bark, chocolate boxes, bones, driftwood shells, bark, old breadboards, trays and miscellaneous objects.

FOUND AND FORAGED OBJECTS

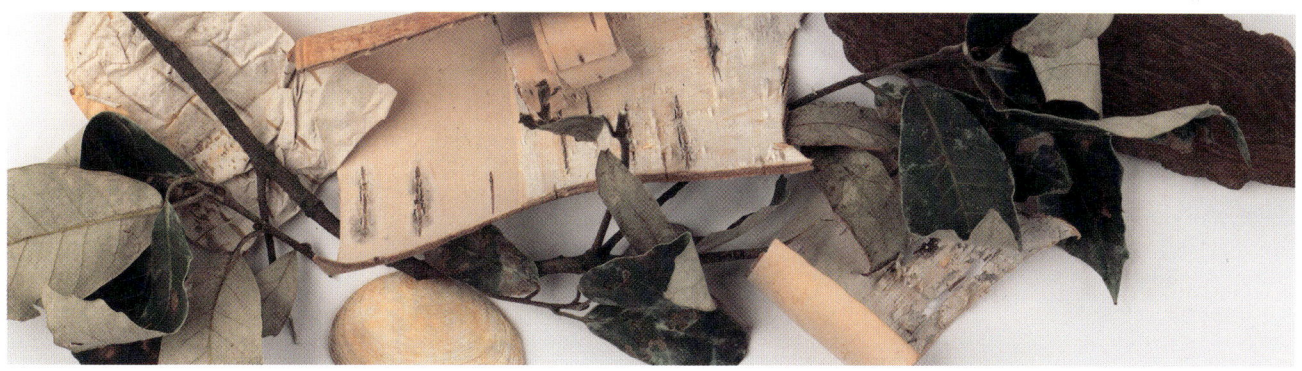

FORAGED FROM YOUR SURROUNDINGS
Birch bark, leaves and shells.

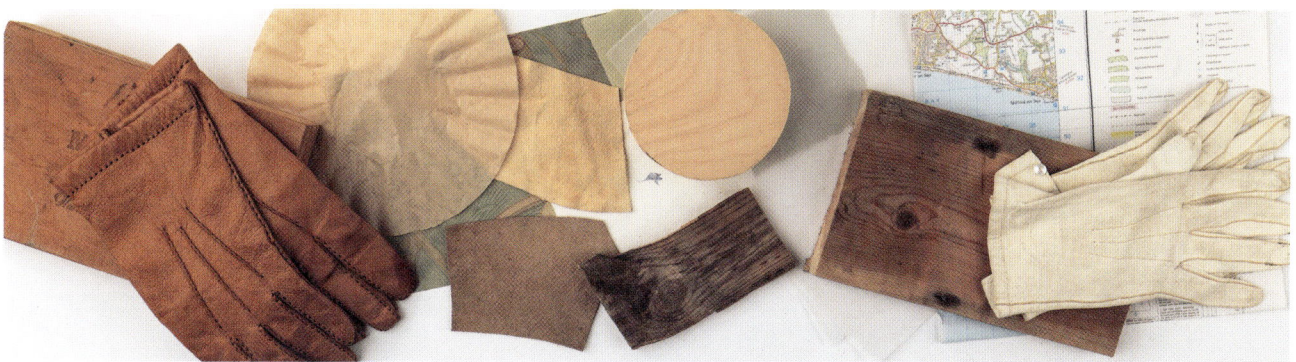

REPURPOSED FROM AROUND THE HOME
Old maps, leather items, chamois leather, wood, coffee filters, sawn wood, tracing paper, writing paper and wallpaper.

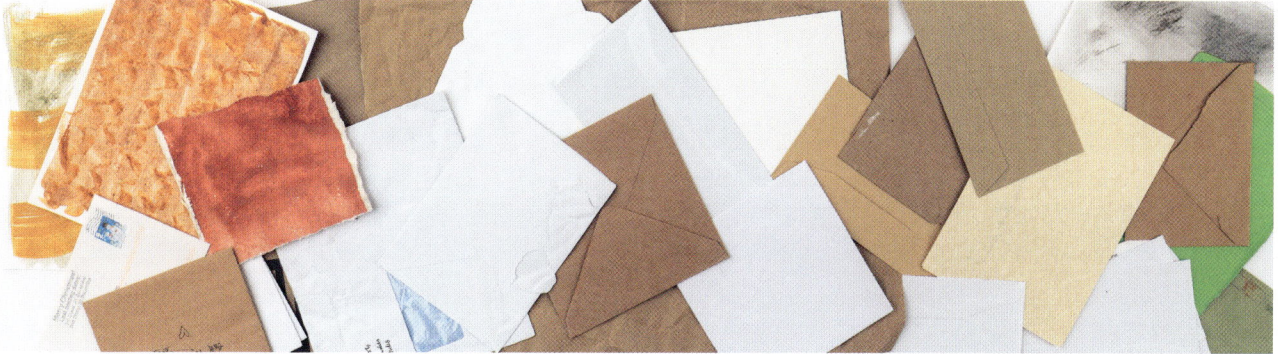

RECYCLED FROM EXISTING SURFACES
Art papers, old envelopes, shopping bags, rubdown sketches, papers that have been used for cleaning brushes, used writing paper and packaging materials.

Ready-to-use surfaces

There really is no end to the materials and surfaces we can draw and paint on and your selection will be as reflective of your locale as the cuisine or local music scene.

Here we look at some artworks on commonplace repurposed and natural materials to inspire you. You might like to try these, or other things from your house or garden.

Ingenious work by Mirella Salamé (see right) and Beke Olbers (opposite page, bottom right) broadens our view of what art can be and when, why and how we can draw and paint. These artists remind us that we do not need expensive canvases or materials to create beautiful, meaningful work.

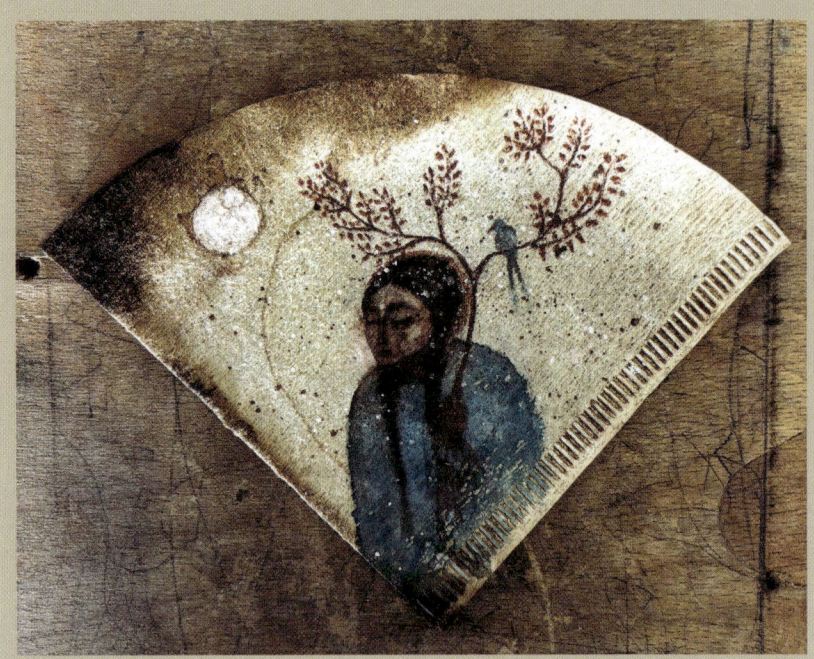

دخلت مرة جنينة (WHEN I ENTERED THE GARDEN) 10.5 x 10 x 14.5cm (4¼ x 4 x 5¾in)
Artist: Mirella Salamé, Lebanon.
Homemade ethically sourced earth pigments watercolour on reused coffee filter.

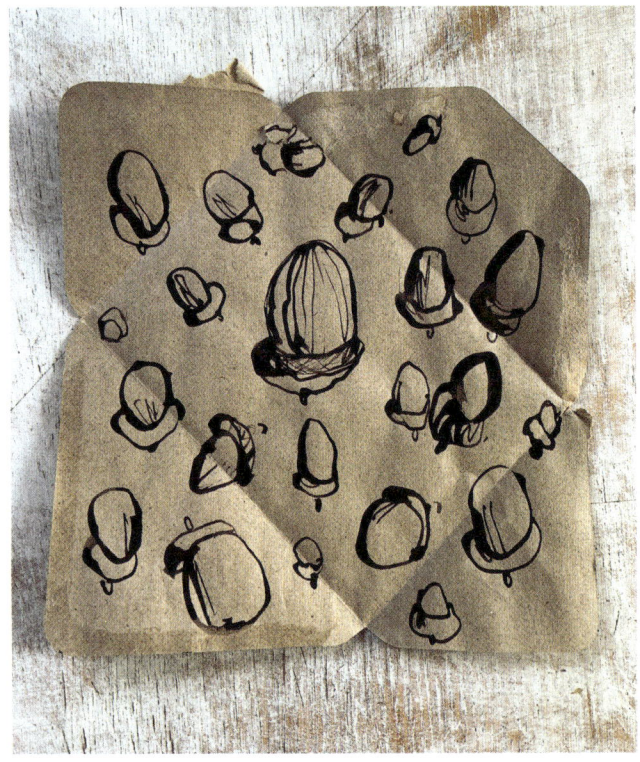

ACORNS 20 x 20cm (8 x 8in)
Iron gall ink on reused envelope. In the collection of Sigrid Verschraeghen

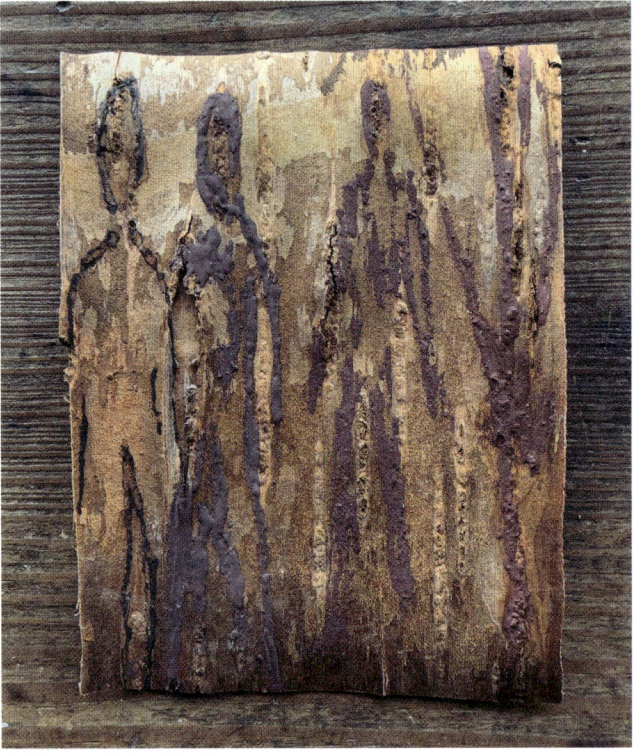

ANCESTORS 15 x 21cm (6½ x 8¼in)
This piece is worked on natural birch bark. Its simplicity suited the paints made entirely from four pure ochres from Clearwell Caves, mixed only with cherry tree gum and honey. It is in the collection of Nina Cadzow.

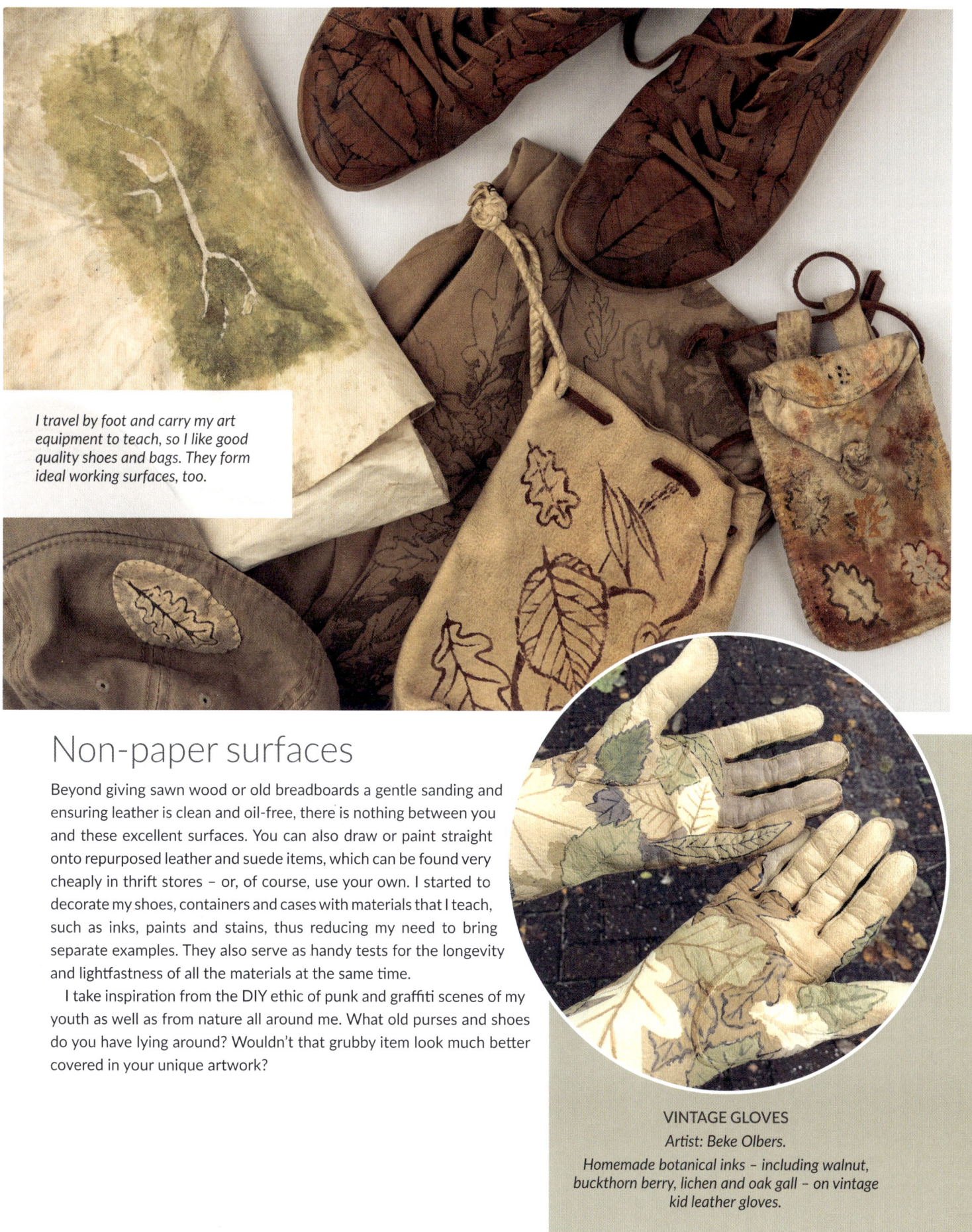

I travel by foot and carry my art equipment to teach, so I like good quality shoes and bags. They form ideal working surfaces, too.

Non-paper surfaces

Beyond giving sawn wood or old breadboards a gentle sanding and ensuring leather is clean and oil-free, there is nothing between you and these excellent surfaces. You can also draw or paint straight onto repurposed leather and suede items, which can be found very cheaply in thrift stores – or, of course, use your own. I started to decorate my shoes, containers and cases with materials that I teach, such as inks, paints and stains, thus reducing my need to bring separate examples. They also serve as handy tests for the longevity and lightfastness of all the materials at the same time.

I take inspiration from the DIY ethic of punk and graffiti scenes of my youth as well as from nature all around me. What old purses and shoes do you have lying around? Wouldn't that grubby item look much better covered in your unique artwork?

VINTAGE GLOVES
Artist: Beke Olbers.
Homemade botanical inks – including walnut, buckthorn berry, lichen and oak gall – on vintage kid leather gloves.

Prepared surfaces

There is no rule to say we should start with a blank white sheet of paper. In fact, for many centuries artists commonly tinted or otherwise prepared their papers in a similar way to how you might underpaint a canvas. Creating a mid-toned background can be a wonderful way to get to work on a charcoal drawing. Rubbing in red ochre dust from cleaning your slab after pastel making makes an evocative background.

I love prepared grounds for two main reasons. Firstly, they use up all the colourful or deeply-toned particles left over from making my own paints, pastels and charcoal, which is a good no-waste habit.

Secondly, they connect me to an ancestral way of drawing and painting, which responds to something already there, such as the shape of a cave wall, or a natural pigmentation or hole in a parchment. By creating a supply of uncontrolled, lively grounds, we can respond intuitively to what we see in the almost random marks.

Fear of the blank page

Over the years, my students have often mentioned not being able to start a drawing due to fear of the blank page. Something about the stark white of a big sheet of paper, or brand new sketchbook, can make us feel daunted. This is one good reason to 'mess up' your paper straight away, with one of these methods. There are a host of ways to get started: make a mark, colour a page, stick a bit of collaged paper down...

Think of the ideas on the opposite page as ice-breakers at a party, helping you get into a conversation which, in this case, is about 'taking a line for a walk' (see page 12).

Rubbing in charcoal

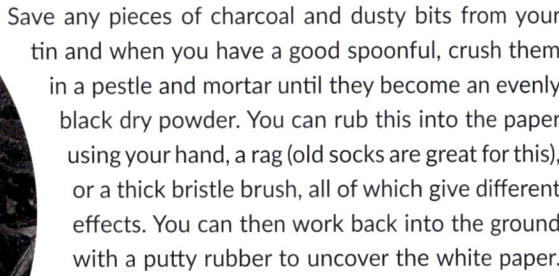

Save any pieces of charcoal and dusty bits from your tin and when you have a good spoonful, crush them in a pestle and mortar until they become an evenly black dry powder. You can rub this into the paper using your hand, a rag (old socks are great for this), or a thick bristle brush, all of which give different effects. You can then work back into the ground with a putty rubber to uncover the white paper. This feels like drawing with light!

You can also mix a little gum tragacanth, glair or veglair (see page 45) with the charcoal dust and paint it on as a wash, which gives a more permanent ground.

Using 'waste' from pastel-making

The same method described above for charcoal waste can be used for pastel and pigment fragments. Experiment with monochrome or multicoloured backgrounds with even coverage, or alternatively with expressive marks to respond to at a later date.

When you have finished making pastels on the slab, instead of taking it straight to the sink, clean off the slab with a brush and a little of one of the mediums in this book and paint it straight into your sketchbook or scrap paper. These pages are inspiring to go back to, and scrap papers suddenly become great collages, impromptu greetings cards or wrapping paper.

Collage

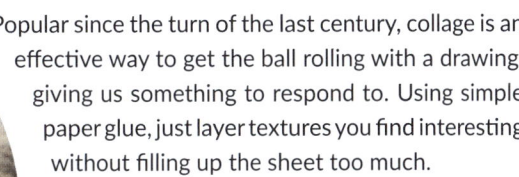

Popular since the turn of the last century, collage is an effective way to get the ball rolling with a drawing, giving us something to respond to. Using simple paper glue, just layer textures you find interesting without filling up the sheet too much.

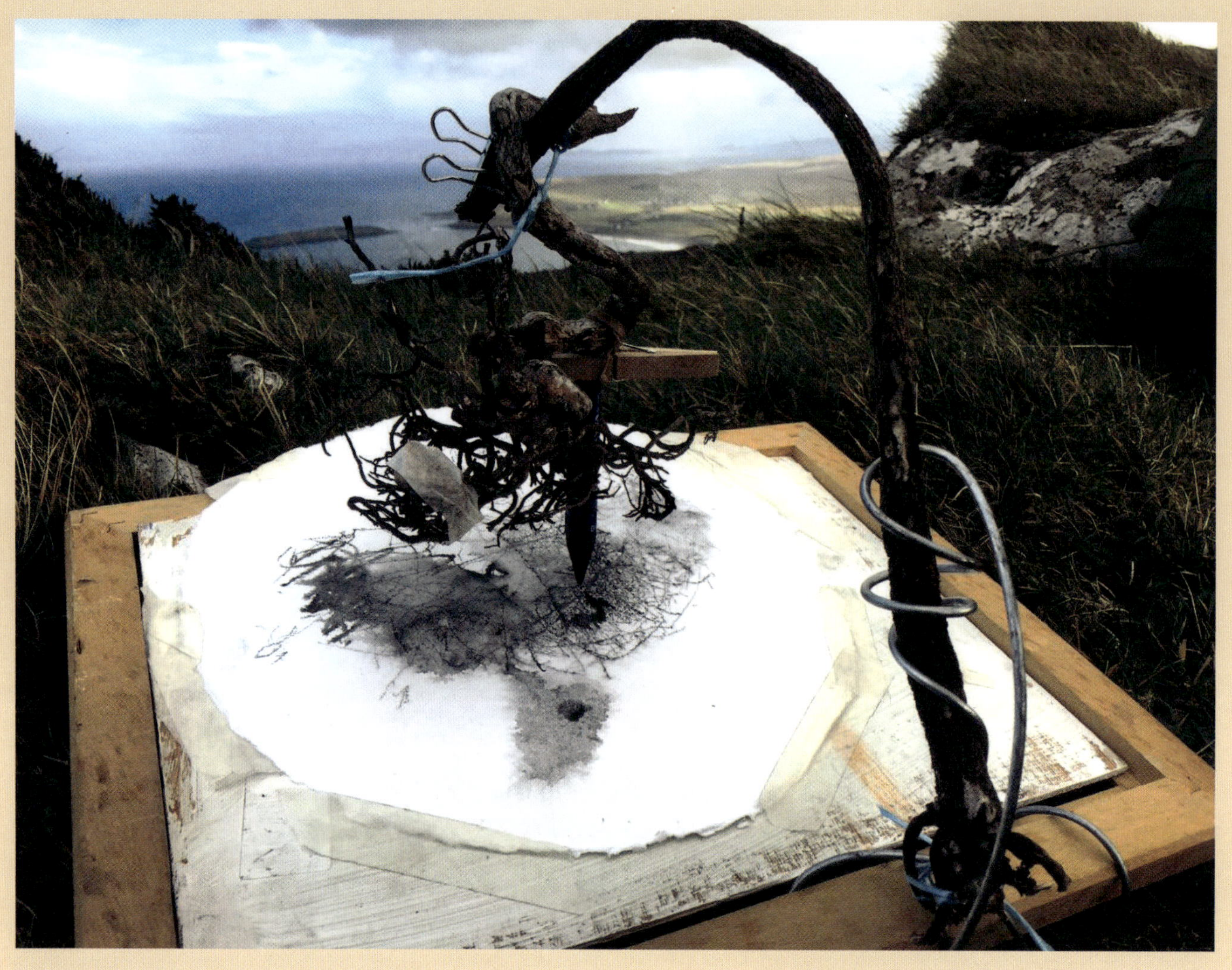

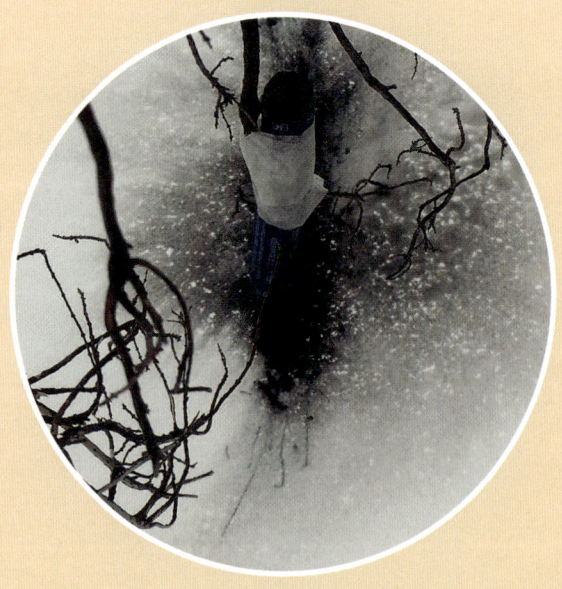

Geraldine van Heemstra's approach

Geraldine's wind drawings are developed in collaboration with nature with drawing devices created from found objects of the land. She records the movement of the wind using naturally sourced earthly materials like branches, driftwood and dried heather, sometimes fitted with pastels made from foraged materials such as peat, red iron earth and pigments found on her travels.

Geraldine's art humbly allows in the influence of the more-than-human world, creating an improvisation with wild nature that a human on their own could never create.

These wind drawing devices translate the subtle forces of nature into unique drawings.

SEISMOPOLYGRAPH #III,
MIXED MEDIA *Dimensions variable.*

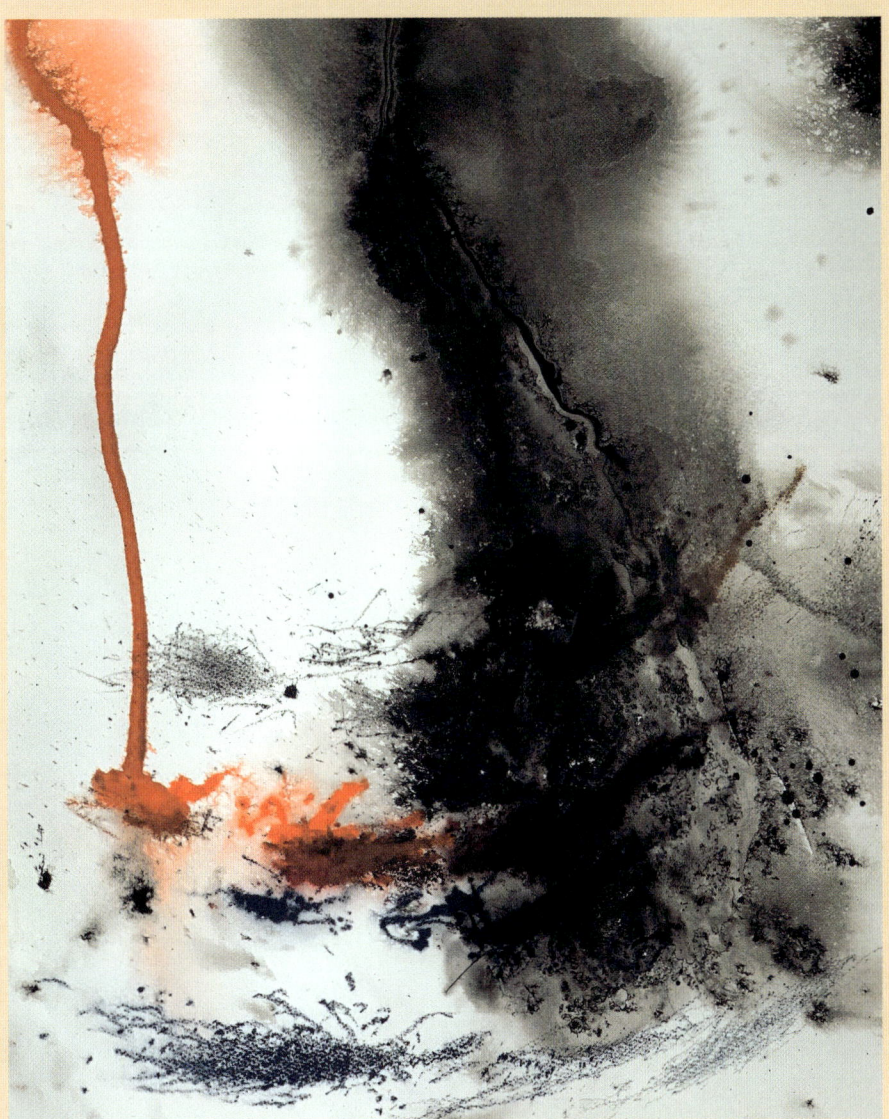

KILMARTIN WIND DRAWINGS SERIES #III
Dimensions variable.

Visible in this close-up detail are great subtleties of mark-making resulting from Geraldine's choices of colour and drawing tools, combined with the improvisational richness of the dancing wind.

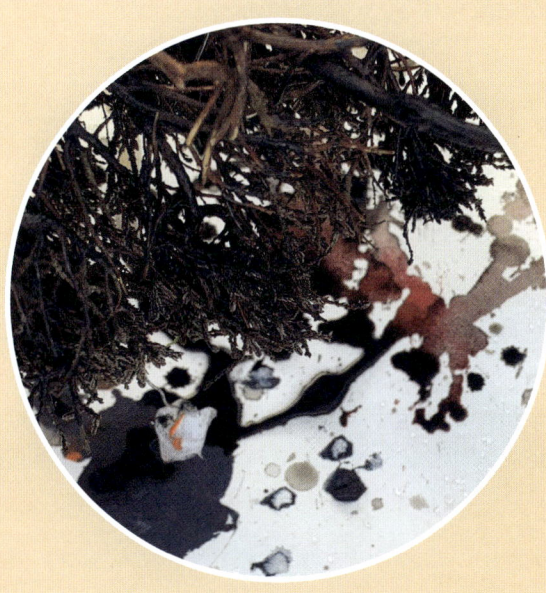

Detail from Seismopolygraph #IV, *another wind drawing device from the same series as the example shown opposite.*

Geraldine van Heemstra was born in Utrecht, the Netherlands, in 1967. She now lives and works between London and the Isle of Skye, where she finds all her inspiration. Captivated by wind and weather, she connects to the changeable landscape through walking the Scottish hills and coastline.

SKETCHBOOKS

By the time I went to do a two year foundation at Shelley Park Art College in the late 1980s, I was already a seasoned scavenger. When fellow students threw away interesting coloured papers that were only drawn upon on one side, I'd whisk them out of the wastepaper basket and fold them into little booklets, chop them up for collage, sew or spiral bind them into improvised sketchbooks. Adding envelopes, the backs of letters and packing papers to this, I found I had an endless supply of notebooks and sketchbooks without having to spend money, which was in short supply as a student.

Later I started to sew little books with my favourite watercolour papers using natural fibres instead of thread. My current favourite way to teach sketchbook-making uses a combination of found and bought papers, sewn with fibre made from long leaves dropped from plants such as New Zealand flax or date palm.

We can sew our books with any strong yarn, thread, thin ribbon, natural or reused fibre that we like the look of. Combine household papers and locally found fibres for a truly unique 'anything-but-common' commonplace book.

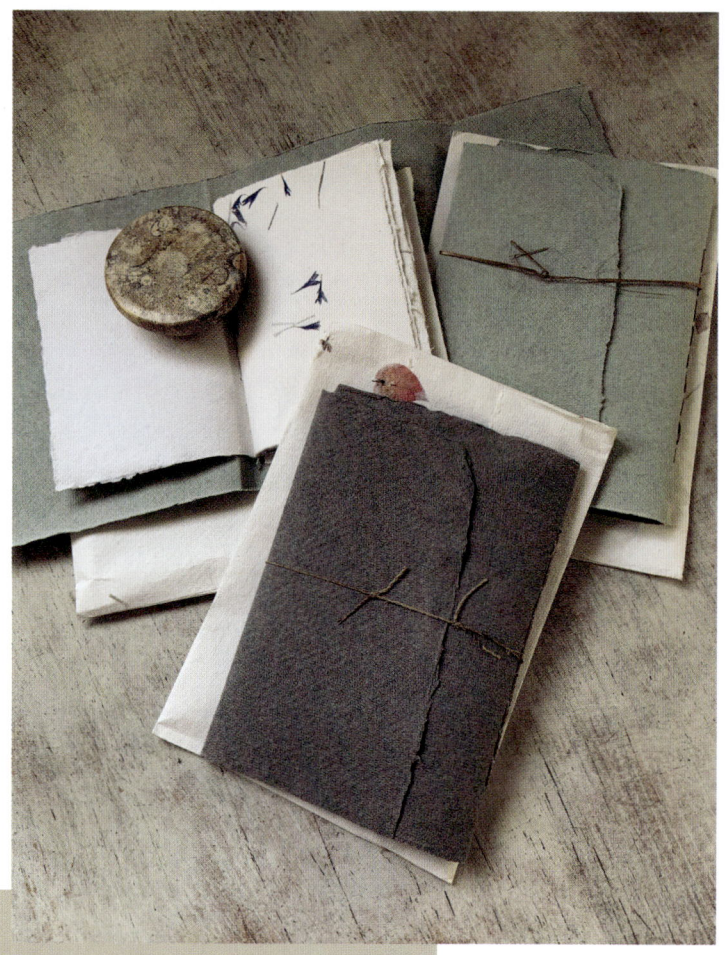

Found threads

There are infinite threads available to find in the home, garden, garage, beach or urban environment. Many fibres such as nettle, dandelion stems and lime tree inner bark are found by the roadside where I live, and are excellent when made into reverse wrap cordage, which is how yarn and string are made. However, I'd need another book to show you that wonderful craft! So look for things that are ready to use: frayed ropes from the shoreline, thin ribbons from gifts, unused embroidery threads, fine crochet yarn, that long colourful string in your kitchen drawer...

You can also pick up long spiky leaves from many semi-arid-climate plants, some of which reach up to a metre long. In the seaside town where I live, no-watering planting is common for environmental reasons, so incongruous palm trees and spiky phormiums are very popular. They shed their leaves all year round and I gather them from the path. The leaves separate easily into fibres and can be waxed and used for sewing without a needle.

Making sketchbooks

This project will teach you to make a simple signature-method sketchbook. You'll need between four and seven sheets of paper, all approximately the same size. These will be folded down to make the 'signature'. I like the final paper size to be around A5 (half-letter) size, so you will need papers twice that size (e.g. A4 or letter); along with another piece of strong paper for the cover, which can be somewhat larger.

You will also need some thread to sew the book: strong waxed cotton or linen thread is traditional, but I have used embroidery threads, sections of leaves from spiky plants, waste plastic threads from ships' ropes or nets removed from the shore. Whichever you choose, make sure they are at least three times longer than the height of your book, longer if possible.

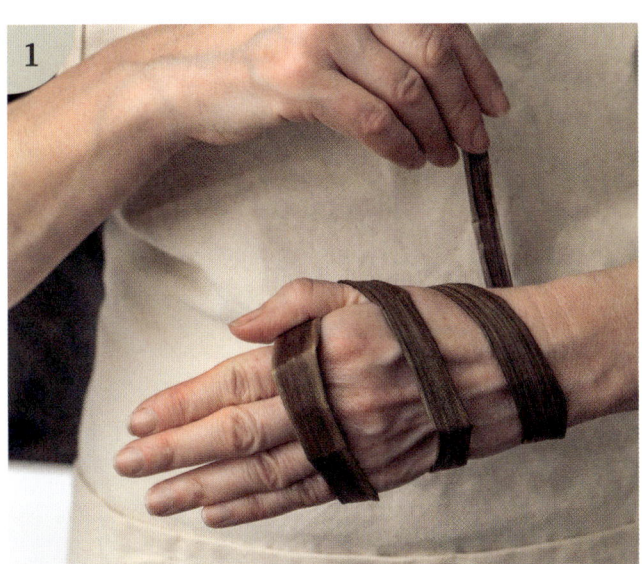

1 Find a fibrous leaf that is at least three times the length you want the spine of your sketchbook, and dampen it in a wet tea towel or dishcloth until it is pliable. Palm leaves, New Zealand flax and yukka are good options, but any leaf that you can wrap around your hand a couple of times without it breaking will be suitable.

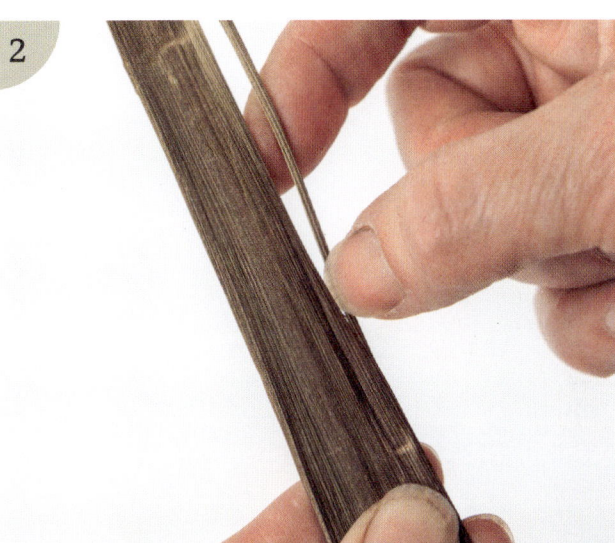

2 Run your thumbnail down the leaf to separate a strand around 2–3mm (⅛in) wide. Cut the hard end to a point – you can use this as a combination of needle and thread. Run the chosen fibre through some wax a couple of times to help it glide through the holes.

Tip

If your leaf feels slightly brittle, you can dampen it again before you begin to sew the sketchbook.

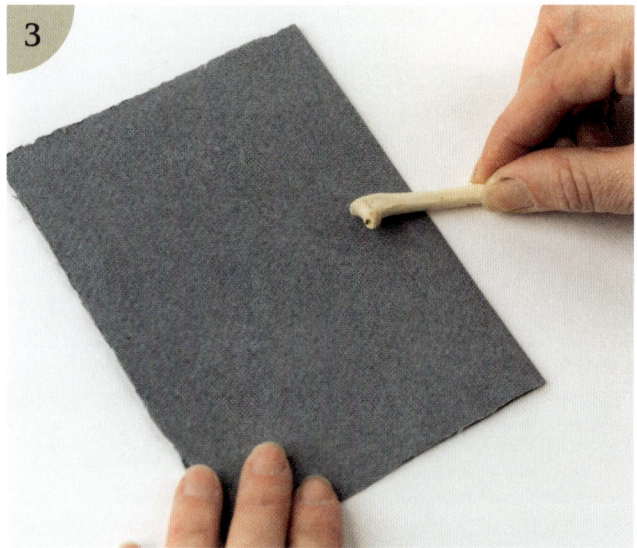

3 Fold your pieces of paper in half, and choose one to be the cover. A cover that is thicker or slightly larger than the other pages tends to be more practical. To save your thumbnail, you can use a bone or a ruler as a tool to help make a sharp crease on each piece.

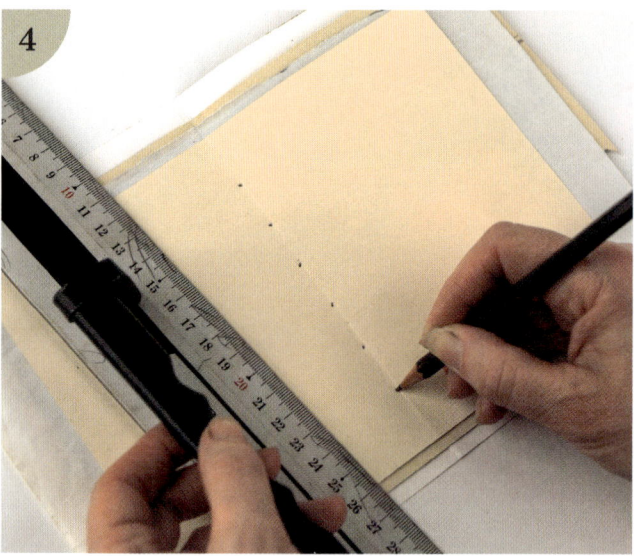

4 Layer the pages within the cover, then use a ruler to mark pencil marks for the stitch holes. Make six evenly-spaced marks, three above and three below the centreline, as shown.

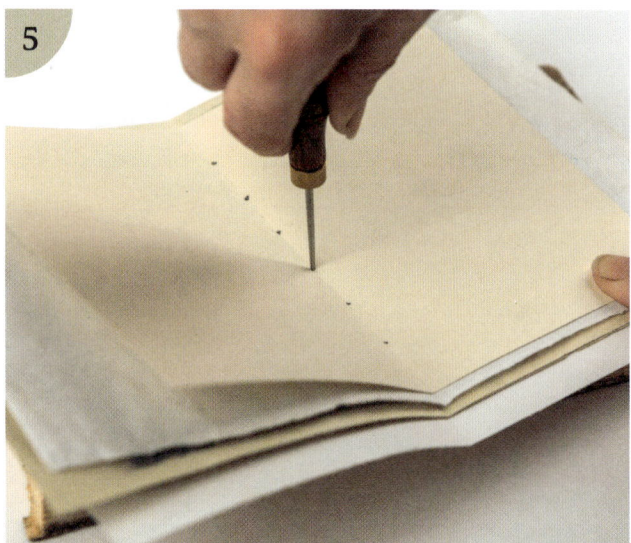

5 Line up the folds of all the pieces of paper (including the cover) and use an awl to gently push through onto a strong board. You can enlarge the holes simply by pushing the awl through further.

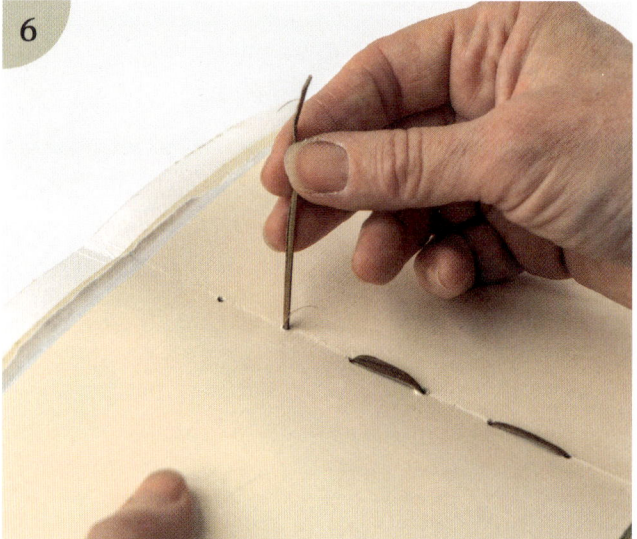

6 Sew the book together using the pointed end of a waxed strand of leaf as a needle. Start from outside the cover, at one end of the holes. Leave a tail of 10cm (4in) and begin working it alternately down and up through the holes.

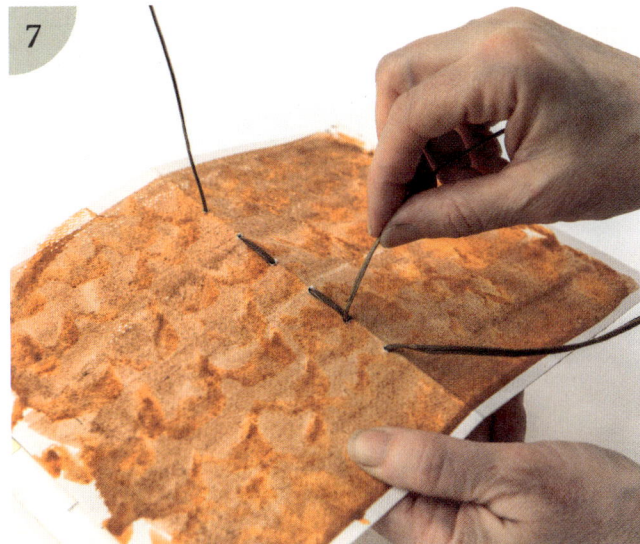

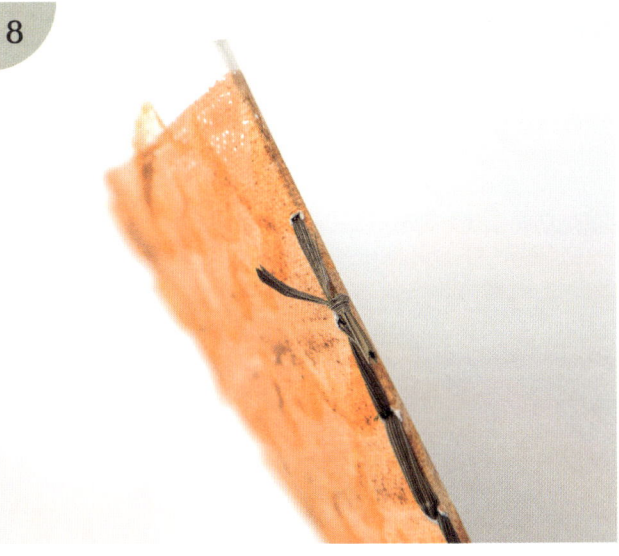

7 When you reach the end, work back the other way. You can further enlarge the holes with the awl if you need to.

8 Tie off using the tail and trim the excess thread. You can now trim the pages (if necessary) using scissors,

THE FINISHED SKETCHBOOK

For this sketchbook, I have used another strand of the leaf to wrap and tie around the book to fasten it.

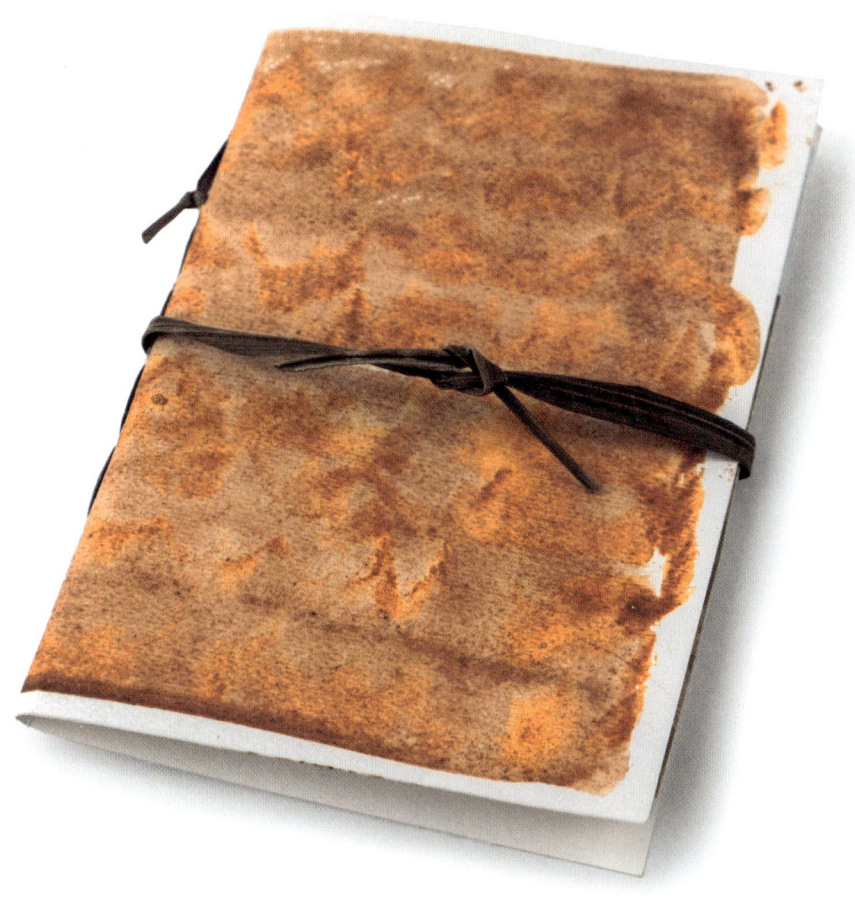

How to use your sketchbook

A small sketchbook is ideal at first, as you can just stash it in your pocket to get into the habit of drawing all the time: you've got somewhere to draw whenever the mood takes you. Sketching outside in nature is most fun, or you could draw friends and family. If they won't sit still for you, draw from magazines, or press pause on your favourite film scenes and draw from the screen.

You could also use it for testing your pastel colours and keeping a record of what you have made, or fill it with coloured grounds and draw on top in charcoal for a lovely layered effect: this is ideal for landscapes.

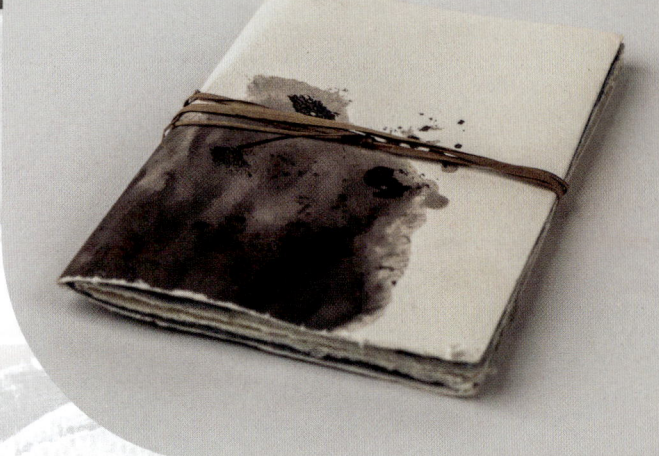

A tiny sketchbook that will fit in the palm of your hand is worth making. Carry a short pencil with you too, and you can surreptitiously draw wherever you are.

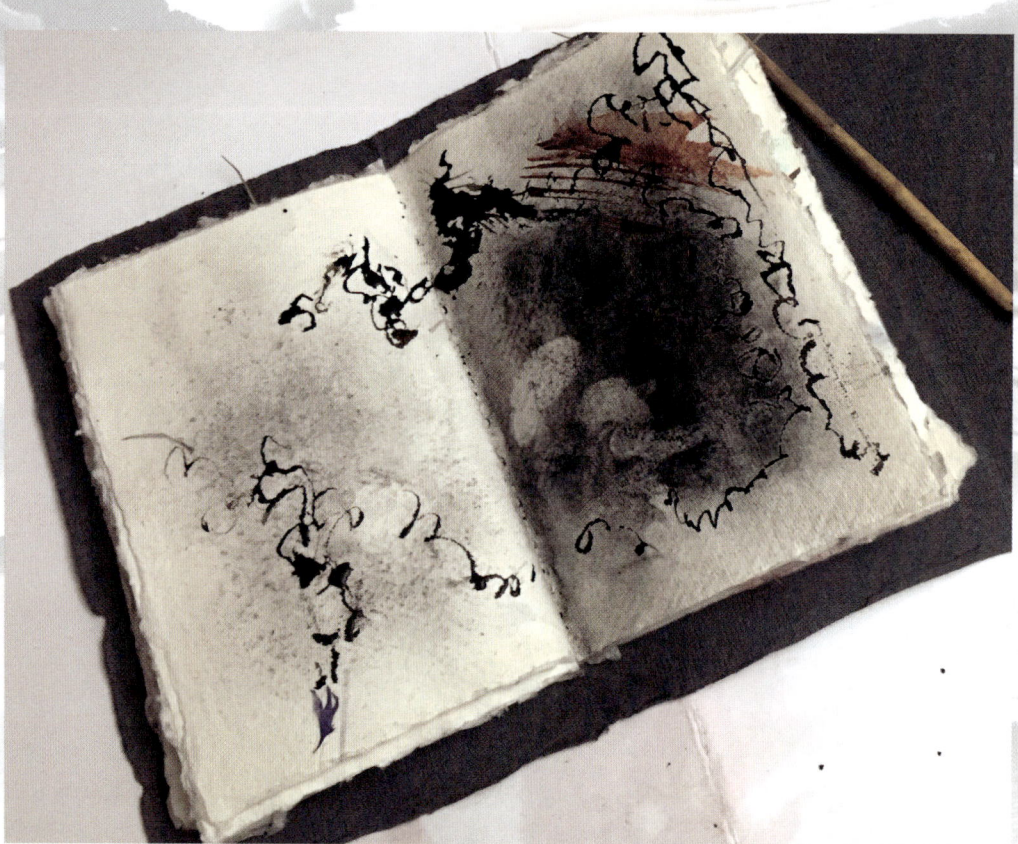

Quick ink and paint swatches become the beginning of a new charcoal sketch.

Emily Burton's approach

Emily's handcrafted sketchbooks are themselves as much works of art as the drawings inside their creatively bound pages. Gathered from a selection of high quality drawing paper, craft paper, found sheets such as envelopes, plus coloured, printed or brown paper, even her empty books are full of life and individuality.

Emily binds the signatures into hardcovers covered with cloth, often printing decorative endpapers or inner covers with hand-cut stamps (as seen at the bottom left, along with some of her bookbinding tools).

I have been a fan of Emily's detailed observational drawings for many years and became rather envious of her beautiful sketchbooks when I first saw them at her open studios several years ago. It inspired me to start folding my own simple books and to explore a completely scavenged and foraged book-practice of my own.

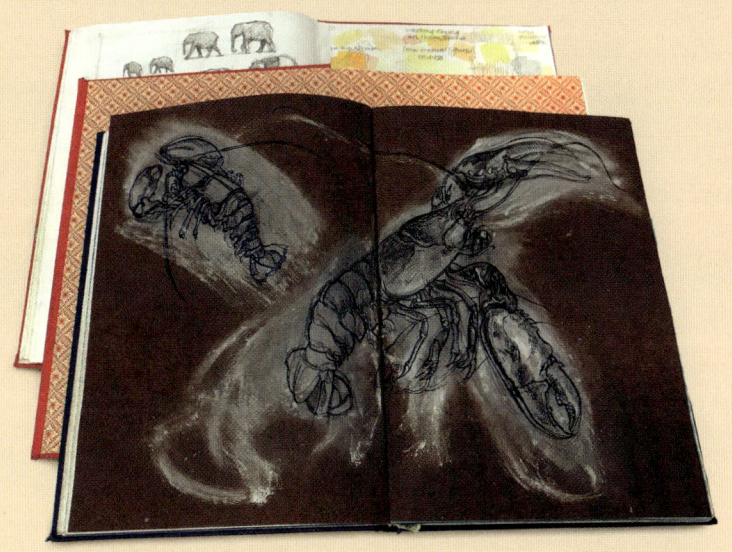

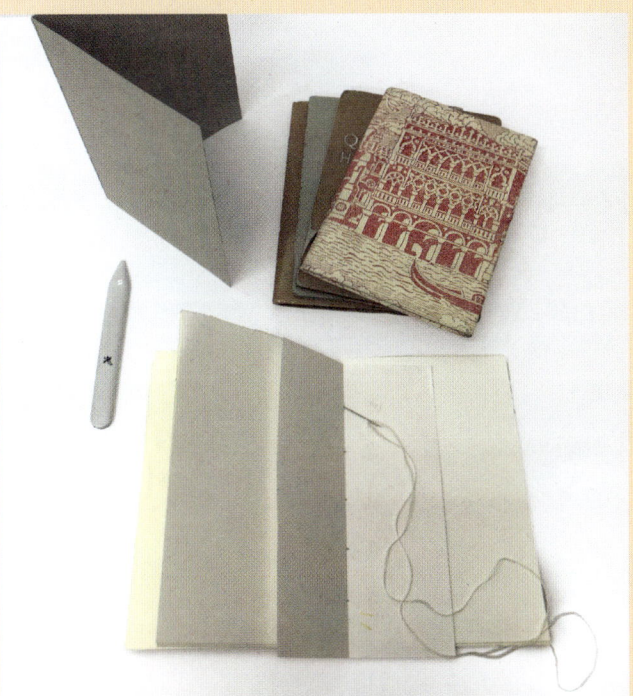

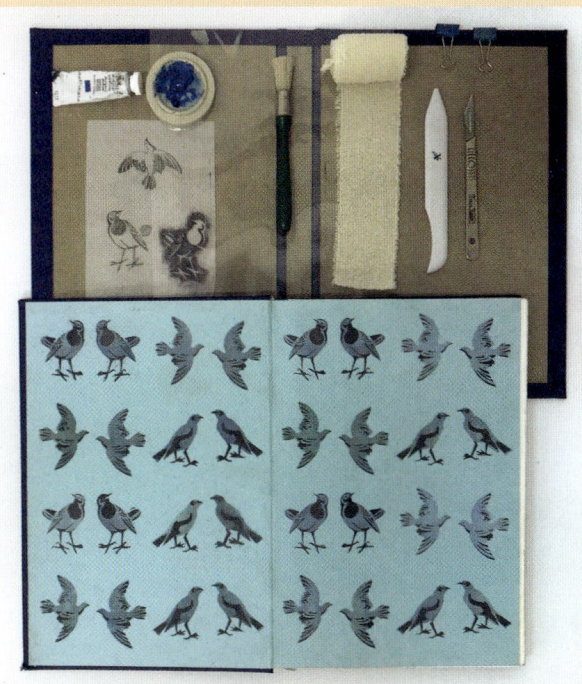

Emily Burton is an artist and drawing teacher. Born in 1977 in Redhill, UK, Emily now lives and works in Kingston upon Thames.

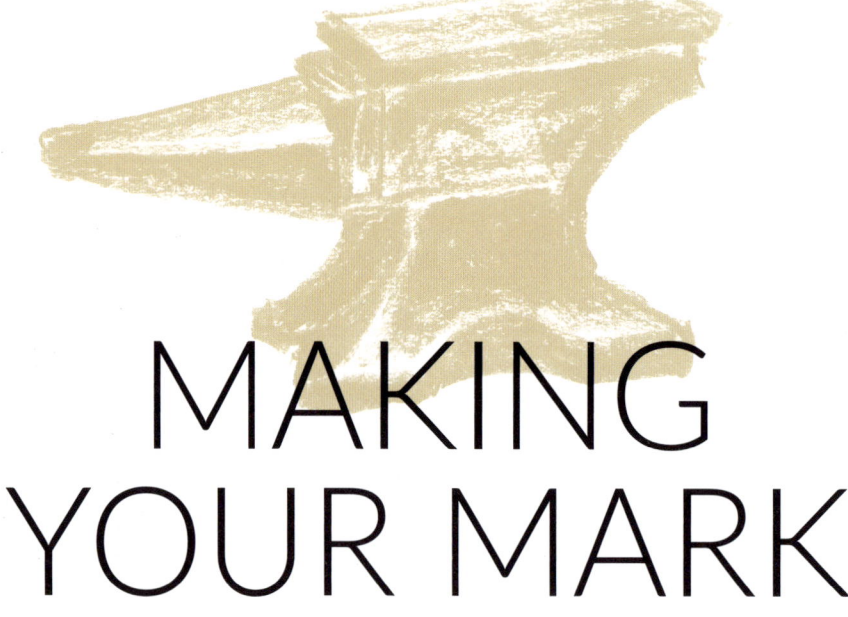

MAKING YOUR MARK

"Fortune favours the bold."

The pen is mightier than the sword, as the proverb goes – but in this particular case it's even made of the same material…

I first came across silverpoint when I was looking at a reproduction of what I thought was a pencil and chalk drawing on a coloured ground – Albrecht Dürer's *Praying Hands*. When I read the caption I was intrigued: what was 'silverpoint'? It was many years later before I could try out the technique for myself in a course entitled 'The Stuff of Drawing and Painting' at The Royal Drawing School, and I quickly found myself hooked! By painting a suitable ground onto good quality paper, to give the surface some 'tooth', we could draw with a silver or gold stylus and leave behind a beautiful pale permanent mark which, in the case of the silver, quickly tarnished to the sought-after warm deep grey. We layered up the drawing to get darker tones by hatching. There was no rubbing out. I loved the boldness required; it was like using a permanent grey fineliner pen but without any pens to throw away when they ran out.

Also included in this chapter is oil charcoal, another little-known historical art technique which gives equally impressive thick black lines, more expressive than any marker pen, and easy to make with the charcoal you have produced.

I believe these near-forgotten materials and methods are due not just for revival but renewal. Whether your style is subtle and detailed or dark and bold, here are some materials you're going to love.

Opposite:
Gifted raw elemental copper.

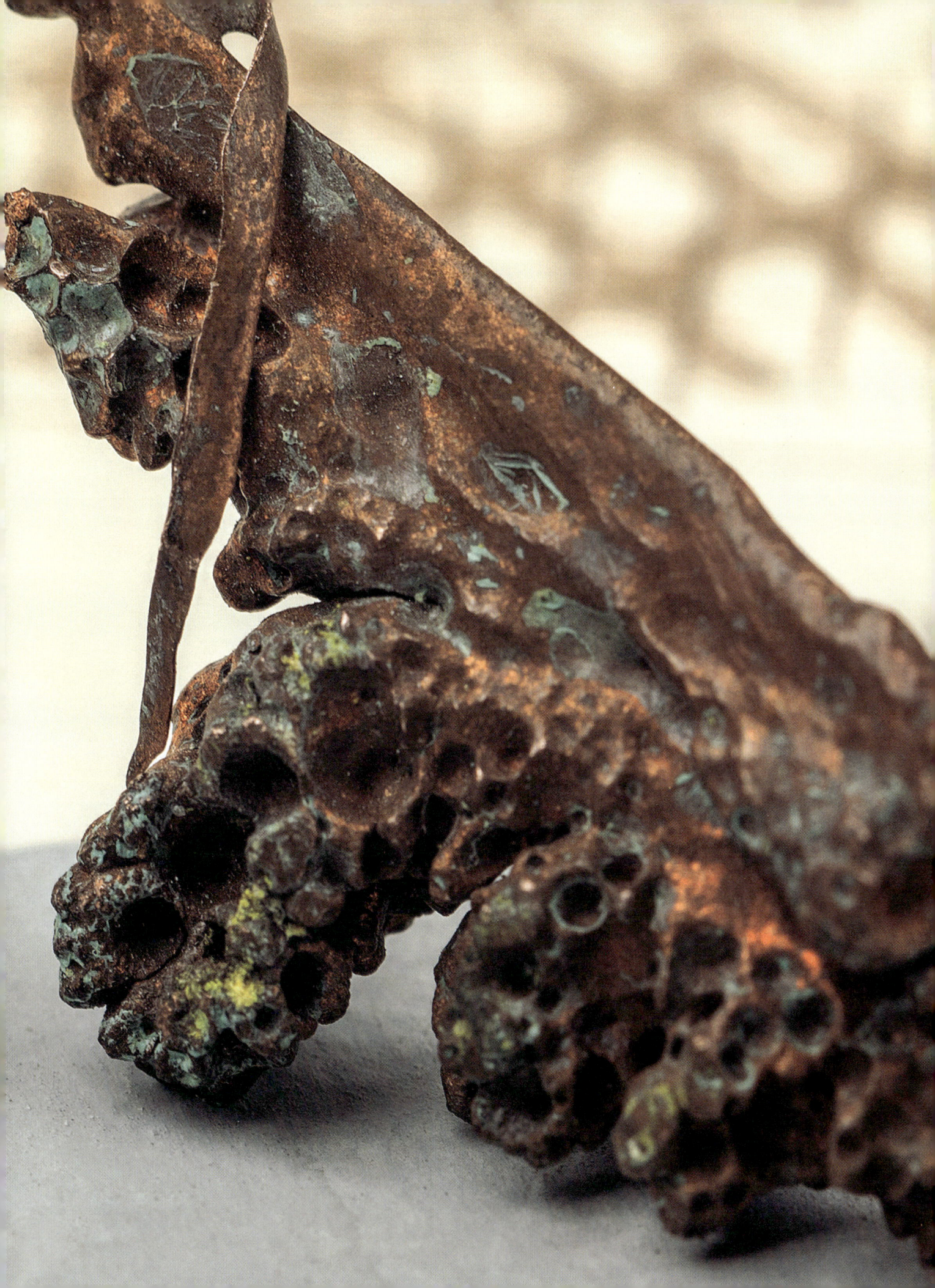

PERMANENCE

Drawing with silverpoint or metalpoint – the terms can be used almost interchangeably – is a wonderful contrast to pastels, say, or ink. You do not need specialist tools for this technique; you can used a variety of foraged metals, which will give different effects. You will be astounded by the range of marks and tones these scavenged metals could leave behind. It is important to note that you should always wash your hands after handling metal, especially before eating.

Metalpoint requires a surface with a slightly rough, abrasive texture, referred to as a 'tooth' – it is the tooth that removes tiny particles of metal from your chosen drawing tool, which are deposited as the line you make. Over the next hours and days, the metal reacts with air and tarnishes, causing the line to become darker. Paper isn't rough enough to remove the tiny particles of metal necessary to leave marks; it needs to be painted with a layer or two of prepared ground.

Bought silverpoint grounds are widely available from art suppliers and work very well. They are, however, usually made with acrylic medium (plastic) as the base, though they rarely state this on the container. If you choose to use these, use a rag to wipe every trace of ground from the brush after using it, before washing it with soap and water in a bucket, to avoid rinsing acrylic particles into the water system. The particulates will drop to the bottom, which can be helped along by precipitating them using washing soda, a method I learned from artist Nina Cadzow. Once it settles, the water can be poured through a cloth and the clear water can return to the earth. The plastic particles are caught in the cloth and can be disposed of in your non-recyclable trash.

Where to find metal

Around the home:

Kitchen drawers (small broken things often live here)
Jewellery boxes
Toy boxes
Sheds and garages
Garden
Sewing kit (metal buttons can be good)
Craft stashes
Waste trim of electrical wires from house remodelling
Old wires from defunct house phones

Around town:

Second-hand shops
Vintage markets
Car boot sales
Garage sales
Hardware stores
Art and craft suppliers
Haberdashers

Suitable metal is less common in most rural areas. Scrap iron is too hard to use, so nails and rusty things aren't useful for metalpoint. Save them for your rust plant to make black ink.

Metals to try

It's worth making up a sheaf of prepared papers (see pages 114–117 for the method) to have stashed ready to try out interesting metal objects. You can also prime each page in a good quality watercolour paper sketchbook and draw in metal while travelling, with no worries about pages getting blotted or smudged on the move, as can happen with ink or pastel.

There's no need to fix the marks once they are made, as all the preparation happens before we draw. Once you know the metals that work, you can think more about the textures of marks they might make as much as the type of metal itself. They can vary hugely in line, density and tone, as shown by the examples below.

FORAGED OBJECT	RESULTING FRESH MARKS
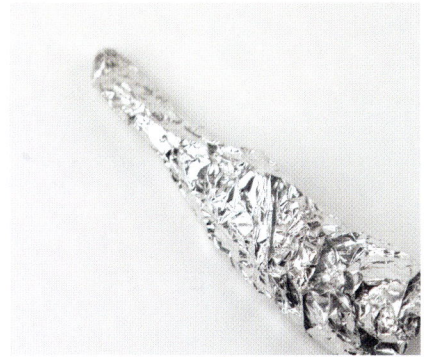 ALUMINIUM FOIL	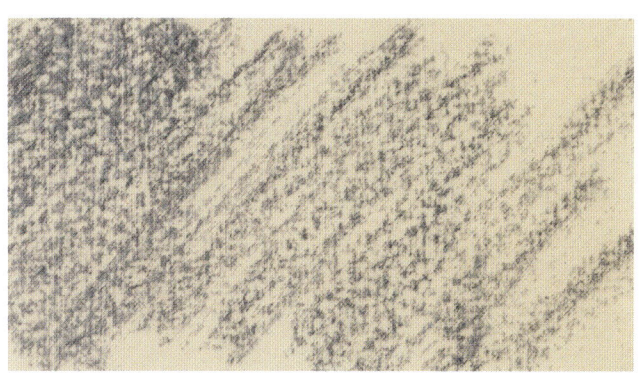
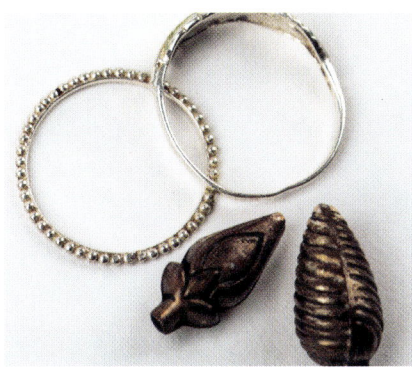 JEWELLERY	
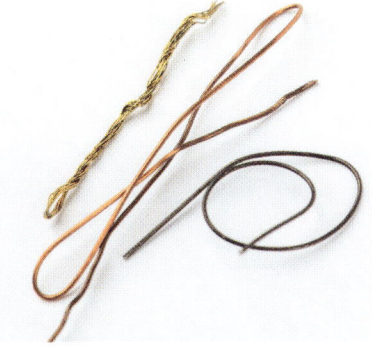 WIRE	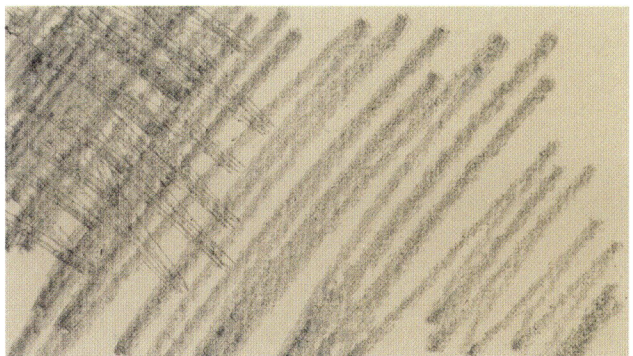

Metal marks sampler

After my early experiences with silverpoint at The Royal Drawing School, I went home with a sheaf of prepared papers, and the recipe to make some more grounds. I didn't have funds for expensive silver or gold tools so I raided my jewellery box and found a few old pendants and beads I didn't wear. Then I gathered up all the random metal wires and objects I could find in my boat, including a pewter tankard, some copper wiring and a piece of aluminium foil that had wrapped my sandwiches, and got to work.

This grid shows just how many wonderful marks can be made with household objects as well as professional silverpoint tools. If you catch the bug for drawing with metal, you can purchase a traditional stylus or modern wire clutch tool from a specialist art supplier. These are a pleasure to use; less unwieldy than a tankard and sturdier than a twist of wire.

You can also improvise your own tools, by attaching your small piece of chosen metal to a stick, much like an arrowhead, or the tools we made for holding charcoal and pastels (see page 56).

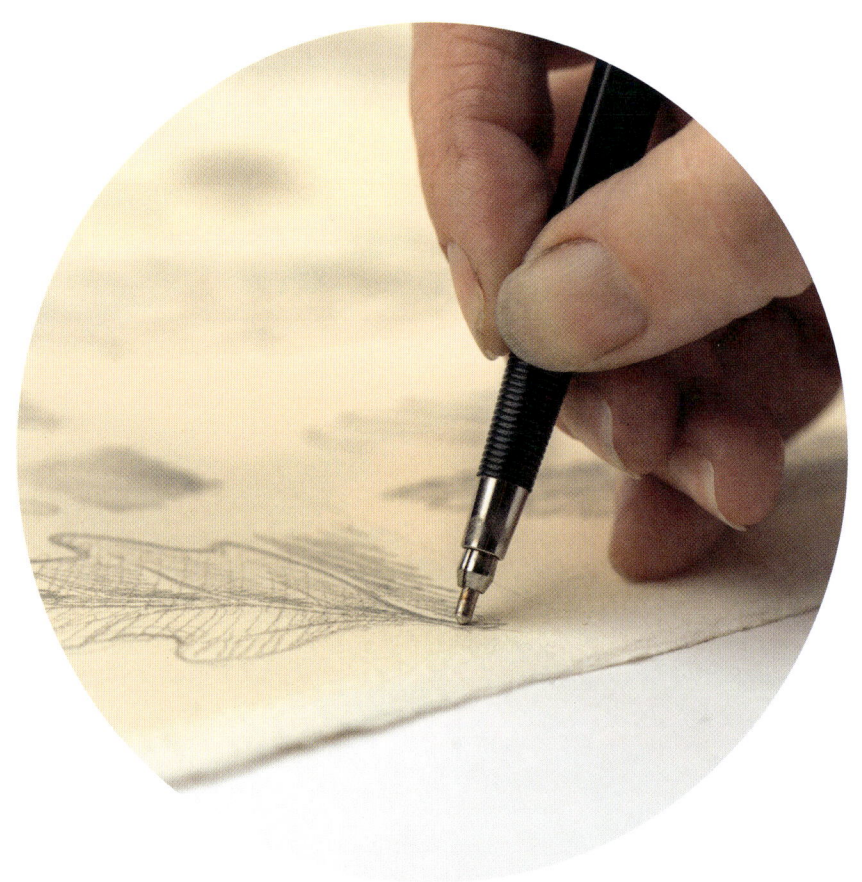

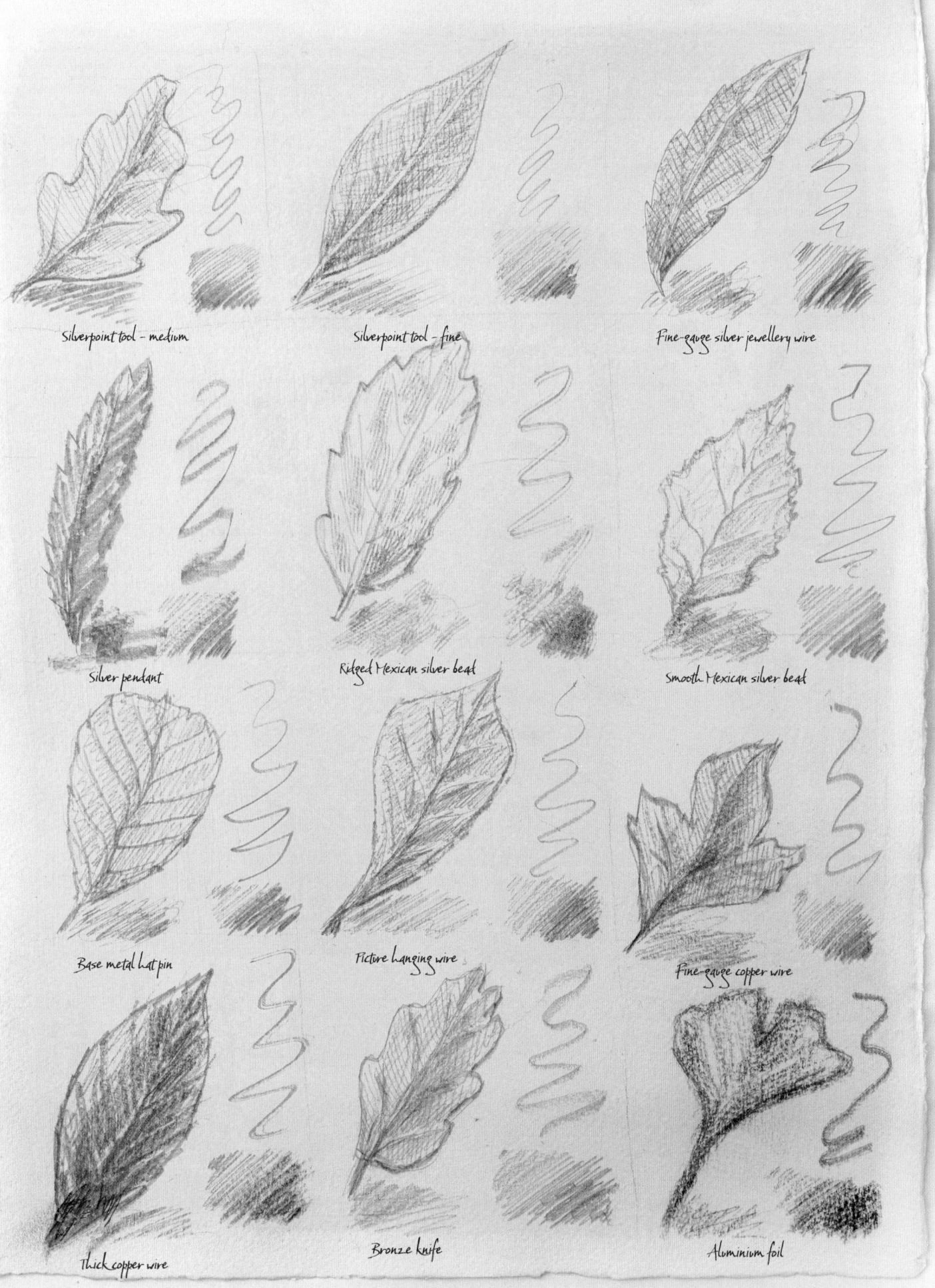

Silverpoint tool – medium

Silverpoint tool – fine

Fine-gauge silver jewellery wire

Silver pendant

Ridged Mexican silver bead

Smooth Mexican silver bead

Base metal hat pin

Picture hanging wire

Fine-gauge copper wire

Thick copper wire

Bronze knife

Aluminium foil

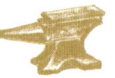

Making grounds for metalpoint

Tools and materials

The traditional ground for metalpoint drawing, as used by Leonardo da Vinci, is bone white mulled in rabbit skin glue. Both of these are traditional uses of waste stream products, and make an excellent ground when a little ochre is added.

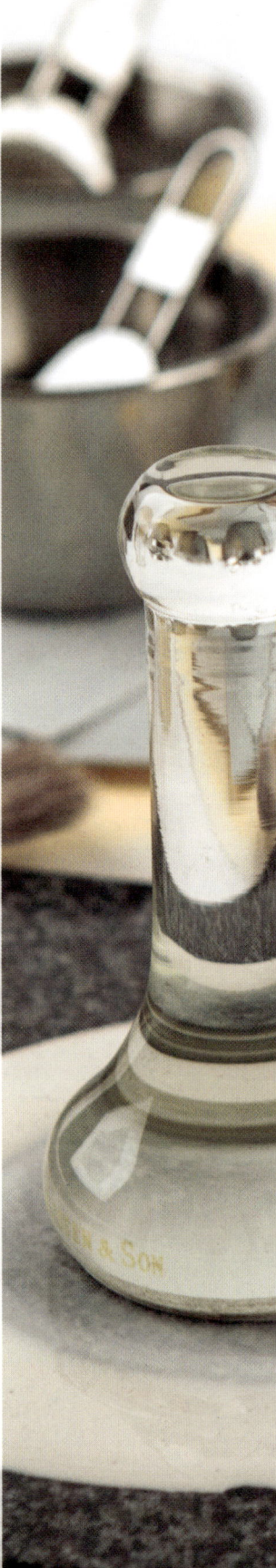

Muller and slab To properly mix grounds and paints, the best tools are a muller and slab, which will last a lifetime. Here, I am using a granite place mat I bought cheaply at a charity shop, and a professional glass muller I bought second hand online. In place of a muller you can use any completely flat-bottomed glass object, such as an old fashioned paperweight.

Pestle and mortar To get pigments and powders to the fine grade we need for grounds and paints, a pestle and mortar are essential. I use stone sets, available very cheaply at most homeware stores for grinding spices. You can also pick them up very cheaply in thrift stores. The heavier the better, as it makes lighter work of the grinding.

Rabbit skin glue Despite the name, rabbit skin glue is made from mixed hides that are waste from the meat industry. It can be bought cheaply in dried granules from any good art supplier as it is still the preferred way to prepare a canvas for oil painting and for making gesso. Soak granules overnight in water, then warm them and stir until completely dissolved. Follow the pack's recommended ratio of granules to water.

Gum Arabic liquid This vegan alternative to rabbit skin glue can be bought ready-made in any art supply shop or prepared by dissolving powdered or lump gum Arabic in a little warm water and soaking it overnight. Stir until dissolved, then sieve through a fine strainer. Add water until it is the consistency of thick cream. I use good quality Indian culinary gum Arabic powder or lumps (*gum gar goond*) interchangeably with art suppliers' (usually north African) gum, with exactly the same results. You can also substitute locally collected cherry, plum or peach tree gum, but will need to make the solution a little thicker than with gum Arabic, as it is not quite as adhesive.

Bone white Cleaned bones are burned in a kiln at 1,000°C (1,832°F) to reduce them to this pure, off-white, powdery ash, which has been added to clay to make bone China for millennia. I buy mine from potters' suppliers, as it is chemically identical (mostly calcium oxide) to the product sold packed for artists, but usually much cheaper, due to the volumes sold.

Powdered chalk Most forms of natural, compressed or even climbers' chalk (or other form of calcium carbonate) can be used as a vegan alternative to bone white – just make sure it is ground finely and evenly, and passed through a fine sieve before use. Work outdoors and/or wear a mask when working with dusty materials.

Other useful tools You'll also need good quality paper, spatula, palette knife, measuring spoons, water and pipette, flat rush, small bowls or deep palettes, cloth for wiping up drips, and natural ochre pigment if you want to tint your grounds.

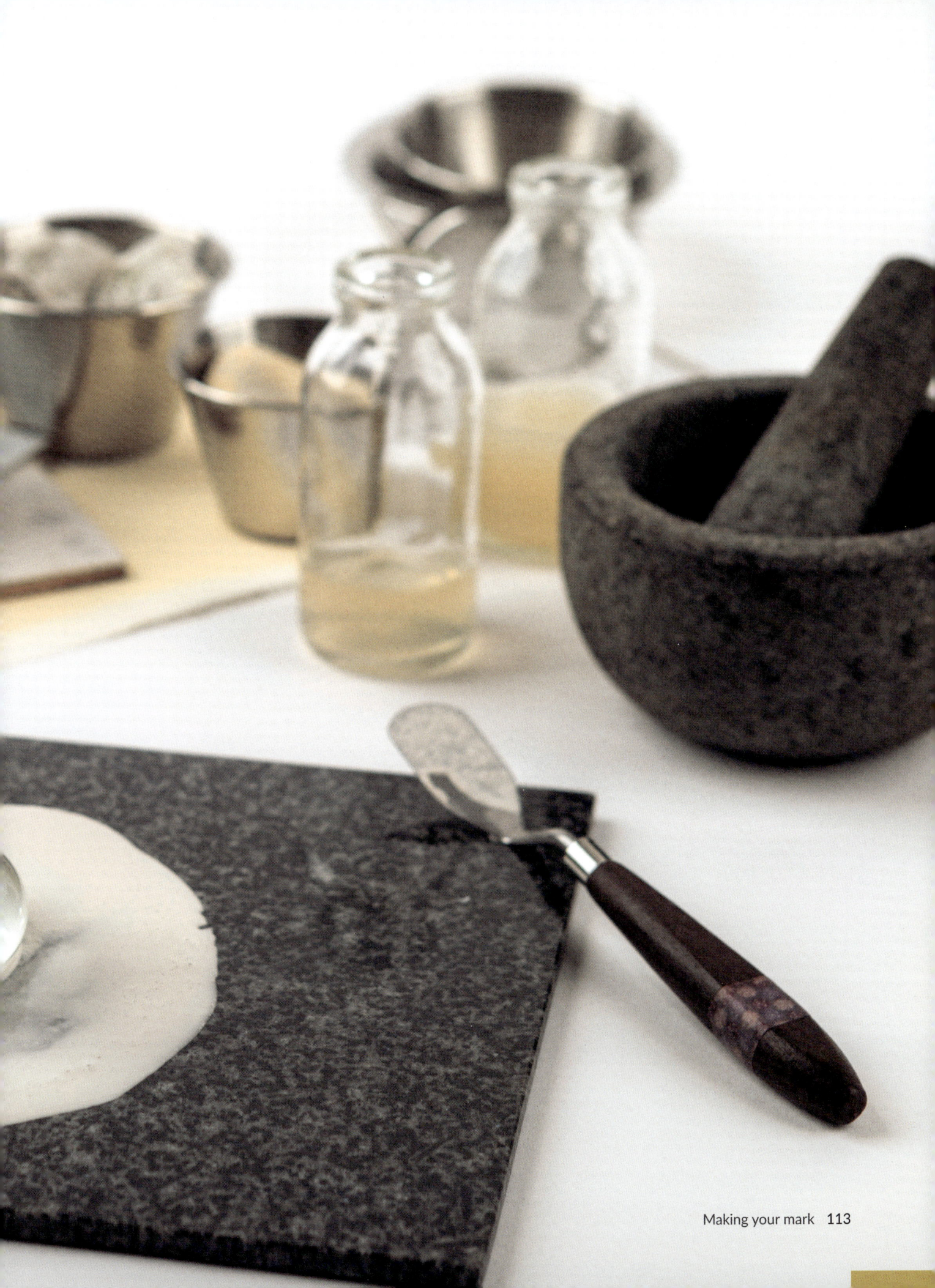

White ground

There are plenty of historical recipes for grounds. Having tried many, I have found several give good results. Natural materials and fine-ness of grind of powders can vary, so tweak your recipes by testing them, until you have consistent results for your choice of medium and abrasive powder. For those who prefer not to use any ingredients of animal origin, even from the waste stream, here is a recipe based instead on gum Arabic, which results in a substance rather like gouache (USA poster paint), an opaque paint that behaves like a thick watercolour.

   If you'd like to skip this phase, you can buy a good quality white gouache paint and tint it with a little ochre pigment, to tone the brightness down a bit.

Tools needed

See the list on page 112

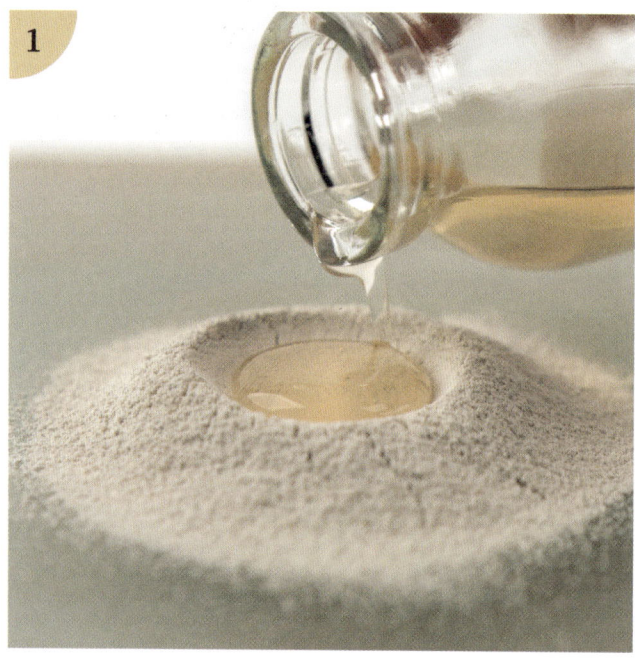

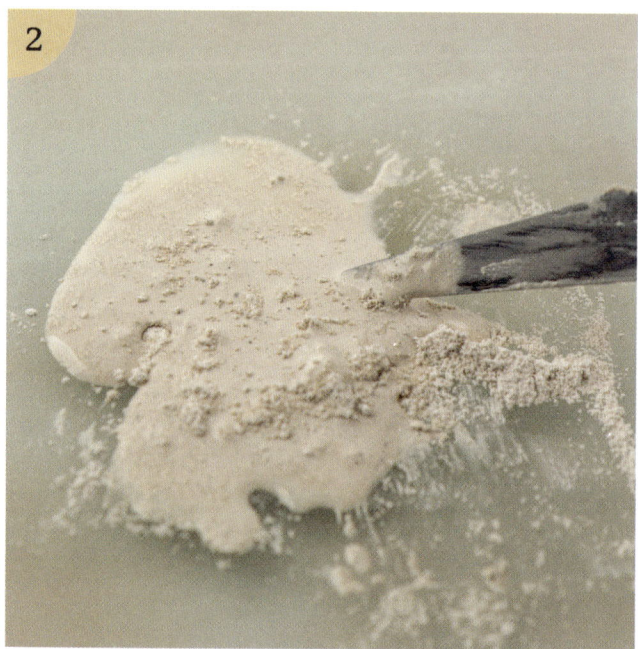

1 Place 1tbsp sieved powdered chalk on the rough side of a slab and make a divot with the bottom of the spoon. Pour in ½tbsp of liquid gum Arabic.

2 Use a palette knife to combine the two – add more gum Arabic or powdered chalk as necessary to reach the consistency of double cream (US heavy cream).

Tip

I crushed the chalk for this in a pestle and mortar. You might try bought white pigment or fine stonedust.

Mulling

The term 'mulling' comes down through French and German variations from the Latin *molere*, 'to grind to a powder', and it has the same root as milling.

When we apply gentle constant pressure and move the muller around the slab, we refine any lumpy bits of powder and coat every particle of solid with the liquid binder. The sound and feel will change as we work – it gets quieter and smoother.

Keep testing your formula by using a wide flat brush to lay down small areas of the ground onto suitable thick paper. When it is dry you can test suitable metal on it to see if it leaves a good mark.

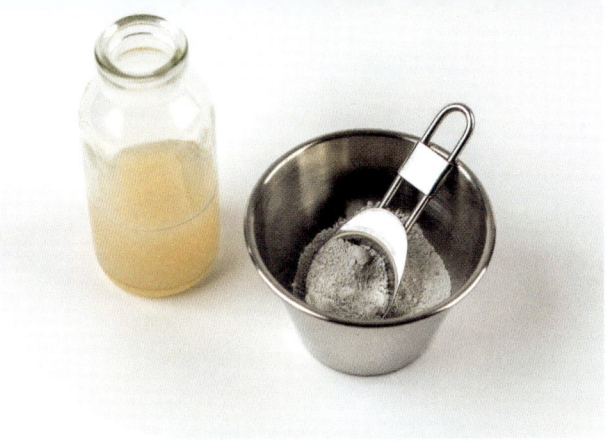

BONE AND RABBIT SKIN SIZE

If you are happy to use bone white and rabbit skin size, you need only mix warmed glue and bone powder in the same way as shown below, and then paint it into the surface.

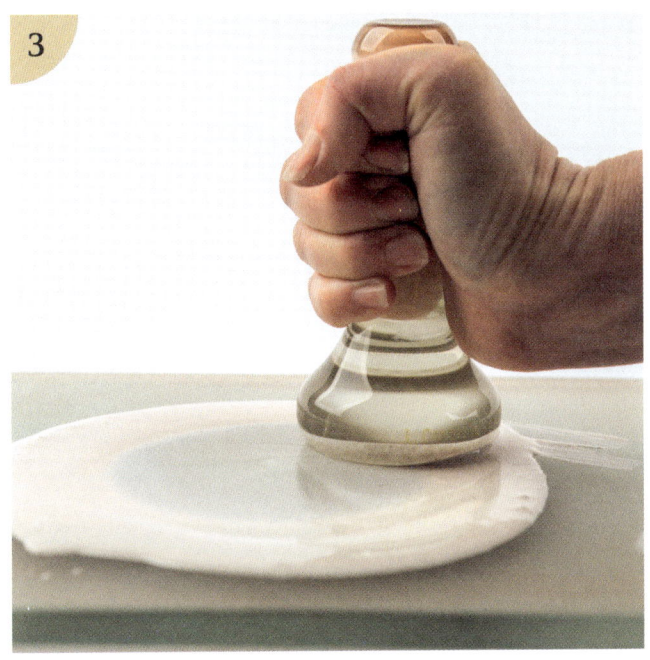

3 Work the muller round in circles to coat every particle of pigment with the gum arabic medium. Keep going until it feels completely smooth under the muller – this can take anything from five to ten minutes. This creates gouache paint. You can use the palette knife to scrape it back into the centre every so soften.

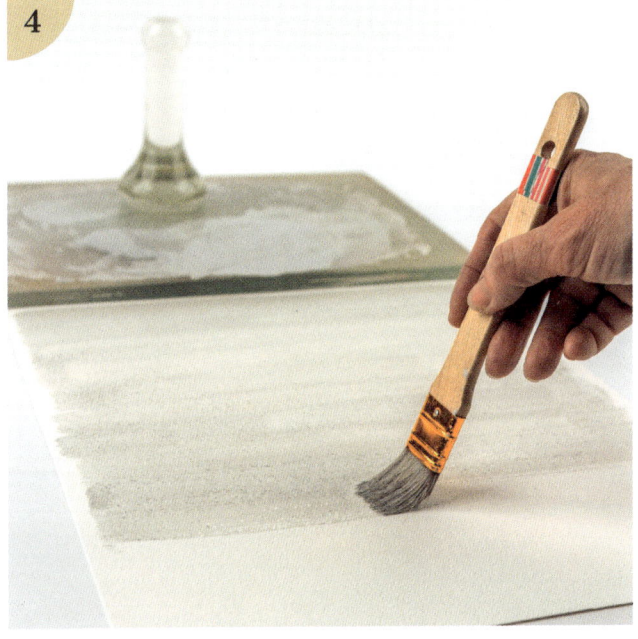

4 Using a pipette, add a little water to the gouache on the slab until it is thin enough to create a smooth, even layer. Use a large flat brush to apply it to your paper. You will want to paint at least two layers, alternating between vertical and horizontal strokes, to get good coverage. Make sure each layer is dry before adding the next.

Tinted ground

Tinted grounds are a wonderful way to add midtones and colour to our drawings. Blue, yellow, pink and red tones have gone in and out of fashion over the centuries.

One advantage of a tinted ground is being able to see where your paper has been primed. When the drawing is nearing completion, you can also work back in with chalk to add highlights, which gives a beautiful three-dimensional quality, highly prized by the Old Masters. Silverpoint looks particularly good in mixed media drawings with chalk and sanguine (red ochre lumps used for drawing), so feel free to experiment with your pastels and other lump media.

The process to make a coloured ground is exactly the same method as for a white ground, except that a coloured pigment is added alongside the chalk or bone white.

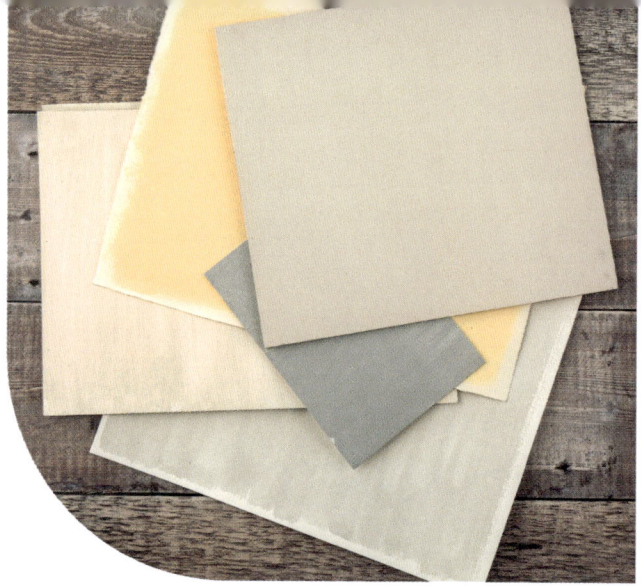

Here is a selection of tinted grounds made by adding small amounts of ochres to the white ground on the mixing slab. They are painted onto good quality paper and salvaged hardboard.

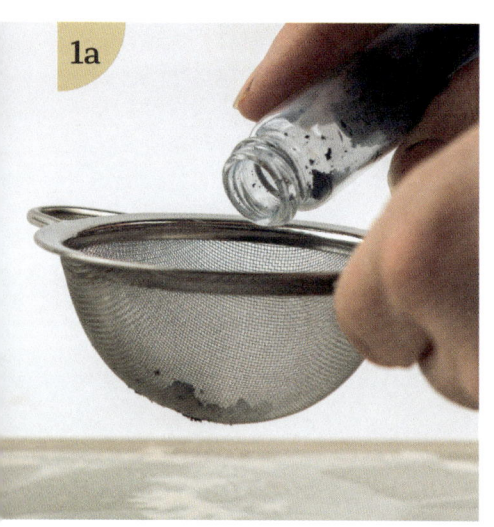
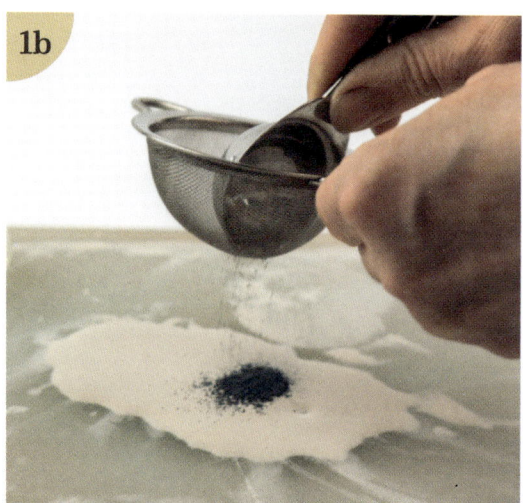
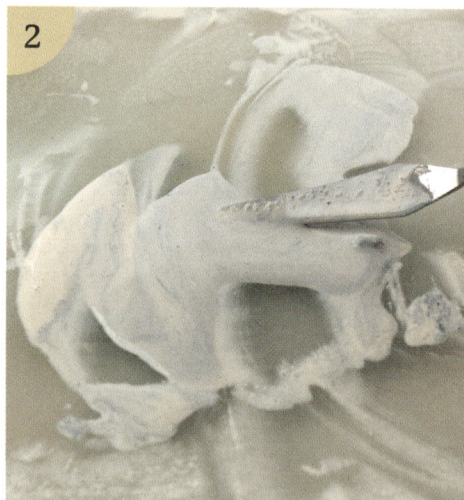

See the previous pages for the step-by-step instructions – the only difference is that you need to add in a second pigment (1a and 1b) alongside the white pigment.

Historically in Europe, indigo, ochre or madder were used to tint the gouache or bone white ground – you can use these or any of your natural pigments. Here I am using vivianite, a gift from a friend, to make a duck egg blue.

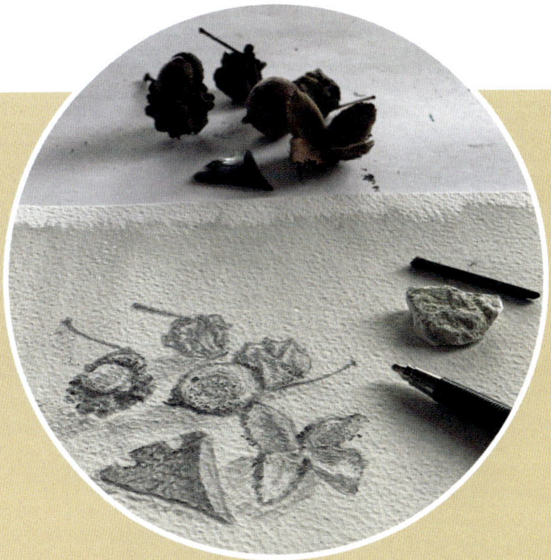

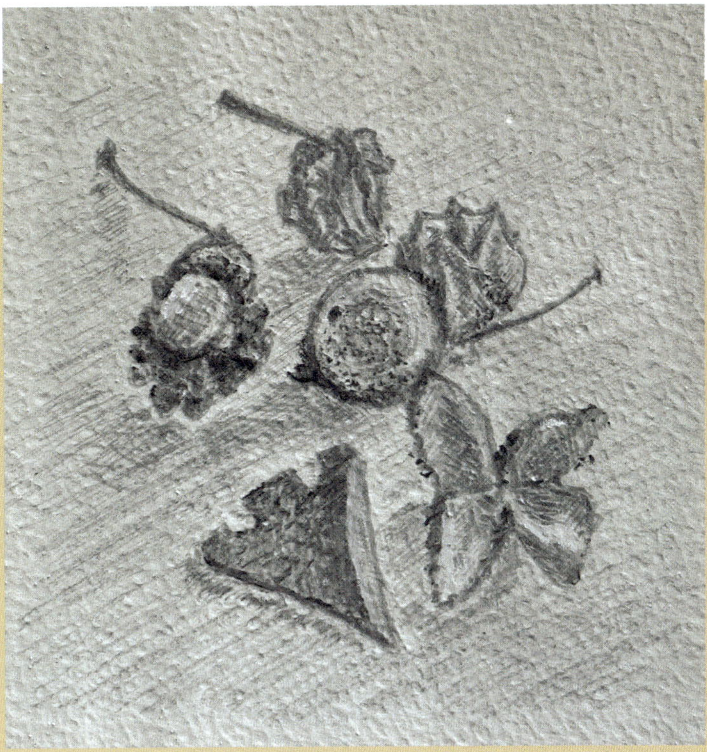

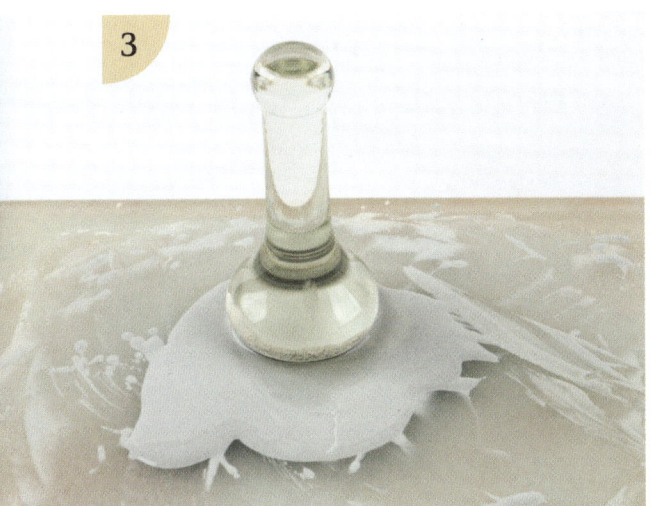

**STILL LIFE WITH OAK GALLS,
ALDER AND FLINT** 10 x 10cm (4 x 4in)
*Silverpoint with chalk and charcoal highlights
on tinted prepared ground on paper.*

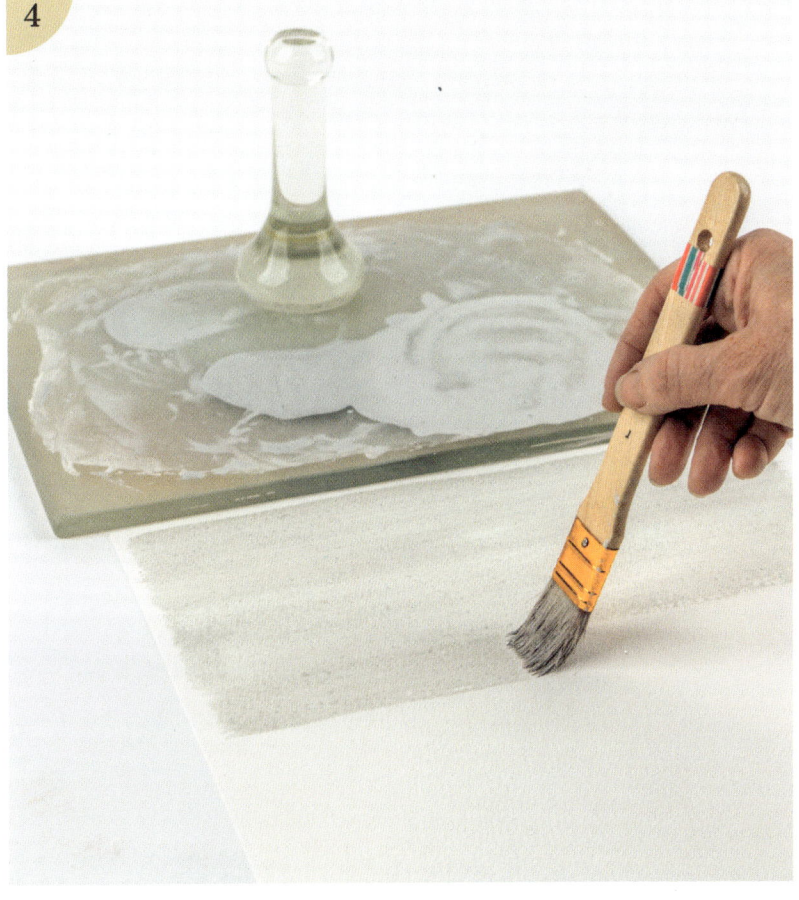

3

4

How to use your silverpoint surfaces

To my mind, for the adventurous contemporary artist, few methods offer more space for new expression than once popular, now overlooked, metalpoint. From early childhood, most people get used to drawing with pencils, not knowing that the central 'lead' holds a clue in its name. Lead, tin, silver, gold and copper have all been used to make fine line drawings on prepared paper, long before modern pencils were invented in 1795. It is also versatile: metalpoint can be worked over in pen and ink or used for preparatory sketches ahead of a final painting.

I always admired silverpoint sketches by the Old Masters, especially those by Albrecht Dürer and Leonardo da Vinci, but it was only after using a silver stylus on prepared grounds that I discovered the possibility of subtle mark-making and building up tones through hatching that this medium offers. I also valued the challenge of not being able to erase my marks as I drew from the life model. The combination of delicate line with boldness of decision-making proved addictive.

As demonstrated on page 110, almost any reasonably soft household metal will leave good marks on your prepared papers. Even used aluminium foil from the kitchen, once shaped into a blunt point, will leave satisfyingly wide, dark, gunmetal grey marks on the prepared paper, and can be scumbled over the surface, too, resulting in an effect like graffiti spray on an old brick wall.

I feel this way of making permanent marks is far more expressive and interesting than anything made by marker pens. It adds a layer of technical challenge to observational drawing that keeps our work from becoming facile or stale.

A future for metalpoint

A hard core of traditional artists have been using metalpoint throughout the centuries, but I would love to see more contemporary abstract work, experimental drawings and expressive portraiture in this medium. With no ink to leak, it's clean and convenient. If you prepare the pages in a small sketchbook in advance, you can even sketch *en plein air*, at the airport or bus stop, or while your family watch a film.

I hope you will accept my challenge and bring this beautiful ancient method into your everyday art practice, especially if it helps you replace the need for buying more unrefillable plastic pens. Metalpoint drawing will be renewed because we'll be reusing metals and improvising from what we find, bringing a whole new ecologically sound slant to the method.

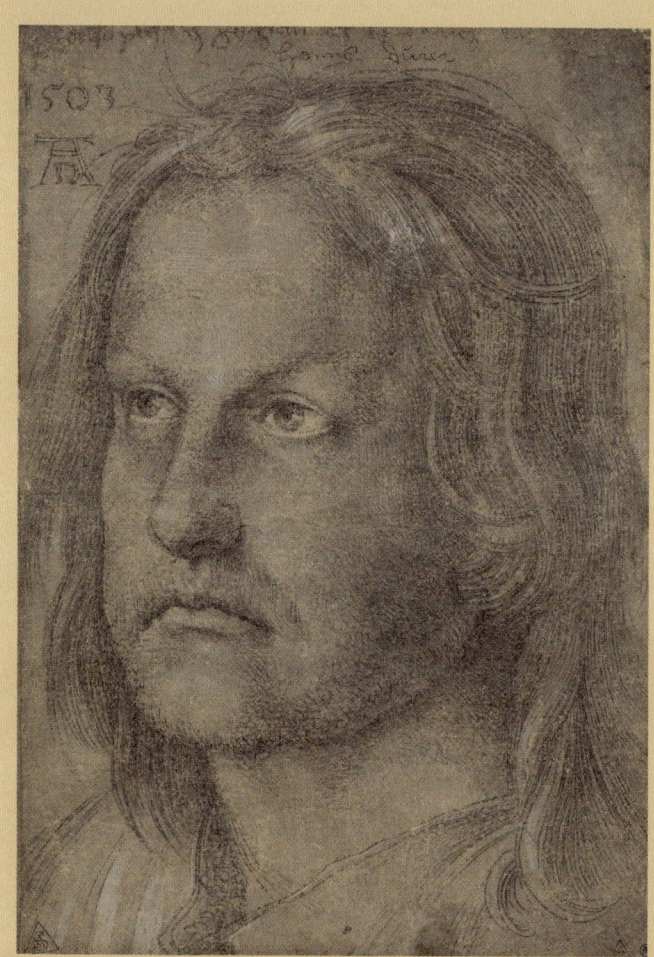

PORTRAIT OF AN UNKNOWN MAN   14.7 x 20.8cm
(6¾ x 8¼in)
Artist: Albrecht Dürer (1471–1528).
Silverpoint heightened with white on brown prepared paper. Rosenwald Collection.

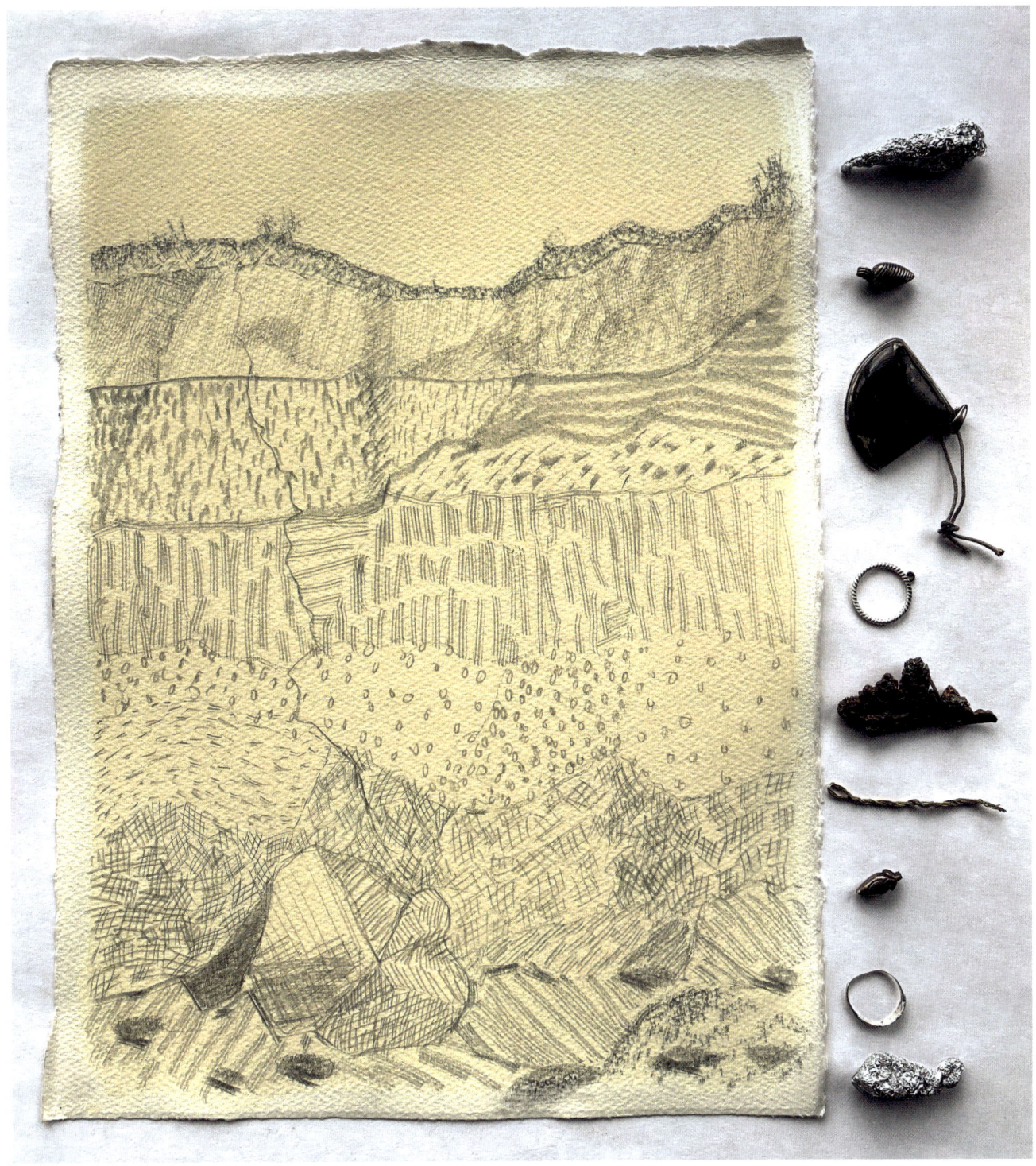

HENGISTBURY HEAD CLIFF STRATA 28 x 42cm (11 x 16½in)

This drawing was made with aluminium foil, Mexican silver beads, a pewter pendant, silver-plated earrings, a lump of raw copper, picture hanging wire, a sterling silver ring and the foil wrapping from a chocolate bar, on a sheet of khadi paper prepared with gouache.

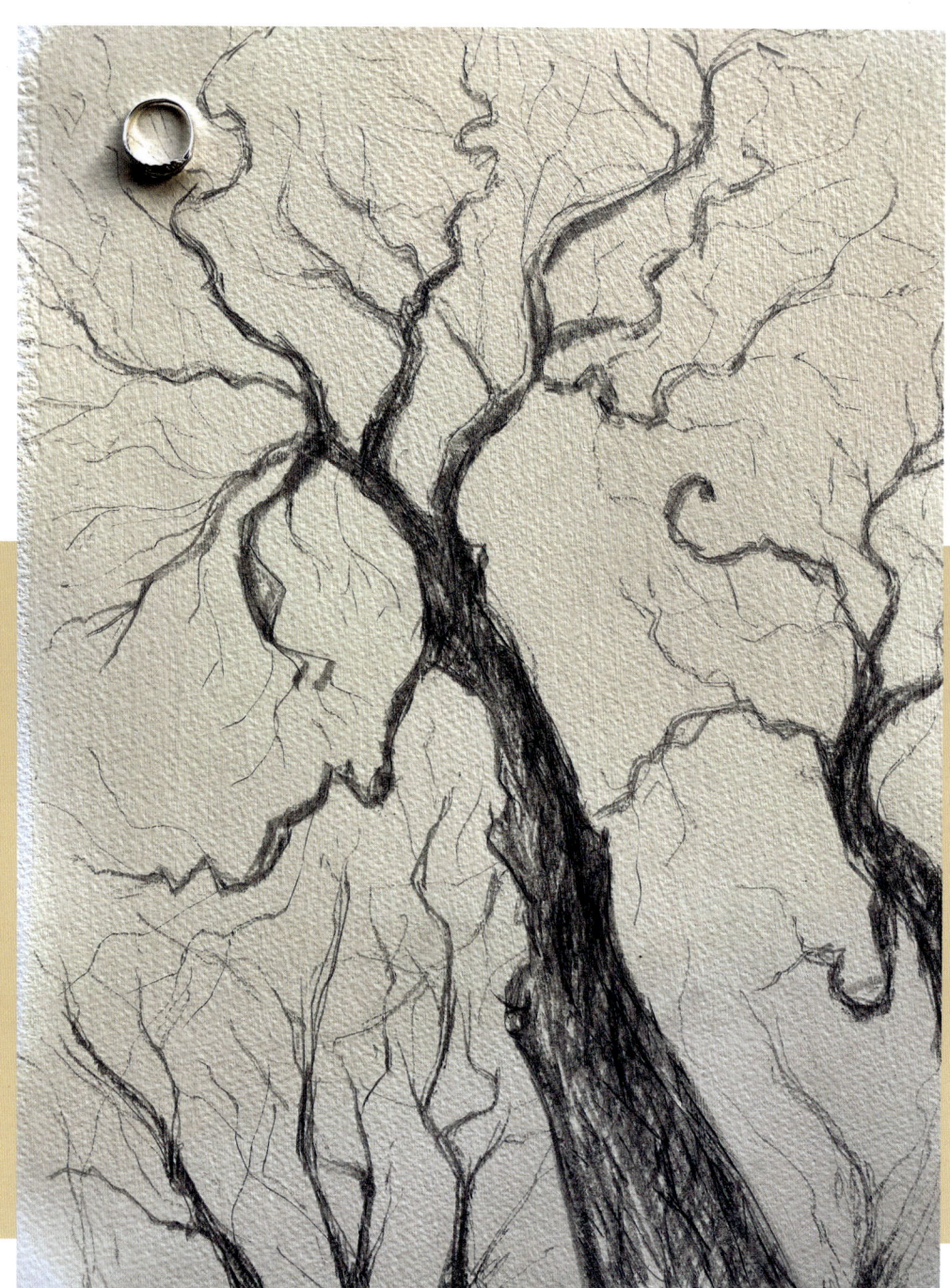

WINTER TREES OF FISHERMAN'S WALK
30 x 42cm (11¾ x 16½in)

Silver ring (seen at top left in the picture) on tinted prepared ground on paper.

Metalpoint is traditionally a delicate medium, but bolder approaches like this are possible with a little ingenuity.

Opposite:
OXALIS   30 x 42cm (11¾ x 16½in)

Cleaned and re-used aluminium foil, rosso ercolano and caput mortuum raw earths on tinted prepared ground on paper.

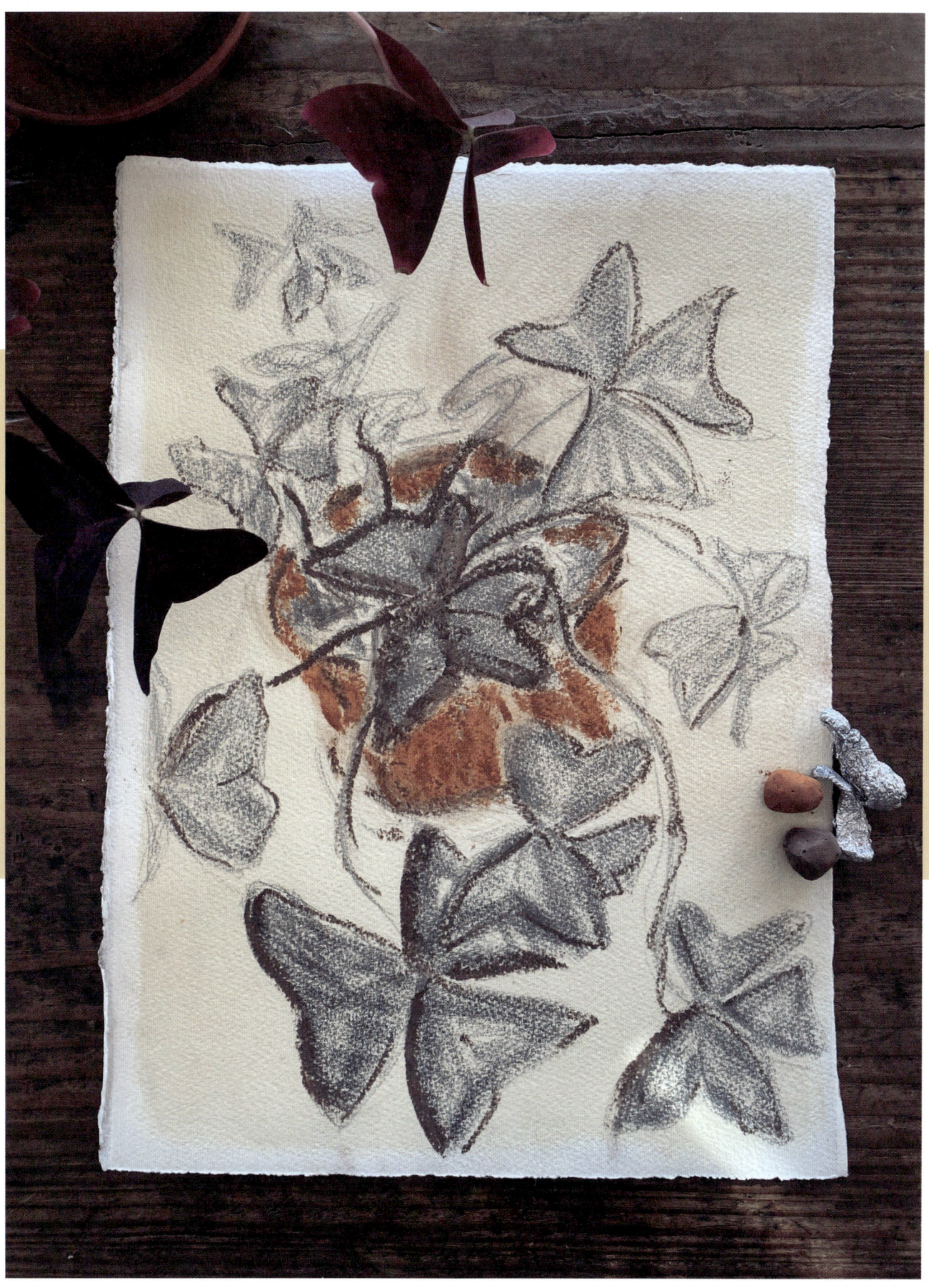

 # Making oil charcoal

Tools needed

Charcoal sticks, bottle of linseed oil

Useful extras:

Tissue for wiping sticks, scrap paper for testing, tweezers for getting sticks out of the bottle

I like making strong black marks when drawing expressively from the model, or when making visual notes from dreams. Oil pastels can be good for this, but they are made with petrochemicals and never dry on the paper, so are always a bit smeary. Marker pens make a host of marks, but are made from plastic too, so I save permanent markers for use when labelling things, often for safety reasons.

Oil charcoal is a little-known medium and is an unexpected delight. I include it as a special extra for those of you who just want to make one simple thing on a rainy afternoon, and get on with making some bold drawings. You'll need a small bottle of artist's linseed oil, the same as we use for veglair medium (see page 45). Keep this bottle aside just for making oil charcoal.

1 Take some sticks of charcoal which will fit in the bottle.

2 Leave the charcoal in the bottle of oil overnight or for a couple of days. Make just a few at a time, as you need them.

3 Remove one stick at a time to use it, and recap immediately, to stop the oil drying. Wipe the stick well on a tissue before use; you can use it as-is or in a holder.

4 Test your marks on scrap paper, then draw on good quality paper that you would use for pastel or watercolour. Your marks will be permanent but still look very much like normal charcoal. Magic!

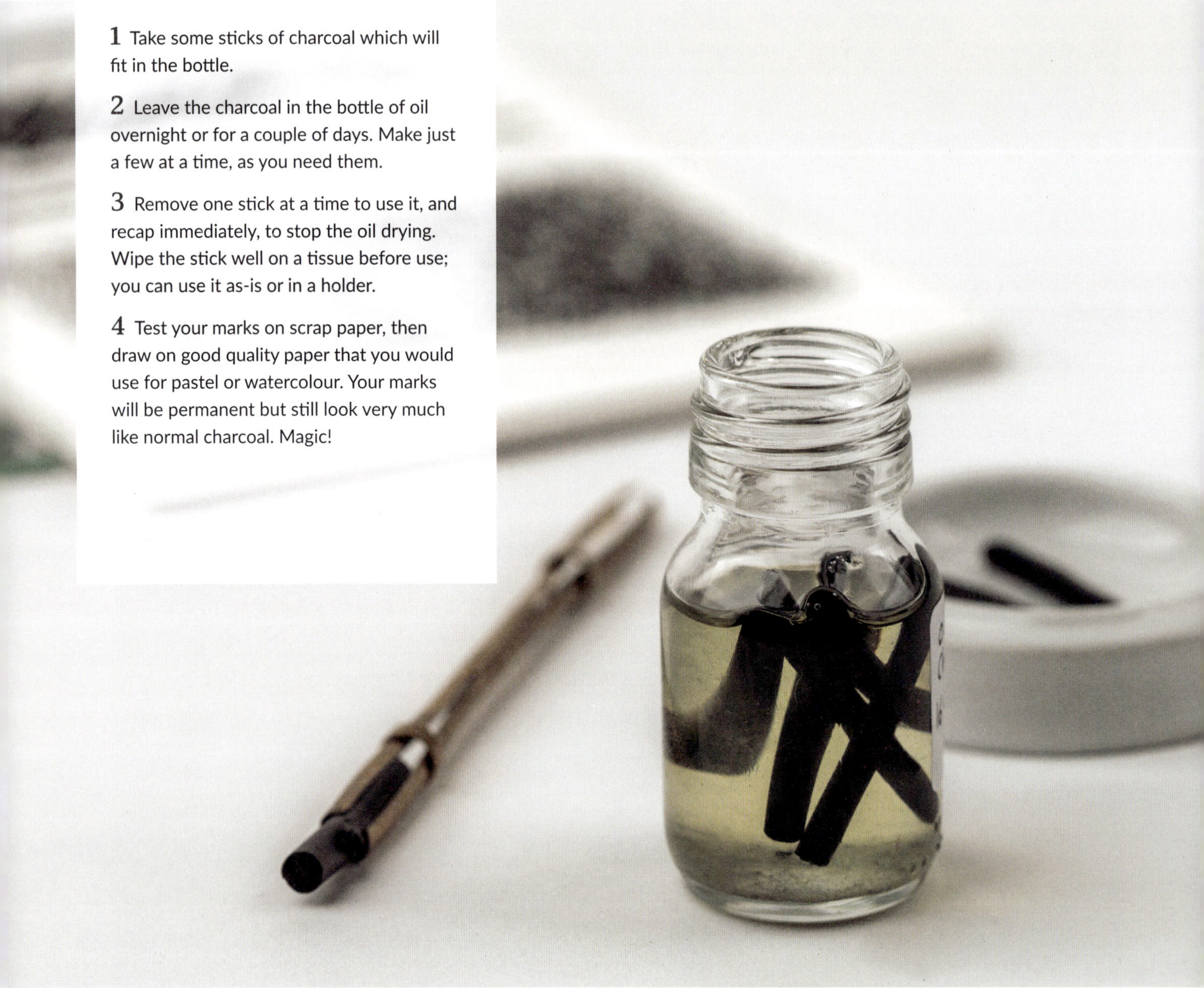

Using oil charcoal

This medium can leave a tiny halo of oil around the marks, which eventually dissipates into the paper as it dries, so make some test sheets of quick drawings if you are thinking of using this technique for drawings you might one day sell or wish to frame. I like to use oil charcoal for quick sketches, or over collage, so I don't see it as a problem.

You can paint over oil charcoal with oil paint, but it will resist water-based paints.

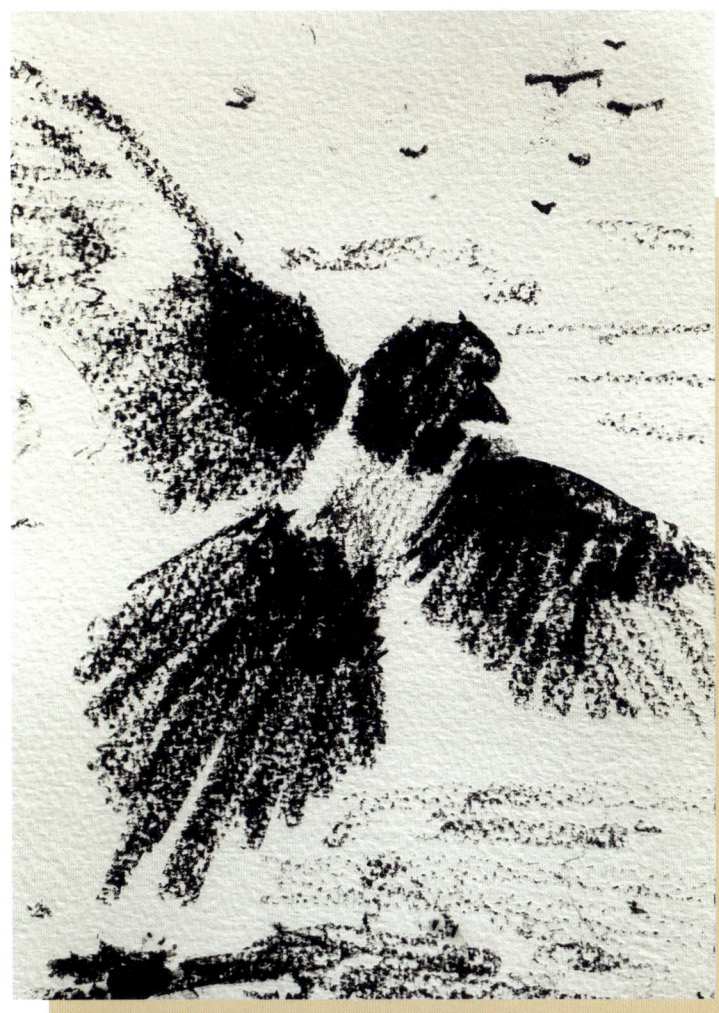

MAGPIE 15 x 21cm (6 x 8¼in)
Worked in oil charcoal.

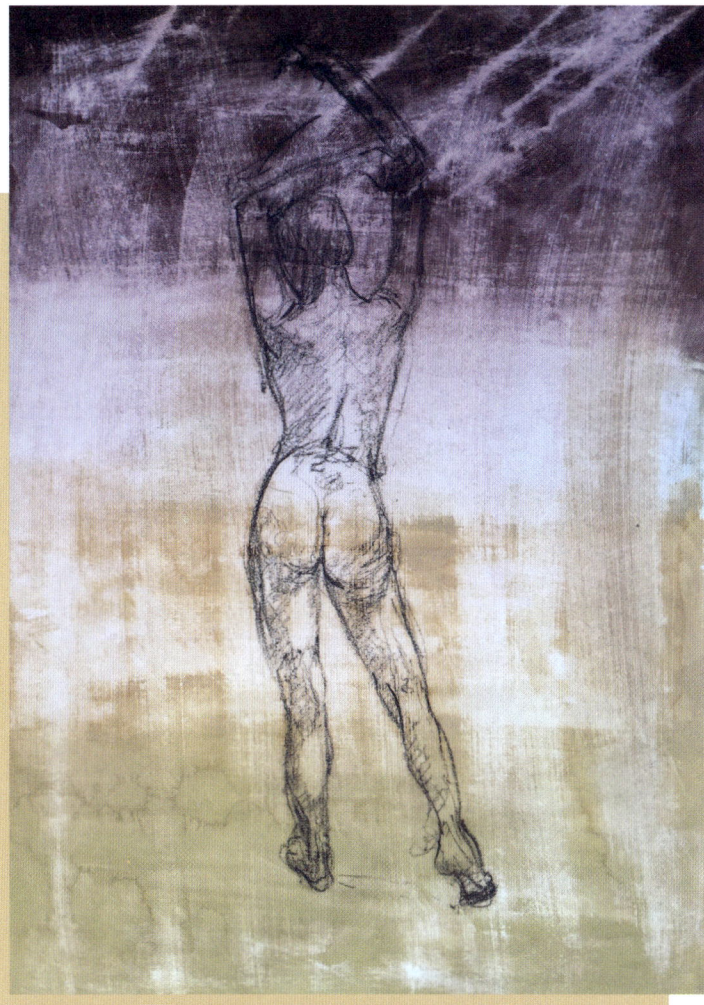

SKETCH FROM THE MODEL 30 x 42cm (11¾ x 16½in)
A ten-minute sketch of a model, made with oil charcoal on prepared ochre ground.

AFTERWORD

> "To make a start, you need only the
> simplest earths, bricks or sticks."

Soon, I'll pick up the quill pens, stash my brushes, gather up my sketchbooks and head off to teach another great bunch of people who hear foraged, natural and ancient art materials calling to them.

I love to teach in person but books are not second best. Indeed, they are just as good a way to pass on knowledge and crafts. Bringing an array of elements together here for you has been such a pleasure, even though there are so many things I had to leave out due to space constraints – another ochre pastel, a way with a feather or an essential ink. Books can reach so many more people, especially those of us who, for reasons such as mobility, family or work commitments, money, or health, cannot make it along to workshops. I hope you have been inspired to try something from these pages and will let it work its way into your art practice.

Transformation

Transformation is at the heart of all my work and in this enterprise, art, science, history and craft are equal colleagues in a team, all coming together to make something new. My superb school chemistry teacher, Mrs Monk, was as much an influence on the path I have taken as any of my art tutors over the years, and her imprint is in this book. She first taught me how to set up experiments, to pay close attention to the method, to note down results and to consider conclusions. Science and art have so much in common: an inquisitive spirit, great attention to detail, the importance of raw materials and the promise of new lines of enquiry even – or especially – from 'mistakes'.

Simplicity aids creativity

One last piece of advice: never feel disheartened by necessary thrift, or local limitations on materials, as they can often be the catalyst for great creativity. To make a start, you need only the simplest earths, bricks or sticks. Remember your ancient ancestors in the landscape, wherever in the world they found themselves, were making art from everything they could find, long before such things as cities or money existed. We can still see their art in every corner of the Earth today, on cave walls, in petroglyphs and artefacts. Let their ingenuity, skill and wildness be your inspiration, as it is mine, and seek to make your art in similar harmony with our wonderful planet.

Wishing you all the elemental best from the Solent seashore, Caro.

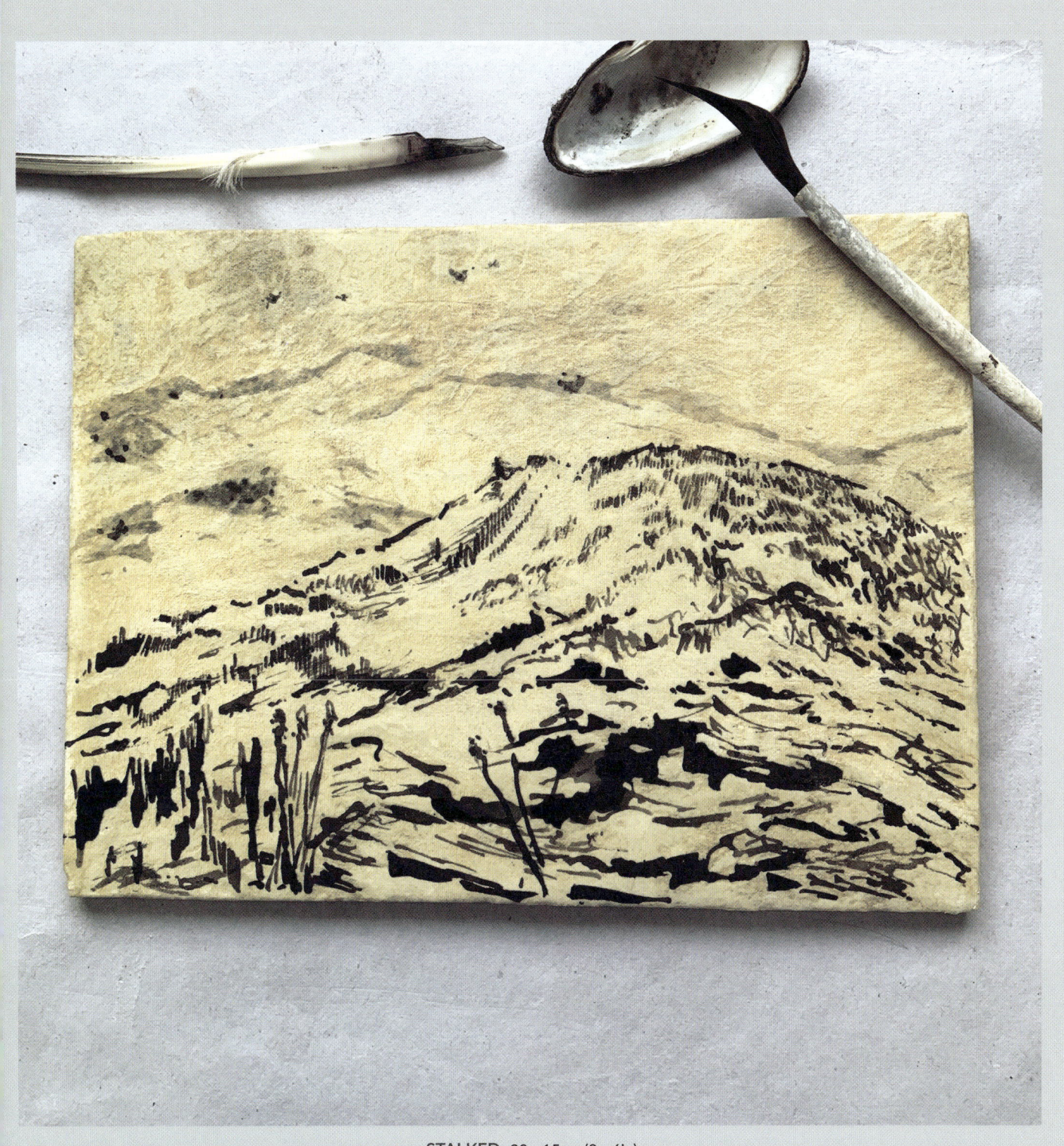

STALKED 20 x 15cm (8 x 6in)

Iron gall ink on buckskin. In the collection of Amanda Short.

Drawn with only a quill pen and feather brush, this was one of four
of my paintings printed alongside Paul Kingsnorth's short story
The Light in the Trees *for Dark Mountain 18: Fabula.*

Recommended reading

The Materials of the Artist Doerner, Max – Harvest, 1984

Gathering Colour Ffrench, Caitlin – Nine Ten Publications, 2024

The Book of Earth Gustafson, Heidi – Abrams Books, 2023

Make Ink Logan, Jason – Abrams Books, 2018

Formulas for Painters Massey, Robert – Watson Guptill Publications, 1967

The Artist's Handbook of Materials and Techniques Mayer, Ralph – Faber, 1991

Inks and Paints of the Middle East Medlej, Joumana – Majnouna.com, 2020

Wild Inks and Paints Medlej, Joumana – Majnouna.com, 2021

The Organic Artist Neddo, Nick – Quarry Books, 2015

The Organic Artist for Kids Neddo, Nick – Quarry Books, 2020

Found and Ground Ross, Caroline – Search Press, 2023

Further reading suggestions can be found on Bookmarked (www.bookmarkedhub.com).
Search for this book by title or ISBN: the information can be found under 'Book Extras'.

Contributors and featured artists

Stewart Lee stewartlee.co.uk

Kauae Raro Research Collective kauaeraro.com

Naimeh Ghabaie instagram.com/colortalisman

Carrie LaChance mmmordere.substack.com

Flora Arbuthnott plantsandcolour.co.uk

Martyn Cross instagram.com/martyncross

Mirella Salamé mirellasalame.com

Beke Olbers instagram.com/bekeolbers

Emily Burton emilyburtonartist.co.uk

Geraldine van Heemstra geraldinevanheemstra.com

Jesse Ajilore jesseajilore.com

Candace Jensen candacejensen.com

Thomas Little instagram.com/a.rural.pen

Joumana Medlej majnouna.com

ACKNOWLEDGEMENTS

Without the deep brown earth of mum's Bournemouth back garden for mud pies, or purple-staining blackberries from the alley behind our house for crumbles and potions, I would never have become a natural materials artist. My greatest thanks go equally to the land of my home county Dorset and my family, both of whom I love without bounds and who continue to form me daily.

For my first book, *Found and Ground*, I somehow completely neglected to write a proper acknowledgments page and only thanked one person, Tilke Elkins, who I thank again here for all she continues to do for Earth and people. So these following thanks are for those who have helped me create both books.

Thanks to my wonderful editor at Search Press, Edd Ralph, for endless good advice and unfailingly cheerful support.

Thanks to the teaching staff of Shelley Park art college in Bournemouth, now sadly closed, where I studied for two years on Foundation, especially the late Eddy Foulstone. Joe O'Leary, of Wilderness Survival Skills whose courses made me realize that 'Art' and 'Craft' need not be separated and that pretty much anything can be done better and more enjoyably when in good company in the woods. Theresa Emmerich Kamper for the skill and beauty in her tanning and leather work, which first gave me licence to resume drawing oak leaves on everything...

To David Knight, for walking into my tiny boat's galley one day asking if I was making glair, when I was making aquafaba meringues, and thereby inspiring an entire range of vegan art media. Thanks also go to him for telling me about the Royal Drawing School, which led me to study 'The Stuff of Drawing and Painting' with Daniel Chatto, who taught me so much. Many thanks also to David Cranswick for his courses on traditional art methods and materials.

Paul Kingsnorth and Navjyoat Chhina, and their children Leela and Jeevan, who hosted me and helped me teach my first courses and classes in Ireland. Nav's original encouragement got me started sharing my 'Pre-Norman' art kit.

Mark Boyle, who hosted my Irish classes at his 'free pub'. Ingrid Rieser, Irja Holter, Schumacher College, Artisans of Now, In Situ Polyculture Commons, Extra Bushcraft and all those who have hosted or helped me run online or hands-on courses, especially Flora Arbuthnott of Plants and Colour, who regularly hosts my online and in-person classes. My colleagues in The Wilderness Art Collective. All my dear friends from the Dark Mountain Project, past and present, especially Charlotte DuCann and Dougald Hine who get me involved with all manner of rewarding projects. Stewart Lee for art, walks, music, laughter, books and conversations over the years, and for noticing the thread running through all my work.

Melonie Ancheta and everyone at Pigments Revealed International for all they do for pigments, people and bringing art and science back together. Prof Linda Hurcombe of Exeter University's Archaeology department for inviting me and my ochres in to the experimental lab.

Friends online from Instagram who sent packages of materials when I lost almost all of mine in 2021: including Thomas Little, Heidi Gustafson, Joumana Medlej, Mona Lewis, Ruthie Siddall and especially Carrie LaChance, who continues to teach me so much and sends me incomparable parcels of bright extracts. To all my colour-friends, including those I have not had space to mention, thank you. You renewed my faith in life and art when I was at a low ebb.

Thanks to fellow ochre heads, rock chicks, dirt fans and pigment people the world over, who write, talk about or share earth colours with me, particularly Nick Hunt, Lucy Mayes, Jonathan Wright of Clearwell Caves and all the artists who graciously allowed me to feature their work in this book.

To all my in-person and online course attendees for wanting to learn what I love to share, and to my subscribers at Uncivil Savant who read what I've been mulling over each week.

To my wonderful partner Jonny Randall who happily gathers nettles, ochres and swan feathers with me. May we always wander the woods and water's edge together.

Lastly, deep thanks for the generosity of the more-than-human neighbours on whom my work depends, including the badgers of woods near Stonehenge for digging chalk, the rooks of Molesey Lock for dropping mussel shells, the swans of Mudeford for moulting feathers, the fallen redwood trees of Dartington for uncovered yellow clay, the earthworms of Wick for purest piles of purple ochre, gall wasps of Tooting for their old homes, the cherry trees of Southbourne for their abundant gum and the lower reaches of the River Stour for path-side reeds and reddest ironstone pebbles. I will never tire of being in your wonderful company.

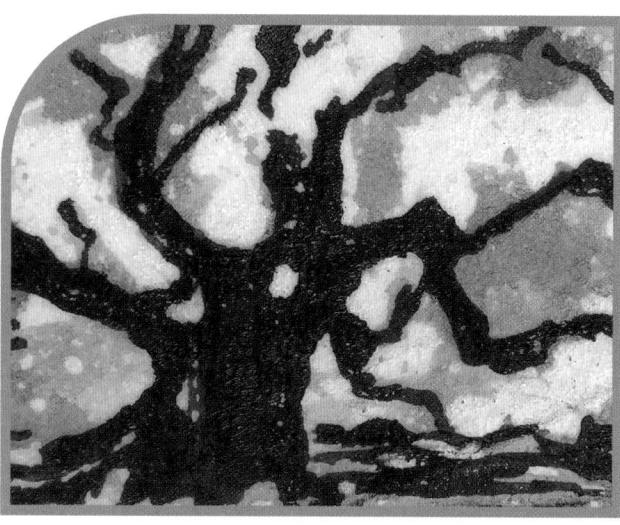

INDEX

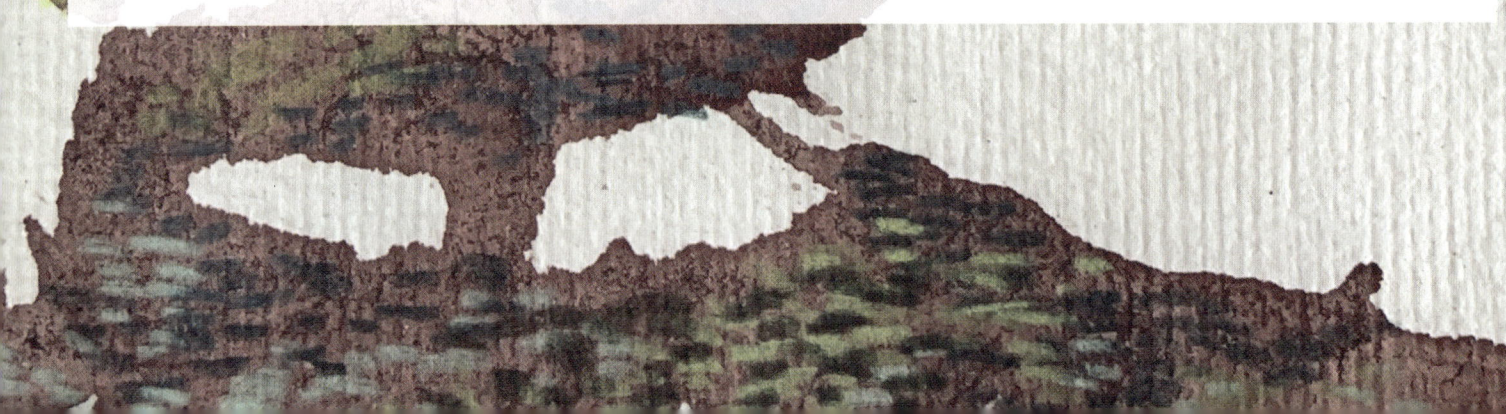